Late Medieval Lodging Ranges

BOYDELL STUDIES IN MEDIEVAL ART AND ARCHITECTURE

ISSN 2045-4902

Series Editors

Professor Julian Luxford
Professor Asa Simon Mittman

This series aims to provide a forum for debate on the art and architecture of the Middle Ages. It will cover all media, from manuscript illumination to maps, tapestries, carvings, wall-paintings and stained glass, and all periods and regions, including Byzantine art. Both traditional and more theoretical approaches to the subject are welcome.

Proposals or queries should be sent in the first instance to the editors or to the publisher, at the addresses given below.

Professor Julian Luxford, School of Art History, University of St Andrews, 79 North Street, St Andrews, Fife KY16 9AL, UK

Professor Asa Simon Mittman, Department of Art and Art History, California State University at Chico, Chico, CA 95929-0820, USA

Boydell & Brewer, PO Box 9, Woodbridge, Suffolk IP12 3DF, UK

Previously published titles in the series are listed at the back of this volume.

LATE MEDIEVAL LODGING RANGES

THE ARCHITECTURE OF IDENTITY, POWER AND SPACE

SARAH KERR

THE BOYDELL PRESS

© Sarah Kerr 2023

All Rights Reserved. Except as permitted under current legislation no part
of this work may be photocopied, stored in a retrieval system, published,
performed in public, adapted, broadcast, transmitted, recorded or reproduced in
any form or by any means, without the prior permission of the copyright owner

The right of Sarah Kerr to be identified as
the author of this work has been asserted in accordance with
sections 77 and 78 of the Copyright, Designs and Patents Act 1988

First published 2023
The Boydell Press, Woodbridge

ISBN 978 1 78327 757 5

The Boydell Press is an imprint of Boydell & Brewer Ltd
PO Box 9, Woodbridge, Suffolk, IP12 3DF, UK
and of Boydell & Brewer Inc.
668 Mt Hope Avenue, Rochester, NY 14620–2731, USA
website: www.boydellandbrewer.com

The publisher has no responsibility for the continued existence or accuracy
of URLs for external or third-party internet websites referred to in this book,
and does not guarantee that any content on such websites is, or will remain,
accurate or appropriate

A CIP catalogue record for this book is available from the British Library

This publication is printed on acid-free paper

For Laura
For Dylan

CONTENTS

List of Illustrations — ix
Preface and Acknowledgements — xi
List of Abbreviations — xv

    Introduction: What are Lodging Ranges? — 1
1. A Room of One's Own — 47
2. Expressions of Individuality and Collectivity — 97
3. The Theatre of Display — 139
4. The Spaces Between — 179
    Envoi: Narratives in Stone and Space — 211

Glossary — 223
Gazetteer A — 229
Gazetteer B — 233
Bibliography — 239
Index — 251

ILLUSTRATIONS

TABLES

1	Provisions recorded in lodging ranges	52
2	Approximate sizes of rooms recorded within lodging, vicarial and collegiate ranges	94

FIGURES

1	Map showing locations of lodging ranges	8
2	Paired garderobes at Thornbury Castle	55
3	The garderobe tower at Haddon Hall	58
4	Paired garderobes at Amberley Castle	59
5	Paired doors and evenly spaced windows at Dartington Hall	64
6	Plan of Dartington Hall	65
7	Engraving of Dartington Hall by S. and N. Buck	67
8	Plan of Dartington Hall's western lodging range	68
9	Entrance with removed north–south stairway at Dartington Hall	70
10	Entrance with removed south–north stairway at Dartington Hall	71
11	Plan of Haddon Hall	77
12	West range of Haddon Hall	79
13	Ground-floor plan of Haddon Hall's lodging range	80
14	First-floor plan of Haddon Hall's lodging range	81
15	A selection of rooms from lodging, vicarial and collegiate ranges	85
16	Simplified depiction of Fastolf's chambers	90
17	Disparity between windows and fireplaces at Amberley Castle	105
18	The three-sided courtyard of Gainsborough Hall	107
19	Phased plan of Gainsborough Hall	109

20	Plans of the ground, first and second floors at Gainsborough Hall	110
21	The uniform external façade at Gainsborough Hall	113
22	Plan of Caister Castle	118
23	The south-west range of Caister Castle	120
24	Plan of Caister Castle's inner courtyard	122
25	North-west range at Caister Castle	124
26	Wingfield Manor from afar	142
27	Plan of Wingfield Manor	147
28	The remains of the stair turret at Wingfield Manor	149
29	Ground-floor plan of the lodging range at Wingfield Manor	150
30	Provisions included within the lodging range at Wingfield Manor	151
31	First-floor plan of the lodging range at Wingfield Manor	153
32	Plan of Thornbury Castle	160
33	Thornbury Castle's cross range	162
34	First-floor plan of the lodging range at Thornbury Castle	163
35	The provisions included in Thornbury Castle's lodging range	164
36	The uniformity of Thornbury Castle's lodging range	171
37	The illusory quality of Dartington Hall's lodging range	172
38	The northern extent of Middleham Castle's lodging range	188
39	The garderobe tower at Middleham Castle	190
40	The remains of the lodging range at Bishop's Waltham Palace including the farmhouse and the bake-brewhouse	194
41	Plan of Bishop's Waltham Palace	196
42	Ground-floor plan of Middleham Castle	200
43	First-floor plan of Middleham Castle showing position of the bridge	201

Full credit details, where needed, are provided in the captions to the images in the text. The author and publisher are grateful to institutions and individuals for permission to reproduce the materials in which they hold copyright. Every effort has been made to trace the copyright holders; apologies are offered for any omission, and the publisher will be pleased to add any necessary acknowledgement in subsequent editions.

PREFACE AND ACKNOWLEDGEMENTS

When I visited Wingfield Manor I found myself winding along Derbyshire's lanes with the great house in sight but with no indication of the road to take to gain access. As it dipped in and out of view, standing above a thicket of mature trees at the base of a natural knoll, I noted the chaos of chimney stacks and garderobe columns. When I left the car and made my way closer still, my eyes were fixed upwards in an attempt to fathom each detail on display. I approached the gatehouse leading to the outer courtyard and was embedded into the shadow of two rooms protruding from either side of the doorway. Eager to get to the lodging range, I attempted to look ahead and into the courtyard. I was faced not with the intact doors which would have confronted the medieval visitor but with dense vegetation; my view was obscured and my movement was slowed. The enclosing shadow gave way to darkness within the gatehouse and I began to deconstruct the space in which I stood. I perceived the gatehouse's unmistakable use – allowing entry – and its functions – forcing a stop and instilling intimidation. The functions were not as readily discernible, rather they were only perceived by looking beyond the utilitarian use.

As I was standing in Wingfield's inner courtyard, the lodging range stood out to me as the part yet to be understood: the *why* behind its construction was unknown. My queries only increased as I viewed its unmistakable uniform architecture: paired garderobes, equally-sized spaces repeated between features, an overall symmetry. This overt *sameness* was at odds with the array of typically heterogeneous medieval features seen elsewhere at the great house. The display before me was almost unique in medieval buildings – what was its meaning? I recalled advice from my studies at university: the only way to understand buildings is to spend time with them.

I have been inordinately privileged to be able to spend time with buildings over the course of my career, in various countries and with colleagues and students, and I have developed a routine, for better or worse. I spend time really looking at each architectural feature – my background in archaeology forces me to focus on the minutiae – what type of arch adorns that window, what is the construction sequence? I draw, photograph, measure. Then I turn to the wider scale, the surrounding landscape, the view outwards from the building. It was during one of these instances of zooming my scrutiny in and out that I noticed the illusory architecture. I was muddled by which of the windows I had drawn and which I had not. On numerous occasions at different sites I started again and recounted: how many identical doors are there? This encouraged me to explore what others viewed when they visited a great house, and my interests extended from architecture to spatial analysis and visuality.

I followed the route a guest to the great house might have taken, leaving the gateway and moving past the lodging ranges towards the hall. As I did so, I contemplated the fact that the befuddlement I experienced was a deliberate tool used by the medieval lords: perplexity was the intention. Spending longer still in these spaces allowed other architectural trickeries to be detected. One was required to turn in certain places, was confronted with the exaggerated heights and widths of particular elements, and denied a view of the final destination. It became clear that the great house was a display of confusion. While we cannot truly step into the shoes of the medieval audience (and I need not quote from Lowenthal's *The Past is a Foreign Country* here), this approach of spending time in their spaces has yielded and will continue to yield new information. It assists our understanding of the past, not as a series of solitary events, births and deaths, but a tangled compilation of experiences, principles, perceptions. And so I embarked upon writing this book.

Many of the great houses included in this book are in private ownership, and my earnest thanks goes to each and every owner. It goes also to the numerous staff working in these buildings, with particular gratitude to Gail at Haddon Hall, Henny at Amberley, and the English Heritage staff at Middleham Castle and Gainsborough Hall. Thank you to the Historic England Archive staff in Swindon, who provided a huge amount of information which took them days to gather; in particular, thanks to Clare Broomfield for organising the archive requests. Thanks to Abigal Gray from Devon Rural Archive for granting access to documents on Old Newnham, and to Mr and Mrs Streeter, who live in Newnham, for inviting me in and showing me their home. Furthermore, to Alan Taylor, editor of the *Edgcombe Family Genealogy and History* for providing information on the Edgecumbe family tree, and to Rachel Hunt, National Trust House and Collections Manager at Cotehele, for information on Cotehele House.

PREFACE AND ACKNOWLEDGEMENTS

Thank you to Colin Johns from Wiltshire Historic Buildings Trust, and Dorothy Treasure from Wiltshire Buildings Record Office, who provided information on Brook Hall. Also to the tenants of Brook Hall, who offered further information on the manor, and to the family at Caister Castle for their generosity. My thanks to Steve Beck, who I met by chance at Brympton d'Evercy, and who sent a selection of reports on the manor house. Further thanks must go to Rob Edwards and Jill Collins from Cheshire Archaeology Planning Service for sourcing and sending reports on Ince Manor. Thank you to the SP Lohia Collection and the British Library for permitting reuse of images, and to Dylan Murphy for his superior photography skills, advice and patience.

Scholarship is a team effort, and this book builds on outstanding work by dozens of people. Whether it was a question (or comment) at a conference or the anonymous review of these chapters, I am grateful for your input. To the buildings folk – Laura Patrick, Karen Dempsey, Rachel Swallow, Kate Weikert, Jeroen Bouwmeester, Duncan Berryman and Martin Huggon – our conversations have always encouraged me and my ideas: I look forward to more of them. Thank you to Keith Lilley, Kate Giles and Colm Donnelly for their feedback on earlier versions of this work. My thanks go to the entire team at Boydell and Brewer, particularly Caroline Palmer, Elizabeth McDonald, Laura Bennetts and Christy Beale. My greatest appreciation is to Mark Gardiner, not only for his comments on an early chapter but for his encouragement in submitting it for review. His support remains something I can rely on: thank you.

Some of the concepts of this book emerged several years ago when I was at Queen's University Belfast. I had a huge amount of feedback, comments and pointers from colleagues there; indeed, too many instances to mention. Therefore I am grateful to the archaeology department for nurturing these ideas when they were just that. Some people in particular provided the metaphorical kicks required to pursue this research: thank you to Heather, Kate, Laura v. d. S., Lauren, Connie, Rachel, Francis, Jj, and especially the dream team: Grace, Dermot and Stuart.

I have been privileged to work with outstanding archaeologists (plus the odd art historian, geographer and historian) in Katholieke Universiteit Leuven, Trinity College Dublin, The University of Sheffield and Aarhus University. So many colleagues have imparted advice, lent a book or an ear: thank you. Individual appreciation is extended to Hedwig Schwall and Mark Hennessy for their guidance and friendship at KUL and TCD respectively.

The support I received from beyond the academy was instrumental in completing this book. Thank you to my family for their love and encouragement from afar: my parents, Carolyn and Michael; Susan, Niamh, Áine, Liam, Isabella, Dan and Nick. And closer to home, thank you to Patricia and Garvan for their enthusiasm, friendship and – often very practical – support.

This book is dedicated to two people who have contributed so much that thanking them alone is inadequate. To Laura, for always championing me onwards and never wavering in your confidence in me. And Dylan, for supporting me every second since we met: I could not have completed this without you.

How lucky I am to know you all.

ABBREVIATIONS

BL	British Library
OED	Oxford English Dictionary
Oxford DNB	Oxford Dictionary of National Biography
PAS	Portable Antiquities Scheme

INTRODUCTION: WHAT ARE LODGING RANGES?

The remains of medieval buildings provide insights into the way in which society lived, to the extent that we can suggest the ways people moved, with whom they interacted, which senses were heightened or diminished, and how buildings simultaneously reflected and shaped medieval life. By exploring the fabric and footprint of a building, archaeologists can attempt to decipher human experience in the past: the medieval lived experience.

This book explores lodging ranges, a type of collective-living building, built as part of the late medieval great house to accommodate middle- to high-ranking members of the household. They were often long ranges, occupying the side of a courtyard and divided into small yet grand rooms that were sometimes divided further into an office and bedchamber. The provisions created a comfortable space in which to live, including windows and fireplaces, often decorated, and a garderobe. Each room was provided with an individual door – a feature almost unheard of in the late medieval great house – that led from a courtyard or lobby into that room and that room only. These were low-occupancy, even single-occupancy spaces, and as such they were some of the most socially separated spaces in the great house, suggesting levels of privacy that would not become commonplace elsewhere in the house for centuries. This created some of the finest spaces within late medieval accommodation, drawing comparison with the suites of the ladies and lords at the head of the household.

The members of the household who occupied the lodging ranges are referred to as retainers: that is, a specific group of people, mostly men, who were tied to their lord by an indenture – a contract with indented top and bottom edges. Their indentures set out their payment in accommodation, bouche of court, livery, and cash in return for loyalty, whether genuine or otherwise, to their lord, and service in times of war and peace, including an obligation to bear arms if needed. Their accommodation provides a better understanding of their service, indicating that their role went beyond military service and superseded their obligation to bear arms. Lodging ranges indicate that retainers had roles integral to the running of the house: they were supporters, followers and servitors to their lord.

In addition to their use as accommodation, lodging ranges had multifaceted functions, from enforcing subtle social meanings to representing multiple identities. Their architecture reveals they were built to construct a sense of collective identity between people drawn from different families, harnessing them to the identity of their lord or lady. The early use of uniform elevations resulted in a strong architectural display of homogeneity, or a sense of sameness, that permeated from the fabric to its occupants.

Within the architectural display of collective identity there were expressions of individualism. Variations between rooms, in both size and provisions, created a hierarchy within the lodging ranges, a household in itself. Distinct differences, in access for example, were at times expressed explicitly; this ensured that the hierarchy was visible, in contrast to the outward uniformity and despite the flexible use of space we expect in medieval buildings. These hints of rigidity in the display of identities indicate that the architecture was one method used to control the occupants of lodging ranges. Control over their daily lives is clear in the ways in which the retainers' movement and sensory perceptions in the great house were curated, and it is likely that this control extended to any broader aspirations of social ascension. At this time of great social mobility, the display of social distance – that is, the distinction between social groups – was a central element of the lived experience. The architecture of lodging ranges, and the space in and around them, played a crucial role in creating social distance and ensuring that it remained static. As the following chapters will demonstrate, the very fabric of the lodging ranges and their manipulation of space were constructed to literally set in stone the identity of the retainer.

This control was administered through the lodging ranges, but it stemmed from the lord or lady at the head of the household. The overwhelming identity experienced when viewing lodging ranges was theirs: their wealth, status, authority. The lodging ranges were positioned within the great house to be seen by guests, and their architectural display was such that it exaggerated what was seen. Repeated doors and windows, equal spacing and overall uniformity were used on the façade to create a visual illusion that made the lodging range seem longer than it was. This bolstered the identity of the lord by emphasising to the medieval audience both their control over a large group of retainers and their wealth. An examination of the architecture reveals that lodging ranges, possibly more than any other element of the great house, displayed overlapping and competing identities and yet were one of the most critical and impactful of the lord's displays.

WHAT IS A LODGING RANGE?

The term 'lodging range' requires some explanation. A 'lodge' or 'lodging', as a noun, is defined as a small house or dwelling, particularly one that is temporary, or rooms leased within the same residence as the owner. 'To lodge', as a verb, similarly describes use of a temporary shelter. The term, deriving from the Old French *logier*, was used in the thirteenth and fourteenth centuries as both a noun and a verb.[1] In previous literature on medieval accommodation, William Pantin, Margaret Wood and Anthony Emery used the term 'lodgings' to define the auxiliary accommodation of the late medieval period, such as chantry houses, academic colleges, vicars choral houses, and household accommodation.[2] As such, the term has lost some of its connotations of being temporary when used in the archaeological context. Jane Grenville uses the term 'lodging ranges' to differentiate the household accommodation from the other types associated with the period.[3] Her definition distinguishes lodgings within a range or wing of a courtyard, which are the topic of this book, from the other small rooms dotted around the great house or other buildings. The distinction is important, as the lodging ranges invariably formed part of a courtyard, with their length contributing to a visual illusion that exaggerated their size. As well as the great houses, rows of lodgings were also found in vicarial and academic contexts. These provide useful comparisons with those of the great houses, as they were architecturally similar. Together, the lodgings created a social identity for an emerging middle class, or 'middling sort'; yet terminological distinction is important, as the meanings of the buildings were not one and the same.

Michael Thompson describes lodging ranges as an 'extended series of cellular lodgings'.[4] The definition used in this volume has avoided the use of 'cellular', as it implies uniformity in the size of rooms, which was not

---

1 OED, 'lodge' (2021) <https://www.oed.com/> [accessed 17 June 2021].
2 William Pantin, 'Chantry Priests' Houses and Other Medieval Lodgings', *Medieval Archaeology*, 3 (1959), 216–58; Margaret Wood, *The English Medieval House* (New York, 1965); Anthony Emery, *Greater Medieval Houses of England and Wales 1300–1500* (3 vols, Cambridge, 2000; 2000; 2006).
3 Jane Grenville, *Medieval Housing* (London, 1997).
4 Michael W. Thompson, 'The Architectural Context of Gainsborough Old Hall', in P. Lindley (ed.), *Gainsborough Old Hall* (Lincoln, 1991), pp. 13–20, at p. 15; Cellular lodging also in Christopher Woolgar, *The Great Household in Late Medieval England* (New Haven, 1999), p. 61.

always the case within a range or across examples. Rather, a key feature is the variety of rooms within lodging ranges, despite overtly uniform architecture displayed on the external façade (facing away from the great house) and particularly on the inner, courtyard-facing elevation. Appreciating that the uniform façades concealed the complex hierarchy within the lodging ranges is crucial for understanding their variety of functions. Thompson may have intended to highlight the small size of the rooms, which was one important way in which they were distinct from the more commonplace larger rooms of the great house. Rooms in lodging ranges varied from around 8m^2 to around 50m^2, which is small when compared to other types of accommodation, such as dormitories. Some of the larger rooms were also subdivided into an office or hall-type room and a bedchamber, as at Haddon Hall, Derbyshire, or into multiple bedchambers radiating from a central communal space, as in the comparable collegiate ranges. The issues of detecting such important divisions are addressed in Chapter 1.

Based on the examination of previous definitions for auxiliary accommodation, and investigation of the extant remains, the following definition of medieval lodging ranges has been created: *Lodging ranges were two- or three-storey, collective-living buildings. They were associated with the courtyards of late medieval great houses and were built to house a lord's mid- to high-status retainers. They are identifiable by repeated architecture, uniform façade and high-status features, in particular individual doors.*

LODGING RANGES AND THE LATE MEDIEVAL GREAT HOUSE

The definition created above for lodging ranges sets out their relationship to the great house. In this book, *great house* is used rather than *manor house* or *castle*. This is in order to avoid the connotations each of these terms carries, particularly that of castle which, despite considerable strides in castellology to provide a more accurate definition of the term,[5] is often taken to imply a defensive structure, which is wholly inaccurate for the time period discussed here. In addition, it is sometimes used indiscriminately when a more appropriate term may exist. 'Manor house' is a more accurate term, although not quite correct either. Manor houses, as defined by Christopher King, were the 'principal residences of the majority of the

---

5   For example: Oliver Creighton, *Castles and Landscapes: Power, Community and Fortification in Medieval England* (Sheffield, 2005); Oliver Creighton and Robert Liddiard, 'Fighting Yesterday's Battle: Beyond War or Status in Castle Studies', *Medieval Archaeology*, 52 (2008), 161–9; John Goodall, *The English Castle: 1066–1650* (New Haven, 2011).

aristocracy', yet the term is used primarily for houses of the gentry,[6] which were much smaller than those of their noble counterparts.[7] As we move through the examples in this book, it is clear that lodging ranges were built as part of the large houses of the principal echelons of society – the upper nobility and, indeed, royals. Descending the ranks, the gentry were socially below the nobility, but there was no clear divide between the nobility and upper gentry, nor, at times, between their houses,[8] and some lodging ranges were built by gentry who were climbing the social ladder. Generally, however, the examples of great houses in which lodging ranges were built were just that: great. They were substantial in physical size, significant in their architectural display, numerous in their occupants, and ruled by a noble lord or lady. As a term, 'great house' is much more suited to the uppermost aristocratic houses, providing a helpful distinction from those built by the lower gentry.

Across England and Wales, there are sixty-five known examples of lodging ranges built between c.1300 and c.1570.[9] Awareness of their existence comes from their descriptions, sometimes with the term lodging range, sometimes without, in the plethora of work published on great houses.[10] Details on the lodging ranges themselves tend to be brief, possibly because the scale and complexity of the house often made it easy

---

6   Christopher King, 'The Organization of Social Space in Late Medieval Manor Houses', *Archaeological Journal*, 160:1 (2003), 104–24.
7   For manor houses both predating and contemporary with the great houses see Gwyn Meirion-Jones and Michael Jones (eds), *Manorial Domestic Buildings in England and Northern France*, Society of Antiquaries Occasional Papers 15 (London, 1993); especially John Blair, 'Hall and Chamber: English Domestic Planning 1000–1250', in Gwyn Meirion-Jones and Michael Jones (eds), *Manorial Domestic Buildings in England and Northern France*, Society of Antiquaries Occasional Papers 15 (London, 1993), pp. 1–21.
8   Peter Coss, 'Knights, Esquires and the Origins of Social Gradation in England', *Transactions of the Royal Historical Society*, 5 (1995), 155–78; Christine Senecal, 'Keeping Up with the Godwinsons: In Pursuit of Aristocratic Status in Late Anglo-Saxon England', *Anglo-Norman Studies*, 23 (2000), 251–66, at p. 252; Jill Campbell, 'Architectural design and exterior display in gentry houses in 14th- and 15th-century England' (unpublished Ph.D. dissertation, Queen's University Belfast, 2012).
9   See the gazetteers on pp. 229–38 for the full list of known examples, extant and lost; Sarah Kerr, 'A study of lodging ranges in late medieval England' (unpublished Ph.D. dissertation, Queen's University Belfast, 2016).
10 Kerr, 'Lodging ranges'; Wood, *House*; Emery, *Greater Medieval Houses*, vols 1–3; Grenville, *Housing*; Robert Liddiard (ed.), *Late Medieval Castles* (Woodbridge, 2016); Charles Coulson, 'Fourteenth-Century Castles in Context: Apotheosis or Decline?', in Robert Liddiard (ed.), *Late Medieval Castles* (Woodbridge, 2016), pp. 19–40; Philip Dixon and Beryl Lott, 'The Courtyard and the Tower', *Journal of the British Archaeological Association*, 146 (1993), 93–101; Philip Dixon, 'The Manor-Houses of the Anglo-Scottish Border', in Gwyn Meirion-Jones and Michael Jones (eds),

to overlook an area which was poorly understood. In addition, certain foci of research have entered and fallen from favour. In response to the nineteenth-century focus on castles and cathedrals, twentieth-century architectural historians and archaeologists, many of them amateurs, turned their attention to smaller buildings, which by the end of the century included peasant housing. Lodging ranges were yet to have their moment.

The study of buildings shifted its emphasis towards discrete features, such as the services or the hall, a change possibly accelerated by archaeological rather than architectural methods, as the former discipline's excavation training developed stalwart attention to detail. Once these features were understood, the focus turned to setting building types in their particular chronological context, as seen most clearly in the vast scholarship on the development of the hall.[11] The granularity of recent archaeological scholarship, alongside the absence of a complete work on lodging ranges, has undoubtedly led to my focus on these buildings. However, Wood and Pantin,[12] and their work from over five decades ago, provide some of the most useful descriptions and analyses of lodging ranges. They both focused on the rooms within the ranges in the context of other auxiliary late medieval accommodation.

The spatial distribution of known lodging ranges is fairly even across England, and there are two examples in Wales. It is highly likely there are more examples to be found elsewhere. For example, Dunluce Castle, in County Antrim, Northern Ireland, retains some evidence of uniform architecture in the outer ward. Despite the different contexts, there may have been similarities in the desire to use architecture to create identities and illusions. In England, where the majority of known lodging ranges exist, there is a slight concentration between the Humber and the Exe, which allows a tentative suggestion that lodging ranges were more commonplace in the area referred to as the Central Province. During the late middle ages, this area was characterised by tightly nucleated settlements and open fields, which were enclosed during the movement away from grain cultivation to more pastoral agriculture.[13] The subsequent

---

Manorial Domestic Buildings in England and Northern France, Society of Antiquaries Occasional Papers 15, (London, 1993), pp. 22–48.
11   Blair, 'Hall'; Mark Gardiner, 'Conceptions of Domestic Space in the Long Term – the Example of the English Medieval Hall', in Mette Svart Kristiansen, Else Roesdahl and James Graham-Campbell (eds), *Medieval Archaeology in Scandinavia and Beyond: History, Trends and Tomorrow* (Aarhus, 2015), pp. 313–33.
12   Wood, *House*; Pantin, 'Lodgings'.
13   Brian Roberts and Stuart Wrathmell, *Region and Place: A Study of English Rural Settlement* (London, 2002); Stephen Rippon, Piers Dixon, and Bob Silvester, 'Overview: The Form and Pattern of Medieval Settlement', in Christopher Gerrard

high rents resulted in an economically prosperous area administered by wealthy lords. Lodging ranges were primarily (but not exclusively) built by the most prosperous in late medieval society, as they required wealth both to construct the buildings and to pay the staff within. Thus a concentration in the affluent Central Province is likely to be a true picture of distribution rather than, for example, the result of uneven survival rates (Figure 1).

A two-storey range at Wells Palace, Somerset, is the earliest extant example of a lodging range suggested in the previous literature.[14] It was built in the early to mid-thirteenth century, although any characteristics of a lodging range are concealed today. The period between the mid-fourteenth and early sixteenth centuries appears to be when the majority of known examples of lodging ranges were built, suggesting that they were fashionable for a relatively short period: they appear in the archaeological record almost abruptly and cease to be built in a similarly sudden way. Any development towards the fully-formed lodging range is absent from the current archaeological record; in fact, progression towards that plan can be traced only through the vicarial rather than the great-house context. It seems that there was no long slow development towards the inclusion of lodging ranges in the great house. Rather, they were not required until the social and cultural context was 'just-so' in the fourteenth century.

Growth of the Household and House

Part of this context is the increase in size of the late medieval household; that is, the number of people who lived and worked together under the same roof. Maryanne Goldberg and P. J. P. Kowaleski set out in their introduction that, in the late fourteenth century, when the term *hous(e)hold* first appeared, it alluded to both the physical house and the relationships among its occupants.[15] For clarity here, however, I will use the term 'household' for the group living in the house rather than for the house itself, as a distinction is important when discussing the growth of one or the other.

The surge in examples of lodging ranges from the mid-fourteenth century onwards suggests that accommodation in this form simply was not required until the great household grew to what Kate Mertes

and Alejandra Gutiérrez (eds), *The Oxford Handbook of Later Medieval Archaeology in Britain* (Oxford, 2018), pp. 171–92.
14 Emery, *Greater Medieval Houses*, Vol. 3, p. 669. See the gazetteers on pp. 229–38 for the full list of known examples, extant and lost.
15 Maryanne Kowaleski and P. J. P. Goldberg, *Medieval Domesticity: Home, Housing and Household in Medieval England* (Cambridge, 2008), p. 2.

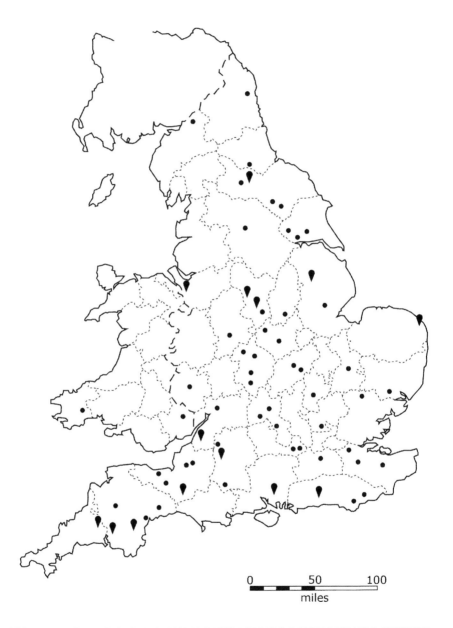

FIG. 1 MAP OF ENGLAND AND WALES, WITH BORDERS OF THE HISTORIC COUNTIES, SHOWING THE SPREAD OF KNOWN LODGING RANGES. THE LARGER ICONS INDICATE THOSE DISCUSSED HERE.

describes as 'monstrous dimensions',[16] although there is ongoing debate on just how monstrously large it became.[17] Christopher Woolgar puts forward a restrained interpretation of the late medieval house. He uses diet accounts to estimate the total size of a selection of fourteenth-century households and suggested that, prior to the Black Death, c.1350, houses of the uppermost elites could have been as Mertes describes. After this, he argues, households generally diminished.[18] There is conflicting evidence to consider, however, and Woolgar concedes that his sample is small; additionally, there were exceptions, particularly amongst the households of the upper nobility.

A number of key broad cultural trends may have driven the growth of the late medieval household. There was a transition in the thirteenth century away from a peripatetic household to a more settled arrangement with longer periods in fewer residences. Mertes suggests that by the fourteenth century households spent up to eight months in one house rather than less than a month, as they had in the previous century.[19] This was in part the result of reduced reliance on the estate's resources and crops and greater use of commerce to obtain food and dispose of surpluses. By the end of the fourteenth century, houses were intended and designed for almost continuous occupation, encouraged by the centralisation of government in Westminster.[20] This meant that households were required year-round and potentially there was a need for more servants and staff to manage purchasing and storage to aid longer occupation in one residence. This was far from an insignificant task; indeed, the officer in charge of the wardrobe (the financial department for the lord's and lady's treasure) was crucial to the running of the house. The wardrober was often a learned man of gentry rank, sometimes a close acquaintance of the family, with command over multiple staff, including clerks and deputies.[21] They dealt with acquiring and maintaining all manner of expensive items, from clothes and jewellery to armour, weapons, crockery, spices and wax.[22] In large households, the management of goods and purchasing was divided

---

16 Kate Mertes, *The English Noble Household 1250–1600* (Oxford, 1988), p. 185.
17 For commentary on specific case studies in the late fifteenth century see Audrey Thorstad, *The Culture of Castles in Tudor England and Wales* (Woodbridge, 2019), p. 92.
18 Woolgar, *Household*, p. 14.
19 Mertes, *Household*, p. 185. See also: Woolgar, *Household*, p. 187.
20 Wood, *House*, p. 49; Woolgar, *Household*, p. 47.
21 Woolgar, *Household*, pp. 17, 38; Anthony Emery, *Dartington Hall* (Oxford, 1970), p. 43; Derek Keene, 'Wardrobes in the City: Houses of Consumption, Finance and Power', *Thirteenth Century England*, VII (1999), 61–80; Emery, *Greater Medieval Houses*, Vol. 3, p. 29.
22 Keene, 'Wardrobes', pp. 61, 66.

between more than one department: for example, cloth and spices would be controlled by a separate department, also called the wardrobe or the Great Wardrobe in the royal household.[23] The importance of the wardrober and the multiplication of financial departments indicate that continuous occupation in one house required constant staffing, and potentially more staff, servants and slaves.[24]

The household was highly and hierarchically organised, with clearly defined staff and roles. As a microcosm of the patriarchal and patrilineal society, it was headed often – but not always – by a male; contemporary court records, devotional manuals, private correspondence, poetry and literature attest that women, particularly widows, did head households, and supported a household community.[25] Women built great houses, generating distinctive patterns and features not seen in other houses.[26] They commanded households at various life stages and, when a woman married, she brought her household to her new alliance.[27] Even when a household was headed by a married male, his wife took control when he was absent. And, due to the frequent absence of men in the household,[28] it has been argued that women did the majority of household administration, or at least the same amount as their husbands.[29] Any person who controlled land, was dominant in a social or political relationship, or held power over others in an elite context, was in a position of lordship. Lordship carried

---

23 Woolgar, *Household*, p. 17. Woolgar reassures that any confusion between departments rests only with the modern reader and not with the contemporary household.
24 For discussion on why the term 'slaves' remains contentious despite growing awareness and scholarship that slavery, and other types of unfreedom, were common during the medieval period, see Hannah Baker, *That Most Precious Merchandise: The Mediterranean Trade in Black Sea Slaves, 1260-1500* (Philadelphia, 2019). In summary, she states that a prevailing Christian amelioration narrative, supported by Marxist historiography, has concealed the prevalence of slavery in medieval Europe. For details on slavery in medieval England see, for example, Allen J. Frantzen and Douglas Moffat (eds), *The Work of Work Servitude, Slavery and Labor in Medieval England* (Glasgow, 1994).
25 Nicola McDonald, 'Fragments of (Have Your) Desire', in Maryanne Kowaleski and P. J. P. Goldberg (eds), *Medieval Domesticity: Home, Housing and Household in Medieval England* (Cambridge, 2008), pp. 232–58.
26 Roberta Gilchrist, *Gender and Archaeology: Contesting the Past* (Abingdon, 1999); Matthew Johnson, *Behind the Castle Gate: From Medieval to Renaissance* (London, 2002), p. 8.
27 Johnson, *Castle*, p. 64.
28 Jennifer Ward, *English Noblewomen in the Later Middle Ages* (London, 1992).
29 Linda E. Mitchell, 'The Lady Is a Lord: Noble Widows and Land in Thirteenth-Century Britain', *Historical Reflections/Réflexions Historiques*, 18:1 (1992), 71–97, at p. 93.

certain responsibilities which needed to be undertaken and, in return, it demanded service, loyalty and respect: this relationship was embedded in the hierarchical society, not in the sex of those involved. Therefore, when the lord or head of the household is mentioned, this might refer to a man or a woman. A lord was male or female; the singular 'they' will be used when speaking in general terms when the sex of the lord is unknown.[30]

It is often suggested that the remainder of a household consisted predominantly of men,[31] regardless of whether there was a male or female at its head. Woolgar uses the accounts of Eleanor of Castile's household to indicate that fewer than 10 per cent of the household were women;[32] however, it is well established that historical accounts were strongly gender biased in favour of men, including in the context of retaining household staff.[33] In addition, archaeological and historical research are not without bias. Margaret Conkey and Janet Spector establish that our knowledge about the past reflects the context in which it is produced; that is, today's patriarchal society whereby white men are privileged above others perpetuates gender stereotypes and androcentric perspectives in the past.[34] The gender imbalance in archaeological research and publication, within both academia and professional practice, has resulted in medieval households being assumed male by default, and any deviation otherwise has to be proven.[35] As such, some research on medieval households is void of any critical analysis of sex and gender while at the same time making presumptions about divisions of labour, social structures and roles, and the presence of women in various contexts.[36]

---

30 Following Mark Gardiner and Susan Kilby, 'Perceptions of Medieval Settlement', in Christopher Gerrard and Alejandra Gutiérrez (eds), *The Oxford Handbook of Later Medieval Archaeology in Britain* (Oxford, 2018), pp. 210–25.
31 Tom McNeill, *Castles* (London, 1992), p. 29.
32 First wife of Edward I: Woolgar, *Household*, p. 8.
33 Gordon McKelvie, *Bastard Feudalism, English Society and the Law: the Statutes of Livery 1390–1520* (Woodbridge, 2020); for an overview of gender bias within archaeological research see Karen Dempsey, 'Gender and Medieval Archaeology: Storming the Castle', *Antiquity*, 93:369 (2019), 772–88.
34 Margaret W. Conkey and Janet D. Spector, 'Archaeology and the Study of Gender', *Archaeological Method and Theory*, 7 (1984), 1–38; Dempsey, 'Storming'.
35 Dempsey, 'Storming', p. 782; Emily Hanscam and Robert Witcher, 'Women in Antiquity: An Analysis of Gender and Publishing in a Global Archaeology Journal', *Journal of Field Archaeology*, 48:2 (2023), 87–101. See sweeping statements in, for example, Anthony Emery, 'Late-Medieval Houses as an Expression of Social Status', *Historical Research*, 78 (2005), 140–61; McNeill, *Castles*.
36 Alison Wylie, 'Gender Archaeology/Feminist Archaeology', in Elisabeth A. Bacus (ed.), A Gendered Past: A Critical Bibliography of Gender in Archaeology (Ann Arbor, 1993).

In the three decades, thereabouts, since Roberta Gilchrist outlined the dearth of knowledge in relation to women and archaeology, much research has sought to rectify this.[37] While this has allowed for the much needed insight into medieval women, it has, as Karen Dempsey says, led to a 'filling in the gaps' approach rather than a re-evaluation of the assumptions on which pre-existing interpretations were based.[38] More recently, supported by social questions and interpretations occurring in archaeology more broadly, buildings archaeology has acknowledged that great houses functioned in multiple, even contradictory ways. The medieval household, even if predominantly male, was not hermetically sealed; rather, it was fluid, with staff and guests coming and going, and it was sexually and socially diverse.[39]

In addition to its sexual composition, the household was a gendered environment; that is, it contributed to the social processes that produced and reproduced distinctions in gender identities.[40] It is well accepted within archaeological discourse, and beyond, that gender is a performance of socially constructed identities.[41] However, Marianne Moen has highlighted that gender archaeology remains a marginalised sub-discipline, and Dempsey remarks that studies discussing LGBTQIA+ perspectives of gender are exceptionally rare.[42] Despite this, archaeology has accepted that gender is fluid, non-binary and non-normative, and it is a growing area within archaeological research.[43] Household members,

---

37 Roberta Gilchrist, 'Women's archaeology? Political feminism, gender theory and historical revision', *Antiquity*, 65:248 (1991), 495–501; also highlighted in Conkey and Spector, 'Gender'; some main works on women and archaeology include Gilchrist, *Gender and Archaeology* and Roberta Gilchrist, *Gender and Material Archaeology: The Archaeology of Religious Women* (Abingdon, 1994); in relation to buildings, see: Karen Dempsey, 'Planting new ideas: A feminist gaze on medieval castles', *Château Gaillard: Études de Castellologie Médiévale*, 29 (2021), 85–98; Amanda Richardson, 'Gender and Space in the Later Middle Ages', in Christopher Gerrard and Alejandra Gutiérrez (eds), *The Oxford Handbook of Later Medieval Archaeology in Britain* (Oxford, 2018), pp. 805–18; and for the Tudor period, Audrey Thorstad, 'Living in an Early Tudor Castle: Households, Display, and Space, 1485-1547' (unpublished Ph.D. dissertation, University of Leeds, 2015).
38 Dempsey, 'Storming', p. 777.
39 Richardson, 'Gender and Space', at pp. 813, 815.
40 Johnson, *Castle*, p. 90; Dawn Hadley, *Masculinity in Medieval Europe* (London, 1999).
41 Judith Butler, 'Performative Acts and Gender Constitution: An Essay in Phenomenology and Feminist Theory', *Theatre Journal*, 40:4 (1988), 519–31.
42 Marianne Moen, 'Gender and Archaeology: Where Are We Now?', *Archaeologies*, 15 (2019), 206–26; Dempsey, 'Storming', p. 778. LGBTQIA+ is an abbreviation for lesbian, gay, bisexual, transgender, queer or questioning, intersex, asexual, and more.
43 For example: Roberta Gilchrist, 'The archaeology of sex and gender', in B.

rather than being a monolithic male cohort, had gender identities which were produced socially, curated, performed, and variable. Their buildings created and reinforced these identities, with spaces within becoming representations of medieval gender ideologies. Despite this, gendered spaces were often transcended.[44]

At its most basic, a medieval household comprised four fundamental departments. There was a pantry and a buttery, in which the staff were responsible for, respectively, bread and napery, and ale and wine. While these were departments, the rooms associated with these departments, located at the low end of the hall, have taken on the same names. In addition, departments of the kitchen and marshalsea were necessary. The more wide-ranging the needs of the lords, the more departments they had, which, in turn, increased the number of staff and complicated the household's hierarchy. Households of the upper nobility consistently included certain departments. For example, as in the royal household, a noble household had officers of gentle background serving as steward, chamberlain, controller, treasurer, cofferer, wardrober, hall marshal and butler. The chamberlain was charged with looking after the lord's private rooms, the treasurer was responsible for the accounts and expenditure, the cofferer controlled the money chests, and the hall marshal controlled all the procedures relating to the hall. Each department was headed by an officer, usually male, who was in charge of a number of staff.[45] So there were numerous small hierarchies within a wider household hierarchy, directed by the lord. This fragmentation into so many administrative departments hints at the household's complexity: this is further emphasised by Mertes's suggestion that each household structure was different and may have changed under a new lord, generation, social situation, or time period.[46] The hierarchical and well defined arrangement of the household may imply – perhaps imprecisely – that households grew in size, thus requiring more stringent structuring, but it would be misleading to conflate, without careful consideration, growing complexity with growing size.

Throughout the late medieval period, even if households did not grow monstrously vast, those of the upper elites comprised a substantial group of people. Woolgar argues that in the fourteenth century the royal household comprised between 400 and 700 staff, servants and slaves, whereas Henry I (d. 1135) had a significantly smaller 150. In 1318, the household ordinance of Edward II listed a minimum of 363 staff, with seventy-six officers in

---

Cunliffe, C. Gosden and R. Joyce (eds), *The Oxford Handbook of Archaeology* (Oxford, 2009), pp. 1029–47; Demspey, 'Storming'.
44 Richardson, 'Gender and Space', p. 815.
45 Wood, *House*, pp. 177–8; Emery, *Greater Medieval Houses*, Vol. 3, p. 28; Mertes, *Household*, p. 57.
46 Mertes, *Household*, p. 18.

roles pertinent to the running of the household, including wardrober, steward, treasurer, chaplain, confessor and almoner. There were further servants assigned to duties relating to food preparation and service, with thirty-nine for the hall, thirty for the pantry and buttery, and forty-two for the kitchen and larder. The department of the marshalsea comprised 129, excluding the grooms and valets for horses beyond the main court.[47] In these instances, the huge numbers of household members were reflected in the size of the houses. At Windsor Castle, for example, the Norman keep was upgraded in 1356, alongside new kitchens, hall, chapel and lodging ranges, creating a sprawling 'castle-palace'.[48]

The growth of late medieval royal households is evident in both the documentary evidence and the architecture. This suggests that the development of the 'castle-palace' or late medieval palace (the terminological issues with 'castle' for this time period transcend social ranks) was in part the product of the growth of the household. Looking slightly lower in the social hierarchy, to the nobility, evidence from the buildings themselves supports Mertes's assertion of vast household growth.[49] Great houses of noble lords were often either added to over generations, or rebuilt on a much larger scale than in previous centuries. The period under consideration here saw great houses built much larger than those before. Indeed, all of the examples of great houses with lodging ranges were considerable in scale. Some, such as Haddon Hall, began as a single-courtyard house. The fourteenth-century courtyard was added to over the course of the fifteenth century in at least two building phases, increasing the scale of the house and enveloping a late twelfth-century church into a new outer courtyard. The construction of Dartington Hall, Devon, was rather different: it was built on a cleared site around the turn of the fifteenth century. It comprised a small inner courtyard preceded by the largest undivided outer courtyard of its time. For Grenville, the scale of the great house meant that there 'can be no doubt that sizes of households were growing in the later medieval period'.[50]

Mertes and Grenville are in agreement that the house and household both increased in size as a result of the emergence of the static household. While it is clear from the archaeological record that the physical houses of the social elites increased in size, this should not automatically be conflated with the household increasing in size, tempting though this is. It is worth considering reasons why the growth of the house might outstrip that of the

---

47 Woolgar, *Household*, pp. 9–10.
48 Tom Beaumont James, 'Medieval Palaces and Royal Houses', in Christopher Gerrard and Alejandra Gutiérrez (eds), *The Oxford Handbook of Later Medieval Archaeology in Britain* (Oxford, 2018), pp. 371–85, at p. 376.
49 Mertes, *Household*, p. 185
50 Grenville, *Housing*, p. 114.

numbers within the household. One such reason is the greater emphasis placed on display across late medieval elite society; in terms of the house, this meant more elaborate and impressive architecture, parks and gardens. This was possible because, with fewer houses to support, more resources could be spent on those that were most frequently occupied: the owners had the means to build on a grander scale than before.[51] Additionally, the lord's frequent travel had been an opportunity to display wealth to those beyond the household, and now the same desire for display shifted onto the house itself, contributing to the expansion of the house plan.

This period also saw the specialisation of space: there were more rooms reserved for certain activities. Wardrobers, for example, had a specific series of rooms from which they carried out their work. The hall, once a 'theatre where many aspects of life were played', as described by Thompson,[52] shifted towards having fewer uses. While a 'decline' of the hall during the medieval period has been sufficiently disputed,[53] by the late medieval period it was reserved for ceremonial rather than everyday activities.[54] The parlour, for the family's everyday dining, was added to the great house plan, or created by converting the room under the solar at the high end of the hall, as was the case at Haddon c.1500.[55] Similarly, semi-specialised spaces for sleeping were emerging for the most elite household members.[56]

Specialised space allowed areas to be ascribed status and purposely gendered. The removal of cooking activities to separate kitchens indicates the creation of female-dominated spaces from the late fifteenth century.[57] Such spaces were not on the periphery: indeed, an elite woman's chambers would be a hive of activity. Their location, access or decorative imagery, however, demarcated these spaces as separate from others. The shift

---

51 Woolgar, *Household*, p. 47.
52 Michael Thompson, *The Medieval Hall: The Basis of Secular Domestic Life, 600–1600 AD* (Aldershot, 1995), p. 15.
53 See the nuanced rebuttal in: Grenville, *Housing*, p. 107; earlier discourse on the hall's 'decline' in Mark Girouard, *Life in the English Country House: A Social and Architectural History* (New Haven, 1978), p. 30; Thompson, *Hall*, p. 146; Wood, *House*; J. T. Smith, *English Houses 1200–1800: The Hertfordshire Evidence* (London, 1992), p. 25.
54 Grenville, *Housing*, p. 114.
55 Woolgar, *Household*, p. 145; Grenville, *Housing*, p. 115.
56 Although slightly beyond the temporal scope of this book, Sasha Handley describes how beds were moved from multi-functional areas into rooms primarily for sleeping and few other activities in the seventeenth century. See Sasha Handley, *Sleep in Early Modern England* (New Haven, 2016); and for progression towards this see: Thorstad, *Culture*, p. 157; Woolgar, *Household*, p. 68.
57 Matthew Johnson, *Housing Culture: Traditional Architecture in an English Landscape* (London, 1993); Richardson, 'Gender and Space', p. 811.

towards designated spaces required more rooms within the house than before: for example, rooms specifically for dancing and chapels for women appeared in the great-house plan.[58] While the use of rooms remained flexible throughout the medieval and early modern periods, more rooms were added or constructed, each with fewer uses.

A third factor to consider in the growth of the house rather than the household is the emergence of hints of privacy: that is, the medieval version of it. Mark Gardiner and Susan Kilby describe medieval privacy as the ability to be alone and remote from public gaze, and the freedom from intrusion. These were options available only to the most elite household members.[59] The lord's and lady's bedchambers were some of the most hidden spaces in the household, distinguished by few entry points and their location at the end of corridors or as the last of a series of rooms. They were low-occupancy spaces, with only the highest ranking staff staying in the bedchamber or the neighbouring room. This shift, which culminated in the separated rooms of the modern house, was intertwined with the specialisation of space. During the course of the late Middle Ages, rooms came to be occupied by fewer people and therefore greater numbers of rooms were required.

Houses grew in size because of the cumulative need for greater display, the specialism of space, lower-occupancy rooms and extra storage. It may be that, as the house increased in size for these reasons, the result was simply more space for each occupant and the activities they carried out, rather than an increase in the number of occupants to reach the same capacity as before. This argument could be extended to suggest that, while the physical size of the house increased, the overall household membership declined, as Woolgar asserts; however, this seems unlikely. If royal houses and households were increasing, as they clearly were, it is highly likely that the wealthiest of the nobility acted similarly, or attempted to. Much like the blending of ranks between nobility and gentry, in some ways (but not others) the same can be said for royalty and the upper nobility. Wood argues that noble houses attempted to reflect those of the royals in terms of administration and structure and comprised 'a vast personnel', simply on a slightly smaller scale.[60] It is highly probable, then, that houses grew in size also because of the growth of the household; it is, however, crucial to consider variability, particularly across social ranks.

58 Woolgar, *Household*, p. 68; Richardson, 'Gender and Space', p. 813.
59 Gardiner and Kilby, 'Perceptions', p. 216.
60 Wood, *House*, p. 177.

DEVELOPMENT TOWARDS LODGING RANGES

The great houses of upper gentry and noble families shared certain features, which were usually laid out in a single, double or multi-courtyard plan. These included the hall, the chapel, and usually the parlour; the lord's suites, along with others for the family; services, including the buttery, pantry and kitchen; a gateway with staff accommodation; stables, barns and storage rooms; and lodging ranges. The shifts and changes in many of these features can be traced from the relatively smaller, pre-fourteenth-century houses to the great houses of the mid-fourteenth century onwards through extant architecture and archaeologically recovered remains. Lodging ranges, however, appear in the great-house plan in the fourteenth century with little variation in their architecture and no indication in earlier houses of their development towards this, as noted above. This begs the question of 'proto-' lodging ranges: why is there a lack of evidence in the architectural record for something similar but not quite the wholly developed examples of later? They emerged and existed fully formed; their architecture and plan, and the ideas behind them, appear to have been completely developed prior to their first construction. The lack of proto-lodging ranges is summarised by Wood: 'A small garrison and staff would reside in the early castle permanently but it was not until the need arose for a larger body of retainers that special quarters were provided.'[61]

Her summary can be dissected into two reasons for the lack of proto-lodging ranges. First, there was simply no need for lodging ranges as, prior to the fourteenth century, there was no in-house retinue nor vast household to warrant their construction. Second, the smaller household of earlier years occupied chambers dotted around the house, for instance in the gatehouse or towers, while lower-status staff occupied spaces close to their place of work, such as corridors and service rooms. She also suggests that staff slept in the hall, an idea built upon by Thompson. His logical, if not evidential, argument suggests that the aisled hall allowed spaces along the long walls for sleeping compartments. He extends this to suggest that the approximate temporal relationship between the cessation of the aisled hall and the introduction of lodging ranges indicates the latter's use as sleeping quarters for household staff.[62] At Conwy Castle, Caernarfonshire, built by Edward I in the late thirteenth century, staff occupied chambers within the towers, with those of the highest rank in the ground-floor rooms of the inner courtyard. Of a similar date is Aydon Castle, Northumberland, which was built by Robert de Raymes c.1280. His smaller household may have lived within ground-floor rooms below the hall. Later, however, possibly

---

61 Wood, *House*, p. 180.
62 Thompson, *Hall*.

after a licence to crenellate granted in 1305, a range was constructed in the outer court. This may have been communal accommodation supporting the household's growth throughout the fourteenth century.[63]

Wood links the emergence of lodging ranges directly to the growth of the household. In particular, she stresses the 'need' for the addition of 'a large body of retainers' within the house,[64] which might be taken to subtly imply that they were required for their military abilities and protection. These overarching military connotations will be overturned later, and for now it should be reiterated that the term 'retainer' is useful for distinguishing a section of the household's hierarchy: as such, their inclusion in the household was one facet of the overall growth rather than the sole driver.

During the household's growth, principally before lodging ranges were built but when the need for them was becoming apparent, groups of auxiliary staff probably stayed in dormitories while smaller groups shared rooms where available: this would have been organised in relation to each person's status. In addition, staff could have stayed in wooden structures, possibly lean-tos, within courtyards or beyond.[65] It seems that there was no dedicated, universally accepted space for high-ranking household members across examples of elite residences prior to lodging range construction, although spaces such as above the gatehouse, above services, and within towers are frequently posited in the literature.[66] In addition, staff may have stayed for only a short time at the house, returning to their own dwellings afterwards.[67] This does not mean that sleeping in the great house was always *ad hoc*. Just as lodging ranges were the socially accepted form of accommodation from the mid-fourteenth century onwards, the various spaces utilised earlier were probably recognised as conventional places to sleep.

The suggestion that dormitories were used in the great house prior to lodging ranges is supported through comparison with ecclesiastical lodgings, specifically those built for vicars choral. Vicarial ranges were constructed from the early fourteenth century; however, unlike secular lodging ranges, they show a clear development from dormitory to individual houses. In their fully realised form they had strong architectural

---

63 Wood, *House*, p. 180.
64 Wood, *House*, p. 180.
65 Wood, *House*, p. 180.
66 Chambers in these places are discussed in: Wood, *House*, p. 137; Nicholas Cooper, *House of the Gentry* (London, 1999), pp. 57, 306; Blair, 'Hall', p. 14; Emery, *Dartington*, p. 170.
67 This was the case during the Norman period, from the second half of the eleventh century, and it is likely that this was accepted practice beyond this period, up to and including the time when lodging ranges were built: Wood, *House*, p. 180.

similarities – indeed, were almost identical visually – to lodging ranges in the late medieval great house. The occupants were vicars: that is, those who substituted for senior clerics. While the term was indiscriminately used for different grades within a cathedral hierarchy, vicars choral were a distinct group who emerged from minor clergy and replaced, in a variety of tasks, the secular canons. The landholdings of the latter were often considerable, meaning that they were regularly absent from the cathedral.[68]

An extensive excavation in York in the area between Goodramgate, St Andrewgate and Aldwark allowed the development of vicarial ranges to be identified, and David Stocker's descriptions of the associated social implications are fundamental to understanding lodging ranges.[69] The vicars choral complex was established in the mid-thirteenth century to the east of York Minster in the form of an enormous, timber, two-storey dormitory, probably seventeen bays long. The archaeological evidence suggests that on the front, north-facing elevation there may have been a staircase leading to the first-floor dormitory, and a reredorter – a communal garderobe – at the east end. In the 1330s and 1340s the range was divided into *cubiculi* accessed from a corridor, each occupied by an individual vicar, as illustrated in the cathedral's documentation. Therefore each vicar had an individual room with an individual door, and possibly an individual garderobe. By the 1370s the vicarial range had reached its final stage: a row of individual two-storeyed houses, with the lower parts of the walls clad, or partly clad, in stone.[70] The individual doors of the *cubiculi* were now on display, as the corridor was removed. A number of vicarial ranges were adapted into vicarial houses over the course of the fourteenth century. By the retention of the range plan, they created a row of terraced houses, such as those of Vicars' Close in Wells, Somerset.

Both Wood and Pantin suggest that the dormitories and *cubiculi* of vicarial ranges were precursors to the ranges found at academic colleges – here referred to as collegiate ranges.[71] Collegiate ranges were also constructed as two-storeyed ranges around a courtyard, and divided into smaller rooms. They differ from the individual vicars' rooms in that they housed three or four fellows of the college.[72] Each room comprised a number of

---

68   David Stocker, 'The Quest for One's Own Front Door: Housing the Vicars' Choral at the English Cathedrals', *Vernacular Architecture*, 36 (2005), 15–31; Barrie Dobson, 'The English Vicars Choral: An Introduction', in Richard Hall and David Stocker (eds), *Vicars Choral in English Cathedrals* (Oxford, 2005), pp. 1–10.
69   Excavation by York Archaeological Trust from 1973 to 1980: Julian Richards, 'The Bedern Foundry', *Archaeology of York*, 10:3 (London, 1993), 149–210; Stocker, 'Quest'.
70   Stocker, 'Quest', pp. 18–22.
71   Margaret Wood, 'Lincoln – 3 Vicars' Court', *Lincolnshire Historian*, 1:7 (1951), 281–6 (after Stocker, 'Quest'); Pantin, 'Lodgings'.
72   Wood, *House*, p. 183; Pantin, 'Lodgings', p. 243.

small studies radiating from a central chamber, the number of the former correlating to the number who lived there. These low-occupancy rooms were reserved for graduate fellows, with the majority of the college students sleeping in dormitories, academic halls, or inns. Winchester College, for example, built 1380–86, had rooms for fellows on the first floor with the rooms following the plan above, whereas the ground floor comprised only six dormitories for seventy boys.[73]

In the earliest academic colleges, prior to the development of the collegiate range, students, both undergraduate and graduate, occupied dormitories, or space in the hall, or rented rooms in the host town.[74] While little evidence of these spaces remains, one such is Tackley's Inn, Oxford, built c.1320. Tackley's was an academic hall: that is, a place for students to live while studying nearby. While this example housed students prior to the construction of their collegiate ranges, other examples were in use right through to the sixteenth century for undergraduates and less privileged graduates.[75] In its fourteenth-century form, Tackley's had two distinct parts, north and south, separated by a spine wall. The northern segment was parallel to the street and comprised street-fronted shops with cellars below and rooms above. The western end of the southern segment contained a hall measuring 10 by 6 metres and open to the roof. To the east of the hall was a slightly smaller chamber measuring 7.5m by 5m, the two separated by a passageway leading from the street. Above the chamber was a further room of the same size overlooking a courtyard to the south. Tackley's was built by Roger le Mareschal; however, it is not known whether it was actually designed to house students or if this simply happened. It may be more likely that it was originally intended to have a different function, as it seems that initially only the southern segment served students, while the north functioned as an inn above the shops. Adam de Brome acquired Tackley's in 1324 and installed the first scholars of the College of the Blessed Mary, which just a few years later would be renamed as Oriel College, Oxford. They occupied the southern section, living together communally within the large chambers. By 1329, de Brome had acquired a house called La Oriole and the scholars were moved there.[76]

Urban centres, therefore, provided housing for graduate students who would later move to the collegiate ranges, and other students who travelled back and forth from their college throughout their education. Similarly, urban accommodation, in the form of inns, may have been utilised by

---

73 Wood, *House*, p. 184; Pantin, 'Lodgings', p. 247.
74 Pantin, 'Lodgings', p. 244.
75 William Pantin, 'Tackley's Inn, Oxford', *Oxoniensia*, 7 (1942), 80–93, at p. 80.
76 Pantin, 'Tackley's', pp. 80–1, 88.

members of the great house. A widespread comprehensive study of inns, their architecture, social role and temporary residents is yet to take place; however, county-specific studies by Edward Roberts and John Hare are useful.[77] They indicate that inns emerged in the early fourteenth century, just before lodging ranges. Their emergence was probably in response to the commercial expansion of the thirteenth century, with, by the fourteenth century, around ten to twenty inns in provincial capitals and county towns, two to five in market towns, and fewer again in small towns and rural areas.[78] Data from Hare's study in the counties of Hampshire and Wiltshire can be extrapolated to indicate that there were almost ten times as many alehouses and taverns as there were inns, suggesting that inns were for wealthier guests.[79] In his summary of alehouses, inns and taverns, Roberts asserts that the differences were tacitly understood rather than explicitly defined; in any case, the distinctions had dissolved by 1600.[80] The fundamental roles were, however, essentially the same: they provided shelter and food for people and their horses.

The temporal relationship between inns and lodging ranges allows a tentative suggestion that the former provided accommodation for retainers prior to the construction of lodging ranges in the great house. That is, during the transition period when the need for lodging ranges was emerging, some household members attended the great house when required and returned to their own house or a nearby urban centre when not. A further hint of the relationship, albeit similarly tentative, is the architectural similarity between ranges and inns. Extant remains of inns of the fourteenth century are relatively scarce, yet the known examples indicate that they comprised a hall, the innkeeper's accommodation, a kitchen, stables, storage and a varying number of rooms. The series of first-floor rooms at both Tackley's in Oxford and The George inn at Salisbury, Wiltshire, had thirteen chambers, while The Chequers in Winchester, Hampshire, had fourteen. Hare describes these as large inns, with the rooms containing three beds apiece, thus meeting the demand for 'relatively private sleeping' which had emerged in the late medieval period.[81] A frequently seen 'defining characteristic' of inns was the construction of the rooms in the form of a range, sometimes around a courtyard.[82]

---

77 Edward Roberts, 'Inns, Taverns and Alehouses in Hampshire 1300–1600', *Hampshire Studies*, 75:1 (2020), 75–87; John Hare, 'Inns, Innkeepers and the Society of Later Medieval England', *Journal of Medieval History*, 39:4 (2013), 477–97.
78 Hare, 'Inns', p. 497.
79 Hare, 'Inns', p. 480.
80 Roberts, 'Inns'.
81 Hare, 'Inns', pp. 480–1.
82 Hare, 'Inns', p. 481.

One such courtyard inn with ranges of rooms, and potentially uniform elevations, is The Angel at Andover, Hampshire, built on a rectangular plot in c.1455.[83] The east range overlooked the High Street and comprised a hall on the ground floor occupying three of the four bays. The fourth bay was the gateway leading to the courtyard. At each end of the east range there was a cross-wing containing what Roberts describes as 'parlours', differentiating these from smaller, less comfortable, lower-status rooms elsewhere.[84] Both parlours contained substantial chimneys and moulded timbers, indicating that they were for 'visitors of quality'.[85] The north range comprised stables on the ground floor and four single-bay rooms directly above. Each room measured approximately 3.5m by 6.7m and was accessed via a partly jettied gallery. There is some evidence to suggest that this created a uniform architectural display which was repeated on the south range. While the south range is lost, there remains the base of one door frame on the ground floor. Roberts suggests that it gave access to a staircase leading to a first-floor gallery and a range of small rooms.[86] The projected plan of The Angel inn, therefore, suggests that the north and south ranges were similar, if not fully symmetrical.

The position of two opposed galleries, facing one another, with the doors of the four chambers visible from the courtyard, would have created a display of uniform architecture. This is similar to that seen in collegiate ranges, and indeed inns and colleges were closely related in their foundation. The Angel was built by Winchester College, as outlined in the 1455 contract by the college's warden, Robert Thurbern.[87] Inns were profitable investments; as such, colleges bought or built inns throughout the fourteenth to sixteenth centuries. Winchester College, established by William Wykeham in 1382, was particularly active in building inns and possessed a portfolio of eight across southern England from Southwark to Wells.[88] Close to The Angel at Andover was The Bell inn, owned by Magdalen College, Oxford.[89] The connection between inns and colleges may have supported an interchange of ideas on architectural forms between those who were initiating their construction. A clear example of communication of ideas occurred in the mid-fifteenth century, when Henry VI gained an understanding of Winchester College through several visits prior to establishing Eton College in 1440. Roberts suggests that these

83 Edward Roberts, 'A Fifteenth Century Inn at Andover', *Proceedings of the Hampshire Field Club Archaeological Society*, 47 (1991), 153–70.
84 Roberts, 'Andover', p. 154.
85 Roberts, 'Andover', p. 159.
86 Roberts, 'Andover'.
87 Roberts, 'Andover', p. 153.
88 Hare, 'Inns', p. 488.
89 Roberts, 'Andover', p. 162; Hare, *Inns*, p. 488.

visits allowed for a reciprocal exchange of ideas, with Warden Thurbern receiving advice from the king's carpenter which he later implemented at The Angel – advice for which Eton's carpenter was compensated in 1455.[90]

Inns may have been used as accommodation for household members prior to the construction of lodging ranges, and their use may have continued after the latter were built. It will be argued later that the introduction of lodging ranges did not render travelling to and from the great house unnecessary; rather, travelling between a retainer's own house and that of the lord was probably routine for those whose roles did not require their permanent presence at the great house. This travelling back and forth was not a serious inconvenience in the late medieval period. Hare shows that William of Worcester was able to travel the country in 1460 with no more interruption from the Wars of the Roses than from the flooding of November the same year, which suggests that road travel was commonplace.[91] Therefore it is likely that there was travel back and forth both prior to the construction of lodging ranges and during their use, and that inns were used for interim stays.

Many architectural similarities existed across the various types of inns, vicarial and collegiate ranges, and to a lesser extent chantry houses,[92] and lodging ranges, including the individual or low-occupancy small rooms, courtyard plans, high-status provisions, and uniform elevations. This allows the suggestion of a broader typology of collective-living buildings, with *collective* an important distinction from *communal*: these were not high-density dormitories.[93] I suggest this with caution, as the conception of and reliance upon typologies can be limiting, with strict definitions sometimes reifying variation or encouraging tunnel vision. This occurs when a typology is adopted with no reflection on the context in which it was created, as the term 'castle' exemplifies.[94] Typologies can be useful, however, when the parameters are set out clearly and the artificiality of such parameters is reflected on before its adoption by others. With this proviso, the collective-living building type can be used to illustrate those aspects of the development of lodging ranges in a way not evident in their extant architecture or archaeological record. Both students of colleges

---

90   Roberts, 'Andover', p. 162.
91   Hare, 'Inns', p. 488; G. H. Martin, 'Road Travel in the Middle Ages', *The Journal of Transport History*, 3:3 (1976), 159–78.
92   Chantry houses are compared in: Wood, *House*; Pantin, 'Lodgings'. See also Simon Roffey, *The Medieval Chantry Chapel: An Archaeology* (Woodbridge, 2007).
93   Sarah Kerr, 'Collective Living and Individual Identities in Late Medieval England,' *Archaeological Journal*, 177 (2020), 83–98.
94   For an overview and critique of the discussion on castle typologies see Sarah Speight, 'British Castle Studies in the Late 20th and 21st Centuries', *History Compass*, 2:1 (2005).

and vicars of cathedrals occupied dormitories prior to the construction of ranges in each of their institutions. Therefore evidence indicates that there was a development from dormitories to rooms within ranges across types of auxiliary late medieval accommodation. What does this emergence of a collective-living building type tell us about late medieval society? The development from dormitories to ranges of rooms is probably demonstrative of a response to, as Wood suggests, 'the same problem of accommodating a number of individuals'.[95] Ranges, as well as being a pragmatic solution to that problem, were a response to society's shift towards specialised use of spaces and more private spaces (these reasons are further explored in Chapters 1 and 2).

The emergence of lodging ranges in the great houses was, therefore, the product of a particular combination of social and cultural conditions. The sharp cessation in their construction, at least as perceived in the extant remains, is, equally, the result of these environments changing. The late medieval house continued to evolve: as it had grown, so it shrank. One of the most significant changes in the house plan, spanning the shift from the aristocratic great house under discussion here to the houses of the early modern period, sometimes referred to as country houses, was the compact form. Andor Gomme and Alison Maguire reduce the complex sequence of change into the following: 'Then suddenly, or so it seemed, sometime in the seventeenth century the "double pile" arrived ... . Country houses were now four-square, tidily compact, symmetrical.'[96]

A number of key changes spurred the development of what Nicholas Cooper describes as the transition into something 'recognisably of the modern world'. The house form shifted away from the courtyard plan, with fewer houses presenting elevations of 'domestic confusion' with varying chimneys, doors and windows.[97] The house became outward-looking, rather than looking inward towards the central courtyard. The high and low continuum of status embedded in the courtyard system, as well as in the inner/outer chambers and the high/low ends of the hall, did not disappear as the size of houses contracted; rather, it was reflected in the social distinction between upstairs and downstairs. This was not novel, as first-floor rooms had often been reserved, higher-status spaces than those on the ground floor, but it became 'universal'.[98] The hall in its medieval form was becoming exceptional, although not absent, as the seventeenth century continued. A hall in the sense of a formal reception

---

95 Wood, *House*, p. 179.
96 Andor Gomme and Alison Maguire, *Design and Plan in the Country House. From Castle Donjons to Palladian Boxes* (New Haven, 2008).
97 Cooper, *Gentry*, pp. 3, 4.
98 Cooper, *Gentry*, p. 55.

room was favoured, alongside a salon, which probably developed from the parlour.[99] The adoption of uniformity as decoration burgeoned from its use on lodging ranges to fully symmetrical façades and plans. It will be discussed later how the uniform elevations of lodging ranges concealed inconsistencies in provisions and status within, and the façades of country houses had a similar function. Their internal layout was utterly imperceptible from the façade, unlike many elements of the late medieval great house, where the organisation was evident from the outside.

Just as the growth of the house was interlinked with the growth of the household, so too was the contraction of both related. The high-ranking staff of the late medieval great house, such as those who occupied lodging ranges, were a crucial layer in the hierarchical household. By the seventeenth century, however, the distinction between the family and the staff was expanding; a wider gap was emerging than had existed between the close social strata of previous centuries. Cooper suggests that this may have been accelerated by Protestant values, particularly the idea that service equalled actual labour rather than mere attendance.[100] In addition, the contraction of the elite house was influenced by the fashions of London. From the early seventeenth century, the capital became the source of innovation in terms of both elite amenities and elite architectural design. Cooper argues that London townhouses – often only one of a number of homes for the aristocracy – influenced the architectural fashions beyond the city limits not only because experimenting with design was the 'vogue' but because of London's confirmed social supremacy.[101]

SOCIAL MOBILITY

Lodging ranges were associated with the great houses of the uppermost nobility, but it was not the case that lodging ranges were built exclusively by the highest elites. The wider social and economic context was more dynamic than in previous centuries, allowing for greater social mobility; that is, movement upwards and downwards through the social ranks. The late medieval wealthy were no longer only those who had inherited wealth and vast land holdings. Rather, the wealthy also included newly appointed nobles, upper gentry and *nouveau riche* who exploited new ways to earn incredible wealth: these groups, too, built lodging ranges.

Social mobility was greatest within the upper echelons of society, as they were able to exploit the factors which allowed social ascension, including the Wars of the Roses, the growth of trade, and bastard feudalism: that is,

---

99 Cooper, *Gentry*, p. 3; Gomme and Maguire, *Design*, p. 2.
100 Cooper, *Gentry*, p. 272.
101 Cooper, *Gentry*, pp. 155–6.

an increase in cash-based service between social ranks.[102] Similarly, there were opportunities provided by the church, law, service during and outside wars, and marriage. Land remained the predominant source of wealth, status and inherited rank, and, as such, families which survived in the male line added to their estates by marrying into those which did not. This promoted the concentration of wealth in the ownership of fewer families; yet, conversely, a failure of primogeniture allowed the upper aristocracy to remain permeable. S. J. Payling discusses the balance of these opposing factors as the rate of social mobility and it has been suggested that this was far greater in the medieval period than it is today.[103] Lawrence Stone and Jeanne Fawtier Stone endeavour to quantify this 'open elite' and conclude that it was not so easily permeated by new money.[104] They argue that families were generally successful in keeping the same surname attached to an estate. Indeed, Christine Carpenter states that 'society [was] looking more open from some vantage points than others'.[105]

One such lord who exploited social mobility to his advantage was Robert Willoughby, patron of the lodging range at Brook Hall, Wiltshire.[106] Although Willoughby was from a noble family, the Brook estate had been confiscated because of their Lancastrian support and handed to Edward Ratcliffe.[107] Willoughby was attained for high treason but escaped to Brittany to join Henry Tudor. When Henry VII ascended to the throne in the late fifteenth century, he restored Brook to Willoughby.[108] Willoughby remained a close royal confidant, fought at the Battle of Bosworth in 1485 and became Lord Steward and Admiral of the Fleet.[109] In 1491, he was created the first Baron Brook and called to parliament in 1492. As he amassed vast wealth and estates, he built the lodging range at Brook and possibly rebuilt other elements of the house. Increased social mobility meant there was greater descent through the social ranks, too: Willoughby's son, Robert,

102 K. B. McFarlane, *The Nobility of Later Medieval England* (Oxford, 1973).
103 S. J. Payling, 'Social Mobility, Demographic Change, and Landed Society in Late Medieval England', *The Economic History Review*, 45:1 (1992), 51–73, p. 51; Gregory Clark, 'Regression to Mediocrity? Surnames and Social Mobility in England, 1200–2009', *Social Science Research Network* (2010).
104 Lawrence Stone and Jeanne C. Fawtier Stone, *An Open Elite? England 1550–1880* (Oxford, 1984), p. 16.
105 Christine Carpenter, *Locality and Polity: A Study of Warwickshire Landed Society, 1401-1499* (Cambridge, 1992), p. 148.
106 Ivor Sanders, *Feudal Military Service in England: A Study of the Constitutional and Military Powers of the Barones in Medieval England* (Oxford, 1956).
107 Elizabeth Crittall, *A History of the County of Wiltshire: Volume 8, Warminster, Westbury and Whorwellsdown Hundreds* (London, 1965), p. 151.
108 West Wiltshire District Council, *Brook Hall Brokerswood: Statement of Significance and Development Brief* (2004).
109 Wiltshire, *Brook*, p. 1.

fared less well in the social snakes-and-ladders; he received none of the royal favour his father had and he died in 1521 without a male heir.[110]

Willoughby's lodging range was modest in comparison to the extensive ranges of Thornbury Castle, Gloucestershire, or Dartington Hall, reflecting his lower social rank. However, the features of uniformity, individual doors and high-status provisions within rooms were a constant throughout the examples, regardless of scale. Lodging ranges were part of aristocratic great houses, regardless of whether the family were established or *nouveau riche*, and regardless of their rank within this social milieu. But this consistency requires examination of whether those of lower ranks were striving to emulate their so-called betters. Social emulation is a frequently-debated concept in archaeological discourse. Sally Smith, for example, uses a Marxist conception of late medieval social structure to examine the use of artefacts from Wharram Percy, North Yorkshire. She argues that the non-elite wore elaborately decorated accessories to construct their identities and subvert the strict social hierarchy within which they lived.[111] Aleksandra McClain, utilising a non-Marxist view, suggests that wearing decorated belt buckles and strap ends may have indicated social aspiration among the lower classes, rather than resistance.[112] As far as the construction of buildings is concerned, Thompson suggests that the inclusion of courtyards in smaller medieval houses represented social emulation; this argument holds some value in the context of a socially fluid late medieval period.[113] By building in the same style as those in the social ranks above, a newly wealthy family may have seemed similar, at least in appearance, to those long-standing families. In turn, the latter may have attempted to create a veneer of longevity to set themselves apart from the upstarts by constructing buildings similar to a royal house. In David Hinton's discussion of the relevance of closure theory to archaeology, a theory borrowed from sociology which contends that social groups exclude others by monopolising resources, he examines emulation through, for example, the construction of houses and the wearing of jewellery. He argues that visual demonstrations were used to emulate those above while maintaining distance from those below, supporting Thompson's assertions. However, he also suggests that people were equally aware of their position in relation to those 'on the same level'.[114] In essence, there

---

110 Wiltshire, *Brook*, p. 1; Crittall, *Wiltshire*, p. 151.
111 Sally Smith, 'Materializing Resistant Identities among the Medieval Peasantry', *Journal of Material Culture*, 14:3 (2009), 309–32, p. 326.
112 Aleksandra McClain, 'Theory, Disciplinary Perspectives and the Archaeology of Later Medieval England', *Medieval Archaeology*, 56:1 (2012), 131–70, p. 144.
113 Michael Thompson, *The Decline of the Castle* (Cambridge, 1978).
114 David Hinton, '"Closing" and the Later Middle Ages', *Medieval Archaeology*, 43:1 (1999), 172–82, p. 177.

were socially-approved parameters of demonstrating status visually which were influenced by both vertical and horizontal associations.

Christopher King argues that social emulation is too simplistic a notion when discussing the organisation of late medieval buildings. He describes the appropriation of common spatial and architectural vocabularies by the mercantile elite in Norwich, Norfolk, in which a variety of influences, including aristocratic, religious and civic buildings, were at work.[115] Rather than having the single aim of emulating the aristocracy, architectural appropriation also structured and maintained shared, horizontal identities. King asserts that buildings had underlying social functions and meanings which were the reason for constructing in certain ways. This is true, too, of lodging ranges: lords of established and new wealth used them to communicate meanings to the medieval audience, among which were the presentation of social, political and economic identities. Evidently, social emulation was a subsidiary factor in the construction of buildings and far from an isolated motivation.

Social Hierarchies

Displaying social identities through architectural manifestations was contingent on a clearly defined social hierarchy; that is, the ways in which society was organised according to people's status was expressed and demarcated clearly, with the king at the hierarchical apex and the peasants at the bottom, and those in between ranked in line with their relative status. This middle group was divided between the nobility: dukes, marquesses, earls, viscounts and barons; and, lower down the scale, the gentry. The nobility had far greater wealth in terms of estates and resources, and probably greater political ambitions. When they looked upwards in the hierarchy of deference, it was to the king. The lower boundary of the nobility is difficult to define, as it blurs with the ranks of the gentry.[116] Pamela Nightingale, in her discussion of the complexity of the gentry, examines its relationship with contemporary merchants.[117] She argues that, in the fourteenth century, the crown saw landowners and merchants as two distinct groups, and suggests an antagonism between the urban mercantile class and rural landowners.[118] This distinction may have derived from

---

115 King, 'Space', p. 113; Christopher King, 'The Interpretation of Urban Buildings: Power, Memory and Appropriation in Norwich Merchants' Houses, c. 1400–1660', *World Archaeology*, 41:3 (2009), 471–88, p. 485.

116 For earlier context see Senecal, 'Keeping', p. 252; Peter Coss, *The Origins of the English Gentry* (Cambridge, 2003).

117 Pamela Nightingale, 'Knights and Merchants: Trade, Politics and the Gentry in Late Medieval England', *Past & Present*, 169 (2000), 36–62.

118 Nightingale, 'Knights', pp. 36–7, 60.

the gentry's military ethos and chivalric code, which set out only three honourable ways of acquiring wealth: service at court, a good marriage, or through war. Consequently, theoretically at least, wealth accrued solely through trade tainted the gentry, hindering them from ascending into the nobility. In practice, however, the gentry and nobility all had economic interests, which only increased throughout the fourteenth century as they exploited their demesnes. By the fifteenth century, they had expanded their urban and commercial interests; indeed, John Fastolf, who built the lodging ranges at Caister Castle, Norfolk, invested his war-acquired wealth in trade as well as in land.[119] Therefore it is impossible to create clear-cut divisions between these elite groups, and, indeed, such partitions are not essential to the topic here.[120] What is pertinent is understanding that social elites, noble, gentle or otherwise, displayed their social position, while greater social mobility increased the emphasis placed on this display.

Social status, as a facet of one's identity, was displayed through tangible and intangible elements of medieval life. The retainers' display included livery and retainer badges; for the uppermost elites, social status was displayed through, amongst other things, their buildings, landscapes, hospitality and their hired retinue. A commitment to expressing status in multiple ways should not be conflated with rigid ranks; the opposite is more accurate during this time of increased social mobility. In response to this mobility, however, it appears that there was a desire to set one's status in stone, whether it was a long-held position or new prestige, in the hope that this would reduce the risk of descending the ranks. One way to instil, or attempt to instil, permanence was through the construction of, or additions to, a great house. For example, William Herbert (d. 1469), son of William ap Thomas of Raglan, began his career as a servant to the house of York. He was rewarded with the earldom of Pembroke after providing support during the Battle of Mortimer's Cross and assisting in the ascension of Edward IV. He displayed this social progression by constructing the substantial hexagonal keep at Raglan Castle, Monmouthshire, between approximately 1461 and 1463.[121]

Some contemporaries frowned upon, or even outright feared, social mobility. The political theorist Chief Justice Fortescue, a loyal follower of Henry VI, warned of those who 'often tymes growe to be gretter than

---

119 Nightingale, 'Knights', p. 61; K. B. McFarlane, *England in the Fifteenth Century: Collected Essays* (London, 1981).
120 If someone called themselves a gentleman, they should be classed as gentry, regardless of whether they held office or how small their sphere of influence: Carpenter, *Locality*, p. 616.
121 Anthony Emery, 'The Development of Raglan Castle and Keeps in Late Medieval England', *Archaeological Journal*, 132 (1975), 151–86, p. 169. It was not built for safety: contra Emery, *Greater Medieval Houses*, Vol. 2, p. 198.

thai be now' and insisted that lords should 'aspire to non hygher estate'.[122] In the sixteenth century, social mobility may still have been a concern, particularly amongst the ranks immediately below the king's. Edward Stafford, the third Duke of Buckingham and son of Henry Stafford, appears to have tested this when he rebuilt Thornbury Castle. The incomplete outer courtyard was an enormous 145 metres diagonally, incorporating extensive lodging ranges and a grand cross-range, both adorned with semi-octagonal, semi-hexagonal and square towers. While it is likely that the house was nothing more than ostentatious self-promotion of his social prestige, to Henry VIII it seemed that he was building on a kingly scale, and the king responded by ordering Stafford's execution.

Fortescue's views were contemporary with the Wars of the Roses: the factional struggles and civil wars which occurred amongst the descendants of Edward III, between approximately 1450 and 1500.[123] They accelerated social mobility: those who backed the winning side were rewarded and ascended through the hierarchy in a way not possible during times of peace. The Pelham, Nirbury and Bromflete families rose to prominence after supporting the Lancastrians in 1399, while Hastings and Devereux benefitted from supporting the Yorkists in 1461.[124] Of course, this could involve great risk, as the Verney family rose rapidly only to fall out of favour again as soon as the crown changed hands.[125]

Bastard Feudalism

After the Battle of Hastings, William of Normandy parcelled out land to secure support from the lords of England, and land was granted from greater to lesser lords in return for service, thus creating a hierarchical political and economic system. This is traditionally considered to be the start of feudalism in England, which became a cornerstone of medieval society. The usefulness, however, of the term 'feudalism' has been called into question.[126] This contribution appreciates that it is a broad label that

---

122 Quoted in Charles Plummer (ed.), *The Governance of England* (Oxford, 1885), p. 130. For a biography see: Margaret Kekewich, *Sir John Fortescue and the Governance of England* (Woodbridge, 2018).
123 Michael Hicks, 'Bastard Feudalism, Overmighty Subjects and Idols of the Multitude during the Wars of the Roses', *The Journal of the Historical Association*, 85:279 (2000), 386–403.
124 Payling, 'Mobility', p. 66.
125 Carpenter, *Locality*, p. 151.
126 For discussions on feudalism in pre-Conquest England see, for example: Chris Wickham, 'The Other Transition: From the Ancient World to Feudalism', *Past & Present*, 103 (1984), 3–36; Hugh M. Thomas, *The Norman Conquest: England after William the Conqueror* (Plymouth, 2008); Frank Barlow, *The Feudal Kingdom of*

overlooks the diversity of relationships which existed and the complexity of the social hierarchy; but it remains useful to describe the tenurial and hereditary relationships between social ranks in the post-Conquest period. In addition, it is useful for differentiating the types of relationship prominent in the high medieval and late medieval periods as, during this time, the tenurial system declined in favour of monetary payments. The later medieval incarnation of the feudal system is known as 'bastard feudalism', a term coined in the nineteenth century by Charles Plummer to highlight the differences between the eleventh-century post-Conquest model and what he saw as a degenerate, or bastardised, system which characterised the Wars of the Roses in the mid-fifteenth-century.[127] Although bastard feudalism has now been stripped of these negative connotations, the term remains fairly contentious.[128] Here it is used to describe the social, political and financial relationships which supported late medieval society and were integral to the late medieval household.

The central and unique feature of bastard feudalism was the use of cash.[129] Inherited land was no longer a prerequisite for establishing a feudal relationship and so monetary payments permitted more men and women to retain and be retained, hence the term *retainers*.[130] With a growing and increasingly cash-based economy, money was the best means of ensuring upward mobility, and it allowed wealth to be spread through the upper ranks rather than being concentrated in royal families. The use of cash, therefore, allowed greater social mobility among, and into, the patriciate. As K. B. McFarlane describes it: 'Nobility was always for sale'.[131] Bastard feudalism and its mechanisms accelerated both social mobility and the growth of the household. It did not cause the Wars of the Roses, despite its exploitation to facilitate unrest. Much like the post-Conquest feudal system, it enabled and represented a social relationship between people of different ranks and was used to hire male and female staff, servants and, to a lesser degree, soldiers.

England: 1042-1216 (Abingdon, 2014). For issues relating to the term feudalism, see: Elizabeth A. R. Brown, 'The Tyranny of a Construct: Feudalism and Historians of Medieval Europe', *The American Historical Review*, 79 (1974), 1063–88; Susan Reynolds, *The Middle Ages without Feudalism: Essays in Criticism and Comparison on the Medieval West* (London, 2012); Michael Hicks, *Bastard Feudalism* (London, 1995), p. 4.
127 Plummer, *Governance*, p. 14; McFarlane, *Essays*, p. 23; Hicks, *Bastard*, p. 12.
128 McKelvie, *Bastard*, p.3.
129 While land was central to feudalism and cash was central to bastard feudalism, these were not the exclusive payments; both were used throughout the medieval period: Hicks, *Bastard*, p. 4.
130 For discussion on female retainers see: McKelvie, *Bastard*.
131 McFarlane, *Nobility*, p. 9.

A greater understanding of bastard feudalism assists an understanding of why the lodging ranges were constructed. Plummer claimed that a system based on money meant that it was easier to wage war, sway governments and thwart justice as people strove to achieve their own personal agendas, resulting in a 'hierarchy of corruption'.[132] This term was popularised by Plummer's contemporary William Stubbs, who, along with other Victorian historians such as James Gairdner and William Denton, shared the former's view of a bastardised system.[133] They believed that the Wars of the Roses were encouraged by the nobility, and particularly by their enormous retinues, with bastard feudalism their mechanism for unrest. This became the consensus amongst historians because, as Michael Hicks demonstrates, Stubbs's work was central to the history curriculum: no other viewpoint was seriously considered until the mid-twentieth century.[134] It was McFarlane who contradicted Stubbs's argument in his 1964 Raleigh lecture to the British Academy. Referring to Fortescue's writing in the *Governance of England* on the 'perils that mowe falle to a king by ovur mighti subgiettes', McFarlane emphasised that 'only undermighty kings had anything to fear from overmighty subjects'.[135] This instigated a shift in the understanding of bastard feudalism, in particular a downgrading of the role of lords' use of it in causing unrest. In two crucial publications, Hicks supports McFarlane's conclusions and exposes the variety of causes leading to the Wars, including England's weak international position and diminished royal revenues. He also extends a nuanced argument, pointing out that some kings were indeed undermighty and some overmighty subjects disturbed the peace and opposed the crown as it bounced between the Yorkists and Lancastrians during the central part of the Wars; but these were not the product of bastard feudalism and the only causes of the unrest.[136] Gordon McKelvie's recent work builds on Hicks's nuanced understanding of bastard feudalism and continues the move away from Plummer's view of a 'degenerate' and highly androcentric system. He argues that, while we no longer consider the nobility to be a disruptive group continually undermining royal power, bastard feudalism was the mechanism by which recruitment for rebellious and lawless purposes was enacted, particularly during the Wars of the Roses. It could, therefore, be a mechanism for both stability and disorder.[137]

132 Plummer, *Governance*, p. 25; Hicks, *Bastard*, p. 2.
133 William Stubbs, *The Constitutional History of England in Its Origin and Development*, Vol. 1 (Oxford, 1903).
134 Hicks, *Bastard*, p. 15.
135 Quoted in Hicks, 'Overmighty', pp. 386–7.
136 Hicks, *Bastard*; 'Overmighty'.
137 McKelvie, *Bastard*, p. 6.

Plummer's assertions, as the accepted word on bastard feudalism for over half a century, influenced the architectural analysis of the late medieval great house. Anthony Emery and William Douglas Simpson subsequently interpreted the developments in the house plan, particularly features such as the double courtyard, secondary hall and central tower, as responses to the instability of this feudal system and the presence of fickle retainers.[138] They considered that there was a constant possibility of retainers, motivated by money, changing their allegiance to the highest bidder. A retainer might be 'bought' by a rival and use their proximity to the lord in the great house to wage an attack. It was suggested that at Ashby de la Zouch, Leicestershire, and Warkworth Castle, Northumberland, the towers were evidence of attempts to isolate and even protect the head of the household from the retainers. At Raglan Castle, the keep was completely separated from the remainder of the house by a moat and included accommodation and services, suggesting that the lord could retreat entirely into the keep should a retinue revolt occur in the courtyard. In addition to Plummer's views, documented instances of distrust between lords and retainers influenced these analyses. The first Duke of Lancaster was wealthy and able to afford huge sums of money to pay his troops. But, when Lancaster was on his deathbed, one of his esquires gave orders to distribute 200 marks to those whom Lancaster had retained during a Spanish voyage. It has been suggested that the esquire was suffering from a guilty conscience and wanted to make amends for the Duke defrauding the army.[139] While this is an interesting aspect of the relationship between a lord and his retinue, false accusations of peculation were easier to make when a lord was on his deathbed.

All aristocratic men, from the king to the gentry lord, were in a bastard feudal relationship, with many being both one who retained and a retainer themselves.[140] Women, particularly those who were heads of households, were also part of the system, hiring retainers and being bound by feudal legislation.[141] Through close examinations of Elizabeth de Burgh, Lady de Clare, Isabella Morely, Joan Beauchamp and Countess Anne of Stafford, Jennifer Ward outlines the important role women played in establishing households and wider retinues.[142] Just as bastard feudalism was a means of social connection between upper- and lower-status men, women

---

138 William Douglas Simpson, '"Bastard Feudalism" and the Later Castles', *The Antiquaries Journal*, 26:3–4 (1946), 145–71; Emery, *Dartington*, p. 229; Emery, *Greater Medieval Houses*, Vol. 1, p. 17.
139 McFarlane, *Nobility*, p. 27.
140 Hicks, 'Overmighty', p. 390.
141 McKelvie, *Bastard*, p. 50.
142 Ward, *Noblewomen*.

too forged alliances through retaining, thus creating and strengthening kinships across the elite milieu.

Widows, more than married women, appear in the contemporary records documenting bastard feudalism, listing instances of both legal and illegal behaviour. This emphasis on widows is consistent with other historical documentation and supports the analysis that widows might have had more freedom and financial capital than married or single women. Women probably retained more than they were retained, owing to the predominance of men in senior household positions, as suggested by the historical records. That in turn suggests where women were more often retained was in less senior service positions, and these were not dependent on their marital status. In 1491, five women were indicted for wearing illegal livery. It was not that they were not allowed to be retained; rather, they were not permitted to wear this particular livery during the months of January and February.[143] The gender favouritism of the historical records needs to be reiterated: they were biased in favour of men, with a strong concentration on the uppermost elites and, in the context of retaining, the records emphasised those who breached acceptable guidelines, creating a very uneven picture. Despite the limitations of the contemporary documents, McKelvie makes clear that bastard feudalism was a system created not by and for secular men but by and for all of society – male, female, urban, rural, secular and ecclesiastic.[144]

The ubiquitous nature of feudalism meant there was not one standard type of feudal relationship: rather, there were a variety of formal and informal mechanisms which tied one person to another. McKelvie describes how informal bastard feudal relationships involved payments and livery, for example, to state officials, or intangible rewards such as hospitality, favours or entertainment. In return the lord would gain a service, whether legal, military or administrative.[145] McKelvie considers that the retinue, that is, all those retained under one lord, consisted not only soldiers, as per Plummer and his contemporaries' interpretations; rather, it included men and women in a variety of service positions. This supports Hicks's broader interpretation of the retinue. He stated that it included all of the household members, tenants and gentle retainers, a group to which more could be added should the retinue be needed for battle. This is the view adopted here.[146]

Armed with this more balanced view of bastard feudalism, we can turn to its components: indentures, maintenance and livery. Its most formal execution involved an indenture, which was the contract outlining the

---

143 McKelvie, *Bastard*, p. 123.
144 McKelvie, *Bastard*, p. 107.
145 McKelvie, *Bastard*, p. 5.
146 Hicks, 'Overmighty', p. 389; Kerr, 'Lodging ranges'.

terms of the relationship. These invariably stated that the retainer had to be an able-bodied man who could serve his lord in times of war and peace.[147] One indenture between Richard, Earl of Salisbury, and Walter Strykelande, a knight, stated that the latter must be 'well and conveniently horsed armed and arrayed, and always be ready to bide, come and go with, to and for the said Earl at all times'.[148] The indenture between William, Lord Hastings, and William Bassett, esquire, in 1465 stated that the latter was 'retained for the term of his life' and was to 'ride and go and him assist and aid against all persons'.[149] This included 'peace and war', as noted in the indenture of another of Hastings's esquires, Ralph Longford, in 1481.[150] The hints of military prowess required of the retainer fuelled the notion of them as a homogeneous group of male soldiers as seen in Plummer's narrative of boisterous boys. The indentures, however, allow detection of other services the retainer was expected to provide, such as travelling with the lord during times of peace. The connection between lord and retainer was not solely based on military or financial need: social, political and familial considerations constructed these relationships. The retainer's peacetime role may have included attending tournaments, parliaments and public assemblies, joining in the lord's recreations, and being in the household at the lord's will. In return, the indenture listed the good lordship they should receive in return for their service, alongside fees, livery, accommodation and bouche of court.

The second element of bastard feudalism was maintenance, or the lord's support of the retainer during disputes. To Plummer, 'maintenance and other kindred evils' involved upholding retainers' 'unjust quarrels'.[151] In reality, maintenance was an agreement that lawful support would be provided *if* misfortune befell a retainer, by their fault or another's, rather than *when* this happened. W. H. Dunham argues that maintenance in a lawful and reasonable dispute was part of the social code, while Nigel Saul makes it clear that this was a reciprocal relationship, stating that retainer and lord were 'under obligation to each other'.[152] This social connection meant that lords would 'stand by [their] man and ... support [them] in all causes and disputes', while, in return, the retainer was expected to

---

147 Emery, *Dartington*, p. 220; Nigel Saul, *Knights and Esquires* (Oxford, 1981), p. 60; Grenville, *Housing*, p. 116; Woolgar, *Household*, p. 8.
148 Quoted in Simpson, 'Bastard Feudalism', p. 162.
149 William Huse Dunham, *Lord Hastings' Indentured Retainers, 1461–1483: The Lawfulness of Livery and Retaining under the Yorkists and Tudors* (New Haven, 1970).
150 Dunham, *Hastings*, p. 132.
151 Plummer, *Governance*, pp. 24–8.
152 Dunham, *Hastings*, p. 68; Saul, *Knights*; Nigel Saul, 'The Commons and the Abolition of Badges', *Parliamentary History*, 9 (1990), 302–15.

be dutiful, faithful and, of course, law-abiding.[153] Maintenance could be exploited through, for example, making fraudulent copies of a lord's livery for the purpose of a lawsuit, thus giving the impression of lawful support that did not exist. McKelvie notes that William Vernon, father of Henry Vernon, who added the lodging range at Haddon Hall, was indicted in 1410, prior to a cluster of unlawful maintenance cases in Derbyshire.[154]

The third element of bastard feudalism is livery. Frédérique Lachaud explains that livery – *liberatio* in Latin or *liveree* in Anglo-Norman – then meant any payment to the retainer, whether money, clothing, or food. Household clerks would specify *liveree de draps*, *liberatio robarum* or *liberatio pannorum*, resulting in a level of clarity in the accounts upon which Lachaud based his research.[155] Livery robes were garments of woollen cloth, occasionally with a silk or fur lining.[156] As with maintenance, livery robes could be exploited. A series of parliamentary acts between 1390 and 1504 restricted the distribution of livery to certain groups, such as the lord's permanent household; however, livery was illegally granted to others for the artificial expansion of the retinue.[157] McKelvie suggests that this enlargement was for violent purposes;[158] although, in this age of great display, it seems likely that social prestige may have been another reason for swelling the ranks.

Livery robes (hereafter 'livery' for brevity) were a visual display of identities and affiliation. They reflected the social and monetary connection between lords and retainers, with a strong symbolic significance which reinforced the personal bond between two individuals of different ranks.[159] However, the relationship indicated by livery was not equal but, rather, an 'outward sign of dependence' and, as such, it was a fundamental reflection of a lord's wealth, demonstrating as it did the number of people they could afford to pay and support.[160] It also reflected the lord's status, as it identified the group in livery as their subordinates. In addition, livery reflected the retainer's identity, both collective and individual. The granting of liveries was a process of uniforming, in the sense of providing a uniform and erasing individuality amongst a group of people hired from

---

153 Saul, 'Commons', pp. 305–6.
154 McKelvie, *Bastard*, pp. 51, 134.
155 Frédérique Lachaud, 'Liveries of Robes in England, c.1200–c.1330', *The English Historical Review*, 111 (1996), 279–98.
156 Lachaud, 'Liveries', p. 279.
157 McKelvie, *Bastard*, p. 1.
158 McKelvie, *Bastard*, p. 1, 163.
159 Lachaud, 'Liveries', p. 294; J. M. W. Bean, *From Lord to Patron: Lordship in Late Medieval England* (Manchester, 1989), p. 17.
160 George Holmes, *The Estates of the Higher Nobility in Fourteenth-century England* (Cambridge, 1957), p. 59.

a variety of different places: they were swathed in sameness. Livery was administered carefully, with quantity and quality, including material and colour, corresponding precisely to the rank of the retainer.[161] Vair and budge (respectively, red squirrel fur and black lambskin) were reserved for the highest ranking retainers, and common squirrel fur or lamb for lower staff, while servants and slaves may have received unlined robes. This created important visual distinctions within the household; the hierarchy was displayed outwardly through varying liveries. In addition, the representation of the relationship with a lord displayed the retainer's status beyond the household. Their prestige would be boosted if they were recognisable as the retainer of a lord from the upper nobility, preferably a great and ancient family, rather than of a mid-ranking gentry lord.[162] There was, therefore, both a 'symbolical and practical function of identification' woven into the livery.[163]

On top of the livery, a retainer may have worn an emblematic retainer pin or badge. There is considerable inconsistency and debate surrounding the terminology of pins and badges, possibly due to the various approaches previous studies have taken. They have been explored through individual case studies, of both the lord and the artefact, and in the context of jewellery. The result is work which sets out to categorise livery badges separately from other badges and emblems on shields or crests. Michael Powell Siddons provides a comprehensive overview of badges and tackles the terminological issues.[164] He establishes that, in all cases, badges proclaimed ownership and identity and were used to denote hierarchy and demonstrate allegiance. The same emblem could be used across a variety of furnishings, plates and monuments for the same purpose as the badge worn on clothes, but with an added decorative function.[165] For example, Richard II played on his name 'rich-hart' when he adopted the white hart design.[166] His supporter and half-brother, John Holland, emblazoned the hart on the central boss of his newly-built porch at Dartington Hall. Its decorative function drew the eye upwards while making Holland's affiliation clear. Additionally, badges were practical in battle or during tournaments, where they could be displayed on standards to act as a rallying point for retainers.

---

161 Lachaud, 'Liveries', p. 288.
162 David Hinton, 'Symbols of Power', in Christopher Gerrard and Alejandra Gutiérrez (eds), *The Oxford Handbook of Later Medieval Archaeology in Britain* (Oxford, 2018), pp. 418–34, at p. 423.
163 Lachaud, 'Liveries', p. 295.
164 Michael Powell Siddons, *Heraldic Badges in England and Wales* (3 vols, Woodbridge, 2009).
165 Siddons, *Heraldic Badges*, p. 2.
166 Hinton, 'Symbols', p. 421.

Similarly, collars could be worn with livery. These were bands of leather or velvet awarded to the highest-ranking servants and worn around the neck. Matthew Ward's focused study of such collars establishes that they were introduced in the fourteenth century but became associated almost solely with royal affinities in the fifteenth century.[167] He states that they created a distinction between those closest to king and the remainder of the retainers with badges.[168] Some collars included metal depictions of armorial devices and could be entirely composed of silver gilt, silver or gold. Caps or hats were yet another element of the late medieval system of livery. These could be awarded in huge numbers, their cheaper material representing the lower status of the wearer. As with livery and badges, the collar denoted the lord's association with, even their 'possession and ownership' of, the wearer.[169]

The clear parallels with livery indicate that badges created a visual relationship between lord and retainer, and cohesion amongst the retainers. However, Hinton suggests that they may in part have fuelled the unrest of the late medieval period, as to not receive a badge would be a mark of disfavour, allowing factions to fester. He links this to the development of the Wars of the Roses and argues that failure to recognise badges led to riots between retinues and even amongst a retinue if a design was identified incorrectly.[170] His summary relies too heavily on Plummer's notion of a truly bastardised feudal system; however, some jealousy amongst a retinue may be a reasonable assumption, particularly as badges, like livery, reflected a hierarchy. For example, a number of copper alloy retainer badges depicting the white boar emblem of Richard III were found in Northamptonshire, Bedfordshire and at Middleham Castle in North Yorkshire. They were created in a mould and then gilded, suggesting that a considerable number were produced. In North Yorkshire, the same design was found made in silver-gilt and in Leicestershire in an even more precious silver version.[171] Thousands would have been produced of fustian cloth for the lower-ranking supporters of Richard III, a process accelerated as cloth-manufacturing technology developed.[172] As a physical representation of the feudal relationship and the household hierarchy, livery and retainer badges were not so distinct from lodging ranges.

---

167 Matthew Ward, *The Livery Collar in Late Medieval England and Wales: Politics, Identity and Affinity* (Woodbridge, 2016), p. 2.
168 Ward, *Collar*, p. 2.
169 Ward, *Collar*, p. 20.
170 Hinton, 'Symbols', p. 422.
171 PAS, 2020: Northamptonshire (NARC-F57226); Bedfordshire (LEIC-F17145); North Yorkshire, Silver-gilt (YORYM-1716A4); Leicestershire (LEIC-A6C834).
172 This also aided the production of liveries: Lachaud, 'Liveries'.

The statutes of livery, a series of rules introduced towards the end of the fourteenth century, seemed to support the disorderly narrative perpetuated by Plummer. They aimed to restrict the illegal use of bastard feudalism, but they were enforced only sporadically and fines were rare. Implementation commenced properly with Henry V, increasing to reach its peak under Henry VII.[173] Cases of breaching the statutes became more regular during the 1450s, not necessarily because illegal retaining was on the rise but because highlighting a foe's wrongdoing was a mechanism for waging a feud. This temporal relationship between the statutes and the Wars of the Roses is another reason for the longevity of the erroneous bastard feudalism interpretation. One particular statute in 1468 aimed to restrict instances of retaining wherein a retainer received only fees and an indenture; that is, they did not receive livery robes. This seems to have stemmed from violence in Derbyshire, a county which already had a 'reputation of disorder'.[174] Retainers of Lord Grey of Condor murdered Roger Vernon, brother of Henry Vernon.[175] At the time the murder occurred, their retention agreement was technically legal, as previous statutes had only restricted the giving of liveries, not insisted upon their inclusion. The statute of 1468 provides an insight into what was deemed an appropriate lord–retainer relationship: lawful service in times of peace.

Recent scholarship makes it clear that, while the statutes are indicative of the concern over the mechanisms of bastard feudalism, they were never intended to bring an end to it, nor even to stop retaining or the giving of liveries. They aimed solely to restrict the practice to the acceptable categories of staff. By indicating deviations from the norm they reveal that bastard feudalism was in essence the hiring of staff for households and wider estates. This is indicated in the indentures' inclusion of service during war *and* peace, and through the contemporary documents, such as a 1399 record which stated that a retinue should comprise 'necessary officers within their households, and ... necessary officers outside their households to govern their lands and possessions'.[176] This suggests that, fundamentally, retaining had its basis in social connections, with maintenance and livery intermittently exploited for illegal means.

The non-tenurial nature of bastard feudalism assisted the expansion of households. Lords could legally swell their household, even monstrously, if they paid retainers according to the statutes, with livery, fees, bouche of court and maintenance set out in an indenture. In its legal form, bastard feudalism formalised existing social connections between people

---

173 McKelvie, *Bastard*, p. 204.
174 McKelvie, *Bastard*, pp. 66, 135.
175 McKelvie, *Bastard*, p. 66.
176 Quoted in McKelvie, *Bastard*, p. 42.

of different ranks. Lodging ranges were built to accommodate these household members and, much like livery and badges, they reflected the hierarchy within the retinue. As an element of the bastard feudal relationship, lodging ranges reveal more of the social connection between lord and retainer and inform the discourse on late medieval feudalism as it continues to move from its bastardised interpretation.

EXPLORING THE *WHY*

As archaeologists explore the past, a central question is always 'why?'. In this case, why were lodging ranges built? The answer is always the same: a complex mixture of cultural and social reasons. Unsurprisingly, this answer leaves most unsatisfied. Chapter 1 provides a description of lodging ranges and examines one of the reasons why they were built: to be used as accommodation. The remainder of the chapters explore functions beyond the utilitarian: after all, function and use are not synonymous.[177] The purpose of distinguishing between these related terms is set out later before the emphasis is placed on function. That focus stems from a relatively recent shift towards considering meanings which has occurred in buildings archaeology.

Early studies of buildings during the nineteenth century were encouraged by William Morris and John Ruskin, who were interested not only in what had survived, but also in its preservation.[178] A surge in the protection and restoration of buildings was accelerated by the establishment of the Society for the Protection of Ancient Buildings in 1877 and the National Trust in 1895.[179] Around the turn of the twentieth century, the study of building fabric was focused firmly on monasteries, cathedrals, great houses and castles, following in the footsteps of the antiquarians from a century before. This was in part due to the availability of extant remains above ground and associated documents relating to their construction, as well as the lure of extravagant and aesthetic architecture. Aesthetics and antiquity were the measures of building value and therefore persisted as a focus of academic interest until the 1970s.[180]

---

177 Kerr, 'Lodging ranges'.
178 Audrey Horning and Dan Hicks, 'Historical Archaeology and Buildings', in Mary Beaudry and Dan Hicks (eds), *Cambridge Companion to Historical Archaeology* (Cambridge, 2006), pp. 273–93.
179 Mark Gardiner, 'What is Building History? Emergence and Practice in Britain and Ireland', in Liz Thomas and Jill Campbell (eds), *Buildings in Society: International Studies in the Historic Era* (Summertown, 2018), pp. 1–8, at p. 3.
180 Gardiner, 'Emergence', pp. 4, 6.

Later, in reaction to this, in the second half of the twentieth century the focus shifted towards smaller, lower-status buildings as well as auxiliary buildings. This was preceded by Pantin's recording of now-lost timber-framed houses in Oxford, which spurred his enduring interest in urban buildings.[181] In the 1960s and 1970s there was a surge in local studies which defined and redefined typologies in order to determine regional variations and traditions.[182] This may have been influenced by Sir Cyril Fox and Lord Raglan's study of fifteenth-, sixteenth- and seventeenth-century houses in Monmouthshire, Wales.[183] They explored *Smaller House-Plans*, approaching each one through a combination of fieldwork and documentary evidence. Much of this work was preoccupied with classifying geographic, temporal and architectural data, with a persistent focus on use.[184] The subsequent compilation of over a century of buildings archaeology was an affliction of dichotomies: high/low status, vernacular/polite architecture, rise/decline, ecclesiastical/secular. This, in turn, imbued the analysis of the buildings' occupants, resulting in similar binaries: gentry/non-gentry, elite/peasant.[185] This scholarship was, however, the foundation for all future work, as it illustrated the fundamentals of terminologies, construction techniques and typologies. What was missing was the reasoning behind these methods and creations: the meaning.

From around the 1980s the reasons for buildings and their distinct variations – the *why* as opposed to the *what* – became the research focus. Buildings were no longer considered merely as shelter, merely as accommodation; rather, they were viewed as something created consciously to represent, reflect and communicate meaning. This is perhaps most clearly seen in the study of castles and the shift from a warfare-heavy interpretation towards a rounder explanation of their role which expressed facets of personhood. The interactions between people and buildings became the centre of buildings archaeology, with complex ideas on everyday experiences contributing to a better understanding of medieval society.[186] This was influenced by the discipline of archaeology more broadly, which accepts that material culture was imbued with

---

181 William Pantin, 'The Recently Demolished Houses in Broad Street, Oxford', *Oxoniensia*, 4 (1939), 171–200.
182 For example: Eric Mercer, *English Vernacular Houses* (London, 1975); J. T. Smith, 'Timber-framed Building in England', *Archaeological Journal*, 122 (1965), 133–58.
183 Cyril Fox and FitzRoy Richard Somerset Raglan, *Monmouthshire Houses: A Study of Building Techniques and Smaller House-plans in the Fifteenth to Seventeenth Centuries* (Cardiff, 1953).
184 Grenville, *Housing*, p. 13.
185 Jonathon Barry, 'Introduction', in Jonathon Barry and Christopher Brooks (eds), *The Middling Sort of People* (Basingstoke, 1994), pp. 1–27.
186 Gardiner, 'Emergence', pp. 5, 7.

meanings and conveyed messages. In turn, these meanings and messages represent a snippet of the culture in which they were made, used and reused, and exploring them allows an insight into society. However, the dichotomies remain present, at times perpetuated by the uncritical use of unquantifiable descriptors with which buildings archaeology and archaeology more generally are replete, such as status and power.

Grenville writes that the stages of development of an academic discipline, such as buildings archaeology, commence with the recognition of a subject's value, followed by widespread collection and classification of data.[187] She explains that the third stage involves attempting to find meaning behind the patterns identified in the second stage, while the fourth stage is a fully mature discipline that develops different and conflicting standpoints with new arenas emerging from theoretical propositions rather than empirical propositions. In 1997 she asserted that buildings archaeology was in stage three and, over twenty years later, Liz Thomas and Jill Campbell argue that the relationships between buildings, society, meaning and culture remain poorly understood and under-theorised.[188] This may be due to the fact that the study of buildings is spread across various disciplines, and the multi-disciplinary roots of buildings archaeology itself, including architecture, art history, archaeology, ethnology and history, have inevitably resulted in a plethora of approaches to the study of buildings.[189] Indeed, Dan Hicks and Audrey Horning suggest that many archaeologists consider buildings to be the remit of architecture, art history and historical geography, and that 'buried remains of structures encountered by archaeologists are often seen as of less significance than the artefacts recovered'.[190]

If buildings archaeology is in stage three of Grenville's disciplinary evolution, it is not stagnant there. There are a number of key approaches and theories which influence the discipline, and so too this study of lodging ranges; one of these is the theory of space. Katherine Weikert sets out the fundamental motivation for integrating spatial analysis within buildings archaeology: 'there are not simply *things* that allow us to see the past'.[191] There is space, within and between buildings, and it too can be read to reveal meanings. The idea that we must consider and analyse space

187 Grenville, *Housing*, p. 13; David Clark, 'Archaeology: The Loss of Innocence', *Antiquity*, 47:185 (1973), 6–18.
188 Liz Thomas and Jill Campbell, 'Introduction', in Liz Thomas and Jill Campbell (eds), *Buildings in Society: International Studies in the Historic Era* (Summertown, 2018), pp. iii–1.
189 Gardiner, 'Emergence'; Sarah Kerr, 'The Future of Archaeology, Interdisciplinarity and Global Challenges', *Antiquity*, 94:377 (2020), 1337–48.
190 Horning and Hicks, 'Historical', p. 275.
191 Emphasis in original: Kate Weikert, *Authority, Gender and Space in the Anglo-Norman World, 900–1200* (Woodbridge, 2020), p. 47.

in order to understand the past emerged in the mid-twentieth century. It has been used in a variety of contexts, and using a variety of different approaches, but its use in the study of medieval buildings was pioneered by Patrick Faulkner.

In two key papers Faulkner uses spatial analysis to posit domestic planning in manor houses and castles constructed before the fourteenth century.[192] An architect, Faulkner started with the now familiar assumption that a building's plan indicates its function and purpose, and that it can reveal the 'mode of living of those for whom the building was designed'.[193] His planning analysis approach utilises circulation patterns to highlight the development of private rooms and domestic comfort from the thirteenth century to the Renaissance house. Through his work it became accepted that the degree of difficulty in accessing spaces within the great house was an indication of the rank of the occupant of those spaces. His argument that the innermost spaces were occupied by the most important people within the household assisted the development of access analysis.[194]

Access analysis is a spatial analysis method that provides a way to determine the accessibility of a building's constituent spaces. That is, it explores 'depth' of space and the degree to which this is penetrable, which can then be used to determine which spaces might be more likely to host social interactions.[195] It is widely used in the study of medieval buildings and, while it certainly originated with Faulkner's work, it is equally indebted to Bill Hillier and Julienne Hanson's theoretical framework set out in *The Social Logic of Space*.[196] Their focus is on contemporary design, but their central premise that 'spatial organisation in society is a function of differentiation' informs the study of space across the medieval period.[197] A building was created in a deliberate manner to organise and demarcate space, which, as Weikert states, was tantamount to organising

---

192 Patrick Faulkner, 'Domestic Planning from the Twelfth to the Fourteenth Centuries', *Archaeological Journal*, 115 (1958), 150–84; Patrick Faulkner, 'Castle Planning in the Fourteenth Century', *Archaeological Journal*, 120:1 (1963), 215–35.
193 Faulkner, 'Domestic', p. 150.
194 Faulkner, 'Castle'.
195 Kevin D. Fisher, 'Placing Social Interaction: An Integrative Approach to Analyzing Past Built Environments', *Journal of Anthropological Archaeology*, 28:4 (2009), 439–57, p. 440; Peter Fisher, Chris Farrelly, Adrian Maddocks and Clive Ruggles, 'Spatial Analysis of Visible Areas from the Bronze Age Cairns of Mull', *Journal of Archaeological Science*, 24:7 (1997), 581–92.
196 Bill Hillier and Julienne Hanson, *The Social Logic of Space* (Cambridge, 1984).
197 John Schofield, 'The Topography and Buildings of London, ca. 1600', in Lena Cowen Orlin (ed.), *Material London, ca. 1600* (Philadelphia, 2012), pp. 296–321; Gilchrist, *Gender and Material Archaeology*; Graham Fairclough, 'Meaningful Constructions – Spatial and Functional Analysis of Medieval Buildings', *Antiquity*, 66:251 (1992), 348–66.

and demarcating people within those spaces.[198] Graham Fairclough summarises that a key point in Hillier and Hanson's work is that social relations became more formal as they became less frequent. Therefore the 'deeper' the space, the more exclusionary and higher-status it was deemed; in turn, this status can be extended to the inhabitants of this space.[199]

Access analysis is not without its critics.[200] In particular, the use of access diagrams, whereby rooms and access are represented schematically with shapes and lines, is problematic. This format eradicates many of the things that make a space, such as the size of a room or the provisions within, which are represented on a conventional plan. With its focus on control over access, the ways in which a space was received through sight and smell are overlooked. Grenville advises that the ways in which different groups perceived the same space should not be ignored.[201] Similarly, this is a weakness in Faulkner's planning analysis approach. By focusing on the designer's brief, there is a rigidity implied that overlooks the recursive nature of space and occupant. Regardless, Faulkner's work is rightly credited by those undertaking spatial analysis of medieval buildings today.

Despite the potential pitfalls of planning and access analyses, they have been used to take considerable strides in our understanding of the past. Work by Richardson, Fairclough and Weikert, for example, does not use access analysis and its stripped-back diagrams in isolation.[202] Rather, it is the foundation upon which more complicated ideas on gender, authority and meaning are built. The fundamental underpinning of both planning and access analysis, namely, that space manipulated communication between groups, is carried throughout this book. This will be combined with an exploration of the elements that make a space: room size, architectural detail and sensory perceptions. As such, conventional floor plans rather than penetration diagrams will be used to aid the discussion.

A further development in buildings archaeology, underpinning some of the arguments that follow, is the application of phenomenology, which, until recently, was more actively employed in prehistoric archaeology. In essence, phenomenology embraces the use of physical senses and experiences of space to understand the past. This way of thinking has been

---

198 Weikert, *Authority*, p. 47.
199 Kim Dovey, *Framing Places: Mediating Power in Built Form* (London, 1999).
200 As identified by Grenville, *Housing*; King, 'Space'; F. Brown, 'Comment on Chapman: Some Cautionary Notes on the Application of Spatial Measures to Prehistoric Settlements', in Ross Samson (ed.), *The Social Archaeology of Houses* (Edinburgh, 1990), pp. 93–109.
201 Grenville, *Housing*, p. 20.
202 Amanda Richardson, 'Corridors of Power: A Case Study in Access Analysis from Medieval England', *Antiquity*, 77:296 (2003), 373–84; Fairclough, 'Meaningful'; Weikert, *Authority*.

criticised for being limited by uncertainty, being overly subjective and lacking rigour. Despite this, when informed by archaeological context and augmented by collective memory, or *lieux de mémoire*, phenomenology can allow for a richer understanding of the lived experience of the past.[203] In addition, retaining some vagueness and uncertainty is useful. In these chapters I describe the gradations of status as blurry, identities as messy, meanings as complex and ambiguous. The medieval lived experience was contingent on cultures which cannot be truly experienced today; therefore attempting to rigidly set these interpretations would be an erroneous over-simplification. There is no one correct 'answer' to understanding lodging ranges: there are many which can be – should be – renegotiated and contested.

CONCLUSION

This examination of lodging ranges attempts to encompass these approaches and binaries. It offers a classification of lodging ranges to fill a terminological gap, and posits the meanings behind the building type. It attempts to explore the in-between: the buildings which were not immediately identifiable as clearly high- or low-status, and the people of middling rank. It is an attempt to embrace meaning, movement, interaction and the senses, including heat, sound and sight. This is not an argument for the removal of commonly-used definitions such as status, power and display from our vocabulary; after all, it could be argued that all these terms are equally abstract. However, this is an attempt to explore the more complex ideas of how people understood the world around them – the lived experience – embedded within status, display, and so on. This work views buildings as expressions of the society in which they were built, but also as actors. They were not merely reactions and reflections; rather, they perpetuated, confirmed and changed elements of society. This shift to focus on meaning allows a deeper understanding of society, but, in this study of lodging ranges, the architecture will not be altogether ignored. This is not an argument for placing the emphasis solely on meaning rather than materiality: they are both crucial in this discussion.

Returning to the question 'Why were lodging ranges built?', I suggest that the answer is considered like a coin. The use is one side of the coin and the function is another. A building was created to serve a series of functions and was used in a number of ways: these need not be the same. Just as former use is detectable in the architecture, so, too, are the former functions. The functions were the very reasons why a building was

---

203 Matthew Johnson, *Lived Experience in the Later Middle Ages* (Oxford, 2017); Gardiner and Kilby, 'Perceptions'.

constructed at that time and in that way, and as such reveal potentially even more about society than does the use. We see here that lodging ranges were built to perform a number of functions, such as displaying tangibly the feudal relationship and presenting the lord's and retainers' identities. This is in addition to, rather than instead of, their use as accommodation. This book will endeavour to focus on exploring the function of lodging ranges to a greater degree than their use, although it will become clear that some functions are more readily available to the buildings archaeologists' eye than others.

1

A ROOM OF ONE'S OWN

STATUS, PRIVACY, AUTHORITY

When approaching the ruins of a medieval building, the first query is often 'How was this building used?' To answer this, we begin by contemplating the fabric and space to determine what features can be identified. These, in turn, are clues to the activities and movements that may have taken place within. This is known as reading the fabric: architecture has a story to tell and the role of the buildings archaeologist is one of translation. Many elements of the architectural 'language' are known, as we perceive the same appearance of features and configuration of space throughout extant remains. This spatial ordering or architectural 'grammar' of buildings, as it is termed by Matthew Johnson, in other words a standardised organisation of space which is employed time and time again, forms part of the basis of understanding medieval buildings in this study.[1] A clear example is the medieval hall, with the cross-passage and services at the low end and the lord's chambers beyond the high end. This plan may have developed as early as the high medieval period and was fully established by the mid-thirteenth century.[2] Representing a remarkable consensus on organisation of space in medieval England, the same hall layout was present in royal, episcopal, knightly and vernacular buildings, with little variation.[3] The concept of high and low ends, reflecting higher and lower status, can be extrapolated to other building types, such as ecclesiastical buildings and courtyards. Provisions such

---

1   Matthew Johnson, *Behind the Castle Gate: From Medieval to Renaissance* (London, 2002), p. 20.
2   Mark Gardiner, 'Vernacular Buildings and the Development of the Later Medieval Domestic Plan in England', *Medieval Archaeology*, 44 (2000), 159–79, p. 179.
3   Gardiner, 'Vernacular', p. 178.

as garderobes, fireplaces and windows contribute to the architectural language. A fireplace or a larger window at the high end of the hall is a feature indicative of a high-status space.

The architectural language of lodging ranges includes lengthy courtyard ranges within late medieval great houses, divided into smaller rooms. The rooms retain evidence for some or all of the following features: garderobes, fireplaces, windows and individual doors. By reading the language we decipher a sense of light, warmth and degree of privacy. This language ties examples together and separates them from other buildings within the great house and elsewhere: that is, it creates a typology. A comparison of this type of building with others suggests that lodging ranges were high-status accommodation provided for members of a lord's retinue.

What do we mean by high status? The study of buildings that fall into the category of 'castle' (as many here do) has focused for decades on whether they were built for war or to demonstrate power and prestige. Far less discussion has examined how problematic these terms are. This contribution will pay no heed to this dichotomous battle, in part because so much has already been said, but also because late medieval great houses are architecturally different from high medieval castles, which are potentially more contentious. There are hints of military uses in these case studies; however, it is clear that great houses were not built to withstand war. There are several studies which have focused on the domestic life of castles; however, status is discussed in a somewhat unnuanced way and the term is used rather imprecisely in relation to the past.[4]

What does 'status' actually mean? It is the social or professional position of a person or group of people. It is an identity: both an identity one wishes to portray, and an identity that is imposed upon one, regardless of whether or not these are aligned. It is an intangible attribute which can be represented through physical things. This chapter explores these physical things. Here, I will describe tangible remains, using them as the basis for deciphering the status of the associated spaces, and explain why these spaces were considered high-status in the late medieval period. In

---

4 For example: Patrick Faulkner, 'Domestic Planning from the Twelfth to the Fourteenth Centuries', *Archaeological Journal*, 115 (1958) 150–84; Patrick Faulkner, 'Castle Planning in the Fourteenth Century', *Archaeological Journal*, 120:1 (1963), 215–35; Philip Dixon, 'The Donjon of Knaresborough: The Castle as Theatre', in Robert Liddiard (ed.), *Late Medieval Castles* (Woodbridge, 2016), pp. 333–48; Philip Dixon, 'Design in Castle-Buildings: The Controlling of Access to the Lord', *Chateau Gaillard*, 18 (1996), 47–57; Philip Dixon and Beryl Lott, 'The Courtyard and The Tower', *Journal of the British Archaeological Association*, 146 (1993), 93–101; Gwyn Meirion-Jones, Edward Impey and Michael Jones (eds), *The Seigneurial Residence in Western Europe AD c.800–1600*, British Archaeological Reports International Series, 1088 (Oxford, 2002).

the next chapter, the argument will be extended to understand how the space represented the status of groups and individuals.

The sense of status detected in the lodging ranges stems primarily from their architecture and the space enclosed by it. The nature of the rooms within the ranges hints that they afforded a degree of privacy not offered to other members of the household. Privacy is another somewhat tricky word, both a blessing and a curse: we must not impose our modern sense of privacy upon the medieval great house and its people, but it is necessary to differentiate between the spaces which were more open and accessible and those that were reserved for fewer people and less activity. Features which afforded privacy in the great house granted a household member a degree of separation from others. This separation has been discussed in several medieval contexts, including the long-standing debate on the first-floor hall, best summarised by Nick Hill and Mark Gardiner.[5] Katherine Weikert and Audrey Thorstad tackle this topic in relation to houses of the high and post-medieval periods respectively.[6] Both build on the work of Diana Webb, who discusses at length the anachronisms embedded in the concept of medieval 'privacy'.[7] Weikert uses access analysis to show how high-status spaces, such as chambers, became more private. It is widely accepted that the lord's chambers, for example, were among the most secluded spaces. These rooms were accessible only to those with whom the lord worked most closely; gentle servants, for example, might sleep within the chamber or nearby. Medieval privacy, then, should be considered as Gardiner and Susan Kilby define it: the freedom to be alone without impromptu intrusion and the ability to be remote from public gaze.[8]

Much of the work on privacy, or, more accurately, social separation, acquiesces that the terminology is imperfect and that we lack an expression to succinctly describe more separate – less accessible, but not quite private – space. Likewise, 'public' is an over-simplification of the spaces which were more socially and physically accessible. We can, however,

---

5   Nick Hill and Mark Gardiner, 'The English Medieval First-floor Hall: Part 2 – The Evidence from the Eleventh to Early Thirteenth Century', *Archaeological Journal*, 175 (2018), 315–61; Nick Hill and Mark Gardiner, 'The English Medieval First-floor Hall: Part 1 – Scolland's Hall, Richmond, North Yorkshire', *Archaeological Journal*, 175 (2018), 157–83.
6   Katherine Weikert, *Authority, Gender and Space in the Anglo-Norman World, 900–1200* (Woodbridge, 2020); Audrey Thorstad, *The Culture of Castles in Tudor England and Wales* (Woodbridge, 2019). See also: Georges Duby (ed.), *A History of Private Life II* (London, 1988).
7   Diana Webb, *Privacy and Solitude in the Middle Ages* (London, 2007).
8   Mark Gardiner and Susan Kilby, 'Perceptions of Medieval Settlement', in Christopher Gerrard and Alejandra Gutiérrez (eds), *The Oxford Handbook of Later Medieval Archaeology in Britain* (Oxford, 2018), pp. 210–25, at p. 216.

grasp the general distinction between 'public' and 'private' spaces. A lord's chambers, for example, were higher-status spaces, socially and physically separated from others, quieter, and with greater comfort. While this may suggest solitude, it was not so; after all, if someone empties your chamber pot, your room is not 'private' to our modern sensibilities. Privacy was not a mark of modesty but a physical representation of status and honour, and, as such, the lord's room reflected a distinction between its owner and the remainder of the household. Privacy in the medieval context should be considered as a representation of the social distance between people.[9] Therefore, 'private' makes sense only in a continuum with 'public'. These meanings were not dichotomies; rather, they coexisted, dynamically in all spaces. As Thorstad summarises, 'a space [was] neither wholly public nor wholly private at any given time'.[10]

This discussion has gone some way to help set out an understanding of status, but it remains a little sterile in terms of discussing people and where they live. When looking at the high-status nature of the lord's chamber, and considering the comfort and social separation, we can detect an authority over the space. The overwhelming majority of household members could not freely enter this space; likewise, guests could enter only when invited. This control is another thread in our understanding of status: it was demonstrated through one's ability to make decisions on others' movements and, crucially, to enforce obedience.

Status, privacy and authority were overlapping continuums maintained through practice in the great house, rather than through fixed, permanent ideals. Each was relational and dynamic; one person's status only made sense in relation to another's. Lords were not 'high-status' in a vacuum; they were of a higher status than their tenants. Likewise, a private space was only a more separate and secluded space than somewhere else. Rather than being perceived as ephemeral or obscure, status, authority and privacy were utterly recognised and accepted by medieval society. They contributed to the social structure of the household and this, in turn, was partly created and maintained by the physical buildings. These elements of the lived experience are detectable in buildings and help us to understand the uses of the various spaces: this is the focus of this chapter.

THE LANGUAGE OF LODGING RANGES

Lodging ranges are identified in the archaeological record as long, two- or three-storey ranges with uniform elevations within courtyards of

9 Sarah Kerr, 'A study of lodging ranges in late medieval England' (Unpublished Ph.D. dissertation, Queen's University Belfast, 2016).
10 Thorstad, *Culture*, p. 155.

great houses. The ranges might be timber-framed or masonry, although the latter was far more common. Gainsborough Hall, Lincolnshire, and Bishop's Waltham Palace, Hampshire, were originally constructed from timber, with Gainsborough later underbuilt to support its warping frame. The predominance of masonry allows the features of lodging ranges to be identified with relative ease, thanks to its permanence, and how these features are identified will be shown here.

The surviving or supposed fabric of lodging ranges indicates that there was no clear development of the form between the mid-fourteenth century and the early sixteenth century (Table 1).[11] Window, fireplace, garderobe and individual door were provided in one of the earliest known examples, at Ince Manor, Cheshire, built in the mid-to-late fourteenth century. Here, only two diminished ranges remain of the former monastic grange, perpendicular to one another but not connected physically. The hall range retains three large windows on its west-facing elevation, indicating that the high end of the hall was to the north. The lodging range comprised four rooms over two floors, each with an individual door. The two ground-floor doors had hood mouldings and were paired together with shared jambs in the centre of the range; the two first-floor doors were at opposing ends. Each room had a garderobe, a fireplace on the rear north wall, and at least three windows. Built almost two centuries later, the lodging range at Thornbury Castle, Gloucestershire, contained at least five rooms per floor, each with a fireplace and garderobe on its rear north wall. The individual doors were on the south elevation, with two-stone elliptical arches and chamfered edges, beside the windows. Table 1 includes the features in each example and shows that similar plans were repeated, with few exceptions, until lodging ranges were no longer required in the great house. This consistency informs us of the following fundamentals. Lodging ranges were a distinct type of building: that is, they were a specifically defined category of accommodation which differed from other types, particularly in the great house. Second, their architectural distinction implies that they were visually recognisable to the medieval audience. Third, their consistency suggests that they had a function and use which remained constant throughout the period of their construction. This use, according to the architectural language, was high-status accommodation. Yet, some justification of this architectural reading is required: why do these features indicate high-status accommodation? This section will demonstrate *how* these features created a high-status space.

---

11   See also the two gazetteers of known examples, on pp. 229–38.

TABLE 1   A SELECTION OF LODGING RANGES AND THE FEATURES RECORDED IN EACH, DEMONSTRATING REMARKABLE CONSISTENCY ACROSS TWO CENTURIES.

Great house	Date of construction	Type	Uniform façade	Window	Fireplace	Garderobe	Individual doors
Ince Manor, Cheshire	Mid-to-late 1300s	Two-storey range	✓	✓	✓	✓	✓
Amberley Castle, Sussex	c.1377	Two-storey range	✓	✓	✓	✓	Probable
Dartington Hall, Devon	1390–1400	Two-storey ranges	✓	✓	✓	✓	✓
Middleham Castle, North Yorkshire	1400–25	Three-storey range	✓	✓	✓*	✓*	✓
Brympton d'Evercy, Somerset	1434–64	Two-storey range	✓	✓	✓	✓	✓
Bishop's Waltham Palace, Hampshire	1438–42	Two-storey range	✓	Probable	✓	X	✓
Wingfield Manor, Derbyshire	1440–56	Three-storey range	✓	✓*	✓	✓*	✓
Haddon Hall, Derbyshire	1470–90	Two-storey range	✓	✓	✓	✓*	✓
Gainsborough Hall, Lincolnshire	c.1480	Three-storey range	✓	✓	✓	✓	✓
Brook Hall, Wiltshire	1491–1502	Two-storey range	✓	✓	X	✓	✓
Thornbury Castle, Gloucester	1510–21	Three-storey range	✓	✓	✓*	✓*	✓
Cotehele Manor, Cornwall	1530–45	Two-storey courtyard	✓	✓	✓	Probable	✓
Old Newnham, Devon	Early 1500s	Two-storey range	X	✓	✓	✓*	✓

*In some rooms only

Garderobes

The term garderobe, in the sense of a latrine, appeared in the written record in the fourteenth century.[12] The amenity itself appeared much earlier: Eric Fernie notes the 'linguistically magnificent' Gold Hole Tower at Richmond Castle, North Yorkshire, built in the late eleventh century.[13] While in buildings archaeology the term is used almost exclusively to mean latrine, this is somewhat misleading, as the great house also contained spaces called garderobes that were, in fact, wardrobes.[14] Indeed, the term was borrowed from the French word for wardrobe.

The majority of garderobes in late medieval great houses were built within towers which jutted from the external wall, making them easily identifiable to the viewer from outside the house itself. As such, garderobe towers were prevalent in late medieval lodging ranges. These were usually square towers, sometimes embellished with decoration, as at Gainsborough, although most are now too truncated to determine if decoration was the norm. Windows, other than narrow slits or cruciform, were uncommon in the towers. Garderobe towers were probably the preferred construction method because, over the course of the medieval period, average wall thickness reduced, meaning that setting garderobes within the wall itself would have been difficult.

There were two main waste-disposal methods, neither of which can be deemed convincingly as higher-status, and both have been found in examples of lodging ranges. Some garderobes deposited waste into cesspits, which were subsequently emptied. This can be identified by an empty space below the garderobes and within the building, as at Haddon Hall and Thornbury. Other garderobes utilised a chute to expel waste beyond the walls. These can be identified by small, usually square, gaps in the fabric with a slanted base to aid the removal of waste from above. Garderobes were often above one another or grouped together on the same floor; consequently, the base of the tower might accommodate a large communal cesspit or numerous chutes from the latrines above. A common form exploited the landscape, with chutes terminating over a moat, river, or natural drop in ground level, as, for example, at Middleham Castle, North Yorkshire, and Amberley Castle, Sussex.

Regardless of the presence of towers, the architecture of garderobes is often easily discernible from within the lodging range. In all cases the

---

12 Margaret Wood, *The English Medieval House* (New York, 1965), p. 377.
13 Eric Fernie, 'Technical Terms and the Understanding of English Medieval Architecture', *Architectural History*, 44 (2001), 13–21, p. 18. See also: Hill and Gardiner, 'Part 1'.
14 Christopher Woolgar, *The Great Household in Late Medieval England* (New Haven, 1999).

garderobe itself was a small space with a stone or wooden seat. When the seat has been lost the chute or drop to the cesspit is visible, as is the case at Middleham, where some garderobes were set within the exterior wall's thickness. This allows some assurance with regard to their prevalence in lodging ranges, with nearly all known examples containing garderobes within the rooms. A further feature that helps in identifying garderobes is the access point: a door, usually rather narrow, from the room to a smaller space on the exterior wall. Articulation of the door was subtle, if present at all. In larger great houses, such as Thornbury, Wingfield Manor, Derbyshire, and Dartington Hall, Devon, the garderobes were paired in twos across the extent of the range (Figure 2). Two doors, side-by-side and with shared jambs, led to two garderobes. Each door connected one room to one garderobe: that is, the rooms and garderobes were divided by a timber partition. In smaller lodging ranges many garderobes were standalone and there was more variety in form, such as the brétèche-style garderobe preserved on the first floor at Old Newnham, Devon, with wooden seat intact and small, decorative quatrefoil vent. It deposited waste directly into the river along the edge of the house, albeit from a height of several metres. Unfortunately, garderobes are little studied in both archaeology and history. Christopher Woolgar refers to cleanliness as a mark of gentility, perhaps supposing, therefore, that considerable efforts were undertaken to maintain chutes.[15] Johnson, however, discusses how – despite best efforts – moats turned into open sewers and great houses on raised ground had waste visible on the sloping land: the view 'must have been striking, to say the least'.[16]

Particularly sophisticated garderobes had systems utilising streams or rainwater. For example, Warkworth Castle's keep, built in Northumberland in the late fourteenth century, collected rainwater in a cistern, while the garderobes at Fountains Abbey, North Yorkshire, which pre-dated lodging ranges, were flushed by a stream.[17] None of the known lodging ranges exhibit this technology, although a battery of garderobes in the north tower at Wingfield, described below, was flushed by rainwater.[18] Even Thornbury, a late example of a lodging range, had cesspits at the base of the garderobe tower.

Garderobes were among the principal representations of individuals' status. They were not provided in all types of household accommodation, so were not available to everyone. When compared with other high-status features, such as windows and fireplaces, the scarcity of the garderobe

15   Woolgar, *Household*, p. 170.
16   Johnson, *Castle*, p . 43.
17   Wood, *House*, pp. 386–7.
18   Johnson, *Castle*, p. 43.

FIG. 2 PHOTOGRAPH OF THE INNER FACE OF THE EXTERNAL ELEVATION OF THORNBURY CASTLE'S LODGING RANGE. TWO GARDEROBES DOORS WERE PAIRED SIDE-BY-SIDE. EACH CONNECTED ONE ROOM TO ONE GARDEROBE. THERE WERE AT LEAST SIX SETS OF SUCH PAIRED GARDEROBES AT THORNBURY. NOTE THAT THE FIREPLACES ARE SIMILARLY PAIRED TOGETHER.

is clear: at Bodiam Castle, Sussex, there were thirty-three fireplaces but only twenty-eight garderobes.[19] It was this relative lack of garderobes throughout the remainder of the great house that demonstrates the lodging ranges' high status, and that of its occupants.

Garderobe towers served to advertise the social position of the lord in two ways. First, they were an opportunity for status-demonstrating architectural flair, strikingly shown at Gainsborough through the unique stepped gablets on each of the four garderobe towers on the lodging range (see Figure 21). Second, as intimated above, garderobes were reserved for use by high-ranking staff, and their presence therefore indicated to the medieval audience beyond the house the presence of high-status household members. This explicit display of the lord's status may have been another reason for building towers, as opposed to concealing the garderobes within the thickness of the walls or using chamber pots.

While garderobe towers were typical occurrences in lodging ranges, they did not always provide facilities to the ground-floor rooms, despite the convenience given the positions of the rooms one above another. This

19 Johnson, *Castle*, p. 20.

indicates that the ground-floor rooms were of lower status than those above and garderobes were an exclusively high-status feature (Table 1). At Haddon, the garderobe tower constructed in the lodging range had garderobes on the first floor only, with the space on the ground floor accommodating the cesspit (Figure 3). A similar arrangement occurred at Thornbury: in this three-storey example of a lodging range, the garderobes on both the first and (planned) second floor expelled waste into the ground-floor cesspit. While the range remained incomplete and the second floor was never constructed, the chutes terminating in the cesspit can be traced to the top of the ruinous first-floor wall, indicating the plan for a second floor complete with garderobes.

Batteries of garderobes elsewhere in the great house act as an indicator of a high-status space. These were groups of garderobes not associated directly with accommodation, but, rather, accessible to a greater number of people in a more public setting. At Wingfield, the ground floor of the west tower comprised a number of garderobes accessible from the courtyard. Similarly, at Middleham a door located on the ground floor of the lodging range's garderobe tower led directly from the courtyard to a single garderobe, whereas the other garderobes therein were accessible only from the adjacent rooms. In both examples the common garderobe(s) were located in the inner courtyard, suggesting use by relatively high-status members of the household working in this area. Much like their inclusion within particular areas of accommodation, here the garderobes were creating a high-status space. Those who were restricted to working in one of the outer courtyards or outside the great house itself were not considered of an appropriate rank to use this amenity. These garderobes were not truly 'public' or communal, but they appear to have been added for use by multiple people working or passing through the inner courtyard. It is of note that the lodging ranges at both these great houses comprised three storeys, suggesting vast households.

The prevalence of garderobes in lodging ranges is of particular interest because both garderobes and chamber pots were used in the late medieval period. While the use of either was not a private affair, there seems to be a development from chamber pots towards the use of garderobes, particularly in high-status great houses. At a time when rooms were becoming more 'private', in the sense of being occupied by fewer people and serving fewer functions, the garderobe may have removed the requirement for another person to enter the room: that is, it was not necessary for a servant to enter when there was no chamber pot to empty. The quasi-private garderobe is part of the development towards the private toilet; by the sixteenth century garderobes had become less frequent in favour of close stools.[20]

20 Nicholas Cooper, *House of the Gentry* (London, 1999), p. 298.

The cessation of garderobe construction was accelerated by the difficulty of adding a tower to an elevation that was becoming increasingly regular and symmetrical.

Individual Doors

Individual doors – that is, one door per room – were one of the most important features of the lodging range because of their consistent appearance and their rarity in other types of accommodation (Table 1). Individual doors are perceptible in remains in the form of the doorway itself – always on the inner, courtyard-facing elevation – and in the configuration of the rooms beyond. The former is the easier to detect: doors invariably have jambs of dressed stone. The apertures maybe be further articulated with four-centred arches, as at Haddon and Dartington, or shouldered or pointed arches. At Middleham, the inner elevation remains as truncated footings, meaning that the door is perceptible only as a chamfer stop at the base of a dressed jamb.

In some instances the inner elevation has been entirely lost or altered, and the presence and position of individual doors must be identified through the configuration of the rooms within the range. At Gainsborough, the survival of the timber partitions within the range indicates the full extent of each room. This is rare, however, and in most cases the positions of the partitions are estimated based on the organisation of space. For example, the paired garderobes described above suggest the presence of a timber partition creating two rooms, which in turn allows an exploration of how these rooms were accessed. At Amberley Castle no inner elevation or room partitions remain. However, a perfectly symmetrical external elevation is retained, with two sets of paired garderobes at the centre (Figure 4). This suggests the position of internal partitions creating two rooms on the ground floor and two above. It is highly likely that there were individual doors into each of these rooms, possibly directly opposite the garderobe doors, as seen at Thornbury, Dartington and Wingfield.

Individual doors differentiated lodging ranges from communal accommodation for servants and other household members, where the door was used by many people. Much like the garderobe, it was the scarcity of the feature that bestowed status upon the space beyond it. However, it also created high-status space through physical separation, which in turn bolstered the social importance of those who occupied the space. It offered separation, something akin to privacy, and a sense of ownership of the space beyond the door. The retainer was ultimately under the jurisdiction of the lord, but they had rights to the space beyond the door, where other household members did not. This implies that the door was a principal status indicator and pinnacle of architectural aspiration in late medieval

FIG. 3 PHOTOGRAPH FACING HADDON HALL. THE LODGING RANGE WAS TO THE SOUTH (RIGHT) OF THE GATEHOUSE, WITH A GARDEROBE TOWER CENTRAL ON ITS EXTERIOR ELEVATION. GARDEROBES WERE PROVIDED ONLY ON THE FIRST FLOOR, WITH THE CESSPIT OCCUPYING THE GROUND-FLOOR SPACE OF THE TOWER, ALTHOUGH THIS DISTINCTION IS IMPERCEPTIBLE FROM OUTSIDE THE BUILDINGS.

FIG. 4 TWO SETS OF PAIRED GARDEROBES IN THE CENTRE OF THE LODGING RANGE AT AMBERLEY CASTLE INDICATE THE PLACEMENT OF PARTITIONS TO CREATE FOUR ROOMS. FOUR INDIVIDUAL DOORS INTO THE ROOMS MAY HAVE BEEN PRESENT ON THE NOW-LOST INNER ELEVATION. WHEN COMBINED WITH THE FIREPLACES AND WINDOWS, THE GARDEROBES CREATED A SYMMETRICAL EXTERNAL ELEVATION.

accommodation, not only in the great house but throughout society, as demonstrated by David Stocker's description of the development from dormitories to vicarial houses at York.[21] The vicars' college was established in the 1250s, with accommodation provided in the north range. This comprised a two-storeyed, timber-framed dormitory of seventeen bays. In the 1330s or 1340s the dormitory underwent considerable changes, with the space divided into individual rooms accessed by corridors: thus each room had its own entrance. The college's contemporary documentation describes these *cubiculi* as occupied by individual vicars.[22] By the late fourteenth century the *cubiculi* range was again renovated, transforming it into a row of individual two-storeyed houses, with the lower parts of the walls clad, or partly clad, in stone. Individual doors, previously hidden from external view by the corridor, were now visible. Stocker argues that the importance of having one's own door, 'the very symbol of the household', should not be understated. It was 'perhaps the individual vicar's most valued badge of his ... social and professional status'.[23]

In lodging ranges, the doors connected the room and the courtyard, either directly or via a small lobby or corridor. There is some evidence to suggest that they were concealed from view in later examples. At Dartington (*c*.1390) each door was visible from the courtyard, allowing one to count the rooms beyond; however, at Wingfield (*c*.1440), Haddon (*c*.1480), and Thornbury Castle (*c*.1510) concealed stairs provided access to some of the doors. Each room still had an individual door, suggesting that the feature was an important social indicator reflecting the status of the occupants, regardless of whether or not it could be seen from outside.

Fireplaces and Windows

Nearly all examples of lodging ranges contained fireplaces and windows, sometimes large and decorated. Fireplaces, and the heat they provided, were status indicators, as demonstrated by their provision and position in the great house. In the late medieval hall, for example, the fireplace was on the long wall, closer to the high end and the lord's family, rather than in the centre of the room as it had been in earlier decades. Notably, within the hall at Dartington it was directly behind the dais, to the disadvantage of the remainder of the hall. Only in the lodging range at Brook Hall, Wiltshire, was there a total lack of fireplaces, despite the presence of all the other commonly found provisions (Table 1). This was a fairly late

---

21 David Stocker, 'The Quest for One's Own Front Door: Housing the Vicars' Choral at the English Cathedrals', *Vernacular Architecture*, 36 (2005), 15–31.
22 Stocker, 'Quest', p. 18.
23 Stocker, 'Quest', p. 21.

example, built towards the end of the fifteenth century by Willoughby, the first Baron of Brook, which may suggest that a desire for more uniform elevations throughout led to the use of braziers. In some instances, fireplaces were provided in each and every room within the lodging range, while in others the provision was omitted from certain rooms, such as the ground floor of Thornbury and possibly the third floor of Middleham. The overall consistency of fireplaces throughout other examples may suggest that their omission is evidence of servant accommodation; that is, for staff serving the retainers.

Fireplaces are discernible in the extant fabric as a large opening in line with the former level of the floor. There was often dressed stone flanking the opening, invariably a dressed lintel, and a flat stone at the base of the firebox. Some decoration may be discernible, such as that in the three-storeyed range at Wingfield. On the first floor there was a chamfered edge to the fireplace's jambs which was not added to the fireplaces in the half-basement rooms. From outside the lodging range, depending on the condition of the range, a chimney may be visible.

Windows in the great house often illuminated a high-status space; for example, a grand window was commonplace at the high end of the hall, where the lord was seated during meals. Gainsborough's six-bay, timber-framed hall was adorned with a stone-built bay window at the north elevation of the hall, illuminating the dais. Most lodging ranges in this study contained at least one window per room: it was the most consistent feature present. Windows can be identified by a gap in the fabric, surrounded by dressed stone. The jambs were often splayed, to allow in more light, particularly where the walls were very thick. Larger windows would include stone transoms and mullions and might be headed by a decorative arch. Decoration and size varied, particularly across floors, with the larger and more elaborate versions on the upper levels. At Amberley Castle, for example, the ground floor of the lodging range had small cruciform windows with extremely wide splays, while on the first floor there were larger, two-light trefoil-cusped windows, with quatrefoil open spandrels under a two-centred arch (see Figure 17). While there is an overall consistency of windows and fireplaces in lodging ranges, variation in these provisions or in their decoration hints at the creation of a hierarchy within the range. In contrast to these intimations of a hierarchy, the external elevation remained overwhelmingly uniform.

Uniformity

Uniformity, as a part of the language of lodging ranges, refers to an elevation's regular architectural display. This is separate from the consistency perceived within the ranges, and thus requires some explanation. There were some consistently-sized rooms in most of the examples of lodging ranges (see Table 2 on p. 94). For example, at Dartington, sixteen rooms in the west range were all 30m^2, while those at Bishop's Waltham Place, Hampshire, were 20m^2. In other examples, however, such as Haddon, the rooms varied between 13.5m^2 and 21m^2. It is apparent that all known examples of lodging ranges were divided into small rooms, but it would not be accurate to state that these were always uniformly sized.

There was also consistency in the presence of high-status provisions in lodging ranges, as highlighted above, yet this, too, varied: not all features were present in all instances and nor were the features always decorated to the same extent. For example, at Haddon, the omission of garderobes in the ground-floor rooms, as well as the provision of fewer windows, differentiated this floor from the floor above it. At Amberley the ground-floor windows were small, sparsely decorated versions of those in the rooms directly above. Lodging-range uniformity, therefore, does not refer to the size of rooms nor the provisions: it relates to the architectural display of *sameness* across the elevations, despite variations in room size or amenities. The consistency of the uniform elevations suggests that it was intended to deliberately conceal the variations within, as discussed in Chapter 2.

Uniformity was created in a number of ways. Pairing, or mirroring, was the placement of two identical features beside one another. The ground-floor doors at Ince Manor, described above, were paired together in the centre of the range. This occurred at Dartington, too, with the ground-floor doors sharing jambs as they did at Ince. Dartington's first-floor doors were also paired together, directly above those on the ground floor. The result was a group of four identical doors (Figure 5). Garderobes were often paired together, as at Haddon, Thornbury, Wingfield, Amberley and Middleham, on the exterior wall. In each example this allowed the creation of a substantial garderobe tower which drew a viewer's eye skywards and bestowed a sense of minusculatity upon the viewer. Similarly, fireplaces were paired together at Thornbury (Figure 2) and Wingfield, spaced equidistant between the paired garderobes. This was another feature which contributed to the uniformity: equal spacing. At Dartington, windows comprising four lights, mimicking the group of four doors, were evenly spaced between each group of doors along the range (Figure 5). A display of uniformity was created by the groups of four doors followed by the four-light windows repeated along the lodging range. These equidistant, repeated and mirrored features created a striking display of uniformity more commonly associated with the Elizabethan period and later.

Many of the ways of achieving uniformity in Elizabethan-era houses appear in lodging ranges, such as symmetry, repetition, pairing and equal spacing. The elevations of prodigy or country houses did not develop directly from lodging ranges, however. Rather, uniformity was developing across the continent during the late medieval and Tudor periods, and lodging ranges, vicarial and collegiate ranges and inns were a product of this. This development culminated in the façades of the late sixteenth and early seventeenth centuries. In the late medieval great house, uniformity was an emerging fashion, and, as such, indicative of high status.[24] Further motives for the creation of uniform elevations are discussed in Chapter 3.

DARTINGTON HALL, DEVON

As one approaches Dartington Hall, not far from the banks of the River Dart in Devon, the massive expanse of the courtyard is belied by the unassuming gatehouse and the surrounding flat land. Once beyond the gatehouse's semi-circular arch of undressed stonework, one is faced with the exceptional courtyard, 4000m^2 in size, built by John Holland, first Duke of Exeter, Earl of Huntington. Once within the courtyard, the porch of the cross-wing stands opposite, with an entrance much more elaborate than the gatehouse. Two ranges flanked the courtyard, probably both lodging ranges. Whether arriving to meet Holland in the fourteenth century, or visiting Dartington today, the eighty-metre walk towards the hall porch leaves one in no doubt regarding his status. The repetition of doors and windows created an overwhelmingly uniform elevation, particularly on the west range, that is still obvious even today despite modern changes. The uniformity creates something of an optical illusion, giving an impression of even more of these features. The sheer size of the courtyard is impressive and an awareness of what the lodging range contained, namely Holland's many retainers, left a visitor aware of the lord's power and assured that he had the following to prove it.

The great house occupied a site near Totnes which had been in use since at least the second quarter of the ninth century. The Martin family owned the manor in the twelfth and thirteenth centuries, and the earliest archaeological evidence dates to the second half of the thirteenth century.[25] In 1962, excavation beyond the hall range, in what was the inner courtyard, uncovered the footings of an earlier rectangular structure, measuring 6 metres by 12 metres, which may have been the hall of the Martin family (Figure 6). It was rediscovered along with a late thirteenth-century French jug and an unstratified Edward I coin.[26] In 1388 the estate was passed

---

24 Jill Campbell, 'Architectural design and exterior display in gentry houses in 14th- and 15th-century England' (Unpublished Ph.D. dissertation, Queen's University Belfast, 2012).
25 Anthony Emery, *Dartington Hall* (Oxford, 1970) pp. 13, 95.
26 Colin Platt, 'Excavations at Dartington Hall', *Archaeological Journal*, 119 (1962), 208–24, p. 223.

FIG. 5 PHOTOGRAPH OF THE NORTHERN EXTENT OF DARTINGTON HALL'S LODGING RANGE. TWO SETS OF PAIRED ENTRANCES CREATED A GROUP OF FOUR IDENTICAL DOORS, A PATTERN REFLECTED IN THE FOUR-LIGHT WINDOWS, JUST SEEN TO THE LEFT ON THE GROUND FLOOR. THERE WERE THREE OTHER WINDOWS OF THE SAME FORM (CONCEALED UNDER FOLIAGE HERE) EVENLY SPACED AROUND THE GROUP OF DOORS: THE PATTERN WAS REPEATED ALONG THE LENGTH OF THE LODGING RANGE.

from the crown to John Holland, who was Earl of Huntington, son-in-law of John of Gaunt, and Richard II's half-brother.[27] Holland's relationship with Richard II helped him ascend to become Duke of Exeter and a leading magnate, and he immediately began building at Dartington.[28] In the rib-vaulted hall porch, the central boss is decorated with the hart of Richard II, an emblem the king adopted in c.1390 before he was deposed in 1399; this allows the construction of the hall range to be dated to this period. Dartington Hall was built on a much larger scale than any earlier or contemporary great house in the region, such as Powderham, Tiverton, Exeter or Bradley Manor.[29] As it stands, Dartington is mainly the work of the fourteenth century, although different window forms and varying roof heights indicate several generations of additions. It is likely that Holland built the outer court with lodging ranges occupying at least the west range

27 Emery, *Dartington*, p. 95.
28 Anthony Emery, *Greater Medieval Houses of England and Wales 1300–1500* (3 vols, Cambridge, 2000; 2000; 2006), Vol. 3, p. 534; Emery, *Dartington*, p. 23.
29 Emery, *Greater Medieval Houses*, Vol. 3, p. 534.

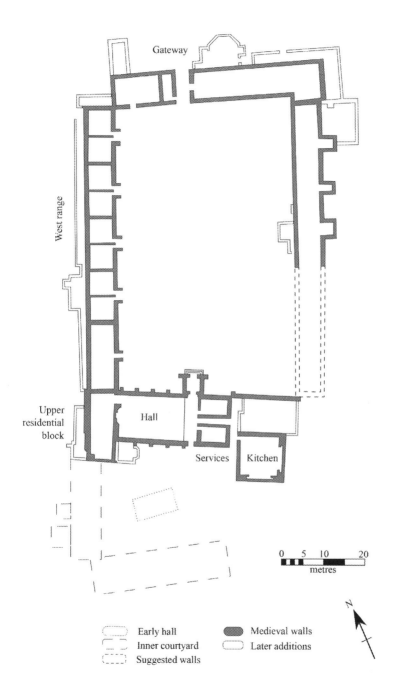

FIG. 6 PLAN OF DARTINGTON HALL SHOWING THE EARLY HALL, WHICH PREDATED THE NOW-LOST INNER COURTYARD, AND THE CONSIDERABLE SIZE OF THE OUTER COURTYARD.

and possibly the east, and it has been suggested that the west range was his last addition before his role in the Epiphany Rising, which resulted in his capture and execution in 1400.[30]

The courtyard is the largest undivided example constructed prior to the sixteenth century, measuring 80 metres by 50 metres.[31] The gateway bisected the barn and stables in the north range. The south range of the courtyard comprised, from east to west: the kitchen, services with the lower residential block above, the hall porch and cross-passage, the hall, and the upper residential block (Figure 6). The range followed the usual medieval plan, with accommodation for the family on the upper floors beyond the high end of the hall. It is currently the private residence of the owners of the estate.

The courtyard certainly comprised a lodging range on the west and there was possibly a second lodging range to the east. The west lodging range, seventy-six metres long, had eighteen evenly spaced doors across two floors, creating an incredibly uniform façade (Figures 7 and 8). Each door led directly from the courtyard into a room. The range was divided into five groups of rooms (Figure 8), four of which comprised four chambers, two on the ground floor and two on the first floor, occupying the full depth of the range. The group at the north of the range remains almost in its medieval form, demonstrating the features that would have been visible across the entire façade. An open porch stood in the centre of the group of rooms. There were two doors under its undressed voussoir archway, each leading directly from the courtyard into a ground-floor room. A stone staircase ascended from the south to the north (left to right) over the porch, leading to a further two doors for the first-floor rooms (Figure 5). The doors retain their four-centred arches, and the jambs, shared between two doors, had chamfer edges ending in a chamfer stop. On the ground floor the shared jambs were later replaced, and on the first floor a pentice was added in the eighteenth century. The plan of four doors leading to four rooms was repeated along the range to create sixteen identical rooms, with sixteen doors and sixteen four-light windows. At the southern end of the range there were two larger rooms comprising the fifth group of rooms (Figure 8).

Each of the sixteen identical doors led into a room measuring 6 metres by 5 metres, each with a window in the eastern façade. The windows were equally spaced along the elevation and consisted of four lights with shouldered arches. The exterior elevation has been much altered and no external evidence remains of the garderobe towers that were once present, although traces have been detected within the interior. The garderobes

---

30 Emery, *Dartington*, p. 98.
31 Emery, *Greater Medieval Houses*, Vol. 3, pp. 534–5.

FIG. 7 ENGRAVING BY S. AND N. BUCK IN 1734 SHOWING THE WEST RANGE OF DARTINGTON HALL BEFORE MOST OF THE ALTERATIONS WERE MADE. THE PAIRED AND EVENLY SPACED FEATURES, REPEATED ALONG THE ELEVATION, CREATED A STRIKINGLY UNIFORM FAÇADE. INCLUDED WITH PERMISSION FROM SP LOHIA COLLECTION AND © THE BRITISH LIBRARY BOARD MAPS K.TOP.11.112.

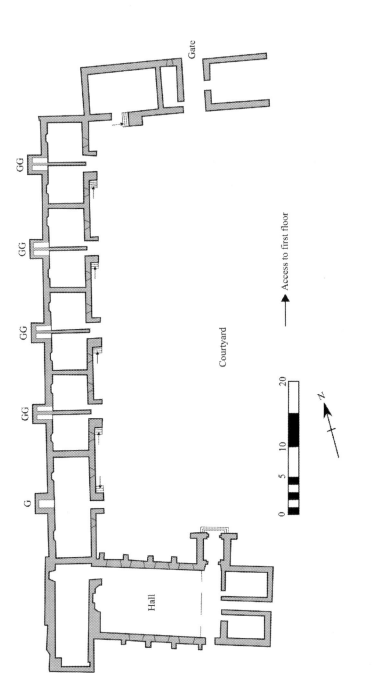

FIG. 8 PLAN OF THE WESTERN LODGING RANGE AT DARTINGTON HALL SHOWING THE GROUPS OF ROOMS ON THE GROUND FLOOR WITH GARDEROBES (G) AT THE REAR. AT THE SOUTH END OF THE RANGE WAS A SINGLE LARGE ROOM ON EACH FLOOR, RATHER THAN TWO PER FLOOR AS ELSEWHERE IN THE RANGE.

were paired together and located directly opposite the entrance doors. The chimney stacks remain, reaching beyond the roof line.

The three middle groups of rooms have had their external staircases removed and apertures altered: together they comprised twelve rooms across the ground and first floors. The fifth group of rooms, located at the south end of the range and abutting the upper residential block, was different from the previous four groups (Figure 8). One ground-floor door was provided under the porch; its undressed relieving arch indicates that it is contemporary with the others. An offset, indicating a staircase which was later removed, declines from south to north, demonstrating that the stairs went in the opposite direction to the other stairs along the range (Figures 9 and 10). The Bucks' engraving shows that the external staircase was removed prior to the eighteenth century, possibly in the sixteenth century, when Arthur Champernowne altered this end of the range to connect it internally to the upper residential block (Figure 7). A first-floor, enclosed, timber-framed porch was probably added at around the same time. The porch has a small, three-light window facing the courtyard, with an ogee arch design at the top of the timber mullions. The internal plan further distinguishes this end of the range from the remainder. Rather than four equal-sized rooms, it appears to have consisted of one large room per floor, suggesting a different purpose to that of the other, smaller rooms. It may have had timber screens to divide the space, or perhaps provided dormitory accommodation. Spatial precedence, that is, the proximity to the high-status space of the lord's accommodation, may make the former more likely.

The east range has been extensively altered, both internally and externally. In 1734, while owned by the Champernowne family, the building was in a state of decay (Figure 7) and a section of the east range was demolished in the late eighteenth or nineteenth century, before the current owners, the Elmhirsts, purchased the estate. Three evenly-spaced towers jutting from the outer, east-facing wall suggest the former position of garderobes (Figure 6). The size of the garderobe towers suggests paired latrines; that is, two on each floor, each serving the adjoining room. This layout is consistent with those at Wingfield Manor, Thornbury Castle and Amberley Castle, and suggests that the east range, too, was a lodging range, possibly with an identical plan to the west range. The west-facing elevation of the east range is much altered from its medieval state and the roof line varies, indicating the different usages over the centuries, in contrast to the Bucks' engraving of a continuous roof line. If the east range once demonstrated the uniform façade still preserved on the west range, Dartington's courtyard would have been one of the earliest examples of architectural uniformity in England and would have exhibited an extremely illusory display to the medieval audience.

FIG. 9 PHOTOGRAPH SHOWING THE FORMER ENTRANCES TO THE ROOMS AT THE SOUTH END OF THE LODGING RANGE AT DARTINGTON HALL, WITH THE OFFSET FROM A REMOVED STAIRCASE JUST VISIBLE ON THE RIGHT-HAND SIDE OF THE PORCH. THE EXTERNAL STAIRS ASCENDED FROM NORTH TO SOUTH (RIGHT TO LEFT), INDICATING AN EXTERNAL DISPLAY OF DIFFERENCE BETWEEN THIS SECTION OF THE LODGING RANGE AND THE REMAINDER.

FIG. 10 PHOTOGRAPH SHOWING THE FORMER ENTRANCES TO THE CENTRAL GROUPS OF ROOMS AND THE OFFSET FROM THE REMOVED EXTERNAL STAIRWAY. THESE STAIRS ASCENDED SOUTH TO NORTH (LEFT TO RIGHT), IN THE OPPOSITE DIRECTION TO THOSE SHOWN IN FIGURE 9.

HIGH-STATUS ACCOMMODATION

At Dartington Hall each of the rooms indicates the presence of high-status features, such as the individual doors and fireplaces within the west range and the garderobes in the east range. This suggests strongly that each room was used as accommodation by those whose status was considerably above that of servants and slaves, yet not quite as elite as the lord and family. However, we are again faced with the vagueness of status. A closer look at the mid-ranking social position represented in the architecture complicates this impression of three levels. The rooms in both the west and east ranges appear grand, comfortable and well-lit, but distinctions – or hierarchies – are perceptible. The majority of the rooms in the west range measured 30m², whereas those in the east range were in general slightly smaller, at 20m². There were further differences within the eighteen rooms of the west range. The two rooms described as the fifth group at the south end of the range were larger than the rooms of the other groups; they were essentially twice the size of others, with one door per floor rather than two. These rooms might initially seem to be dormitories, that is, rooms shared by larger groups; but spatial precedence suggests a different interpretation. These rooms abutted the upper residential block and were situated closest to the hall. This proximity to the epicentre of power within the house – the lord, the lady, and the space they occupied – could suggest that these rooms were reserved for the highest ranking retainers. There are indications of this in other great houses. At Thornbury, Gainsborough and Haddon there was a social hierarchy embedded in the lodging range's architecture, and at Wingfield, Middleham and Bishop's Waltham that hierarchy was reinforced through spatial manipulation. This is discussed in the following chapters.

The amenities provided in lodging ranges allow a tentative comparison with the lord's accommodation. At Middleham, for example, Ralph Neville built his chambers on the first floor of the south range, perpendicular to the lodging range, within the older curtain wall. A series of at least two rooms was built, with garderobes, a substantial fireplace, and considerable fenestration on the external elevation. Timber was probably used to divide the space further, as a duplication of garderobes may indicate at least an inner and outer chamber, which would be expected.

At the other end of the comfort spectrum offered in the great house, dormitories were common. At Bishop's Waltham, a dormitory was inserted by Bishop Wykeham into the first floor of the bake-brewhouse, perpendicular to the lodging range. There is evidence for one entrance and one fireplace and little else in the substantial space. Lodging ranges are somewhere in between these levels of comfort. This might seem a little vague, but it should not be considered as such. Rather than considering lodging ranges as absolutely high-status, their *betweenness* reinforces the relative aspect of status. The status of lodging ranges only makes sense in a contextualised view of the late medieval great house.

The relative nature of status is true of spaces in the past and present; however, medieval space was considerably more flexible than its post-medieval counterparts. This adds another layer of dynamism to the status of medieval spaces. Anthony Quiney argues that spaces were utterly fluid in the high medieval period.[32] In his research on post-Conquest houses, he shows that, with a simple change of furniture, an upper hall could be transformed into a chamber. Weikert also stresses the importance of furniture in creating and changing the use of space, suggesting that we must 'shed ideas of static typology of buildings or rooms'.[33] Quiney states that the use of space was determined by the user, extending the ideas of Dominique Barthélemy, who argues that some rooms were 'whatever men and women wished to make of them'.[34] During the high medieval period, there were far fewer small spaces when compared to the period in focus here, and the houses themselves were smaller overall, whereas in the Tudor period, houses were larger, with compartmentalised spaces and far fewer uses per room. Thorstad argues that rooms became more specialised with regard to sleeping and that this was one of the most private activities for the elite in a Tudor household.[35]

The late medieval period can be considered a transition period between these systems of organisation. Great houses became larger, continuously occupied residences, with a greater number of rooms than those of preceding centuries. Therefore the variety of uses per room decreased; that is, they evolved from versatile to more specialised spaces for fewer individuals. The period of lodging-range construction, from the mid-fourteenth to the mid-sixteenth centuries, was precisely when this development occurred, with lodging ranges contributing to this shift. Their inclusion extended the great house outwards in plan, creating courtyards with a greater number of smaller rooms than before. The small rooms provided low-occupancy accommodation when compared to dormitories. However, dynamic use of space did not cease. We must consider the late medieval period as the time when space was becoming more specialised, which is not the same as it being stringently demarcated. Therefore, when we assign a use to the rooms within lodging ranges – that is, use as accommodation – the caveat is that the rooms were somewhat flexible. The evidence for flexible

---

32 Anthony Quiney, *Town Houses of Medieval Britain* (London, 2004).
33 Weikert, *Authority*, p. 89.
34 Dominique Barthélemy, 'Civilizing the Fortress', in Georges Duby (ed.), *A History of Private Life II*, (London, 1988), pp. 397–424, at p. 418.
35 Thorstad, *Culture*.

and multiple uses is supported by the presence of timber partitions at Haddon Hall.

Divisions: Partitions and Screens

Internal divisions are an elusive yet important element of buildings archaeology. While many hints of previous amenities are preserved in the masonry, such as fireplace jambs, garderobe chutes and the footprints of doors, the presence and position of internal divisions are extremely difficult to trace. This is particularly true in buildings in continued use, although in some buildings, post-medieval divisions have fossilised the position of earlier designs, allowing an insight into former layouts. In lodging ranges there were two types of internal divisions: partitions which divided the range into rooms, and, at least in some examples, screens which divided the rooms further into separate spaces.

Partitions between rooms could be constructed of stone, cob, cloth or timber, and this variety is reflected in lodging ranges. At Ince Manor, the lodging range was constructed of roughly worked sandstone, which was also used within to create two ground-floor and two first-floor rooms. Curiously, the sandstone partition was not quite perpendicular with the south elevation; instead it deviates off to the east. Gainsborough was a timber-framed lodging range and retains the timber partitions used to demarcate rooms. The range was divided in line with its four bays, creating one-bay rooms, except on the ground floor, where an open truss indicates a two-bay dormitory. Any other timber screens dividing the rooms further, if they were ever present, cannot be inferred from the remains. It was not necessarily the case that the material used for the internal partitions reflected the material used in the remainder of the lodging range; rather, based on the extant examples, it appears that timber was preferred in stone-built ranges.

Timber was used widely throughout all manner of medieval buildings for floors, roofs and trusses, stairs, and a variety of decorative elements. In partitions, timber could be used in the form of stud-and-panel screens or studs filled with wattle-and-daub.[36] It is difficult to trace the presence of timber partitions for a number of reasons. Unlike masonry partitions, which can be detected through masonry scars, timber has a poor survival rate and its traces are far more ephemeral, particularly in masonry buildings. Margaret Wood describes two timber partitions, used within the halls at Rufford and Samlesbury, both in Lancashire, that separated the

---

36 N. W. Alcock and Michael Laithwaite, 'Medieval Houses in Devon and Their Modernization', *Medieval Archaeology*, 17 (1973), 100–25; Karen Dempsey, 'Understanding Hall-Houses', *Medieval Archaeology*, 61 (2017), 372–99, p. 388.

main space from the services.[37] She argues that their considerable weight kept them vertical, although they were supported further with right-angled foot projections. Therefore, even in these timber-framed halls, there was no connection between wall and partition. A further obstacle to deciphering their former presence, as N. W. Alcock and Michael Laithwaite assert, is the fact that some fifteenth- and early sixteenth-century partitions were less than 2 metres in height: that is, they did not reach the ceiling, and thus left no traces there.[38] In the development towards fully compartmentalised rooms, stud-and-panel partitions were added to late medieval townhouses, farmhouses and priests' houses in Devon, including Cotmead, Pinhoe. A substantial three-bay, three-room house, Cotmead comprised a central hall, an 'inner room' at the high end of the hall, and a further room at the low end.[39] There was a contemporary first floor above the inner room only, while the remainder of the house was open to the rafters. Two timber partitions created the ground-floor plan; however, they did not communicate with the bays. At the high end of the hall a stud-and-panel partition with a shoulder-headed door did not reach the truss; the gap was filled with stud-and-daub, creating a multi-material partition.[40] At the low end of the hall a second stud-and-panel partition, again with shoulder-headed doorway, was not in line with the truss and nor did it have daub at the top. While this may be a local trend specific to Devon, it demonstrates the flexibility of timber partitions in their materials and their placement independent of the trusses.

There is thus little evidence for timber partitions within the surviving masonry of lodging ranges. The lack of socket marks in the masonry suggests that fixed partitions were attached to the timber floors and ceilings, which have not generally survived. This is highly probable, as, at Gainsborough, where the timber floors are intact, the internal partitions remain affixed to these. All partitions, including the internal corridor, were connected to the floors and ceilings with mortise and tenon joints in this timber-framed example. In masonry lodging ranges, it is possible that partitions were extremely lightweight, such as those described by Alcock and Laithwaite, requiring only minor marrying with the remainder of the fabric; or, conversely, as Wood describes, heavy enough to stand alone. Luckily, in most lodging ranges the position of timber partitions to create rooms is clear due to the organisation of the provisions. For example, to divide a space with two garderobes into two rooms with individual garderobes, a slim timber partition would have been placed at the latrines'

---

37 Wood, *House*, pp. 142–3.
38 Alcock and Laithwaite, 'Houses'.
39 Alcock and Laithwaite, 'Houses', p. 123.
40 Alcock and Laithwaite, 'Houses', p. 105.

shared jambs (Figure 4). This occurred within the otherwise stone-built lodging ranges at Amberley and Thornbury. Likewise, in examples with paired entrance doors, such as Wingfield, a timber partition would have created two rooms with one door each; in an identical layout at Dartington, a stone wall was utilised at the point of the paired doors.[41] Therefore there was a necessary spatial connection between the partitions and the provisions. The permanency of the provisions (a garderobe cannot be moved, after all) suggests that the timber partitions, regardless of their ephemerality, were installed fairly permanently, or at least for the duration of the lodging ranges' use as accommodation.

Detecting the presence of timber partitions is challenging, and identifying the use of timber screens to divide a room further into separate spaces is even more so. Timber screens lack permanency within a building. This is not only due to material durability but also to the portable nature of the screens – they were simply easier to move or remove over the course of the building's life. They may have been a temporary feature, intended to divide part of a room off for a certain use and be easily removed at a later date; as such, they allowed for the flexible use of space in the house. Their temporary nature meant there was no reason to follow roof trusses or bays. For ease of movement they may have been lightweight and thin – perhaps just stud-and-panel screens. Across the ruinous examples of lodging ranges, there is little evidence for the position of internal screens. However, the size of some of the rooms within lodging ranges argues for some sort of division during their use, thereby contradicting this negative evidence (Table 2). There is, however, one known example of a lodging range in which there remains evidence of a timber screen dividing a room into separate sections: Haddon Hall.

HADDON HALL, DERBYSHIRE

Located near the River Wye in Bakewell, Derbyshire, Haddon Hall was owned by Henry de Ferrars, a knight who was granted a total of 114 manors in 1086.[42] The manors were divided in 1170 between Richard de Vernon, who acquired Haddon, and Simon Basset. Richard de Vernon married Alice Avenell, daughter of William de Avenell, then obtained a licence to crenellate in 1195.[43] The parish church of Over Haddon and

---

41 In these two examples the paired garderobe doors were opposite the paired entrance doors, which probably occurred also at Amberley.
42 John Timbs and Alexander Gunn, *Abbeys, Castles and Ancient Halls of England and Wales* (3 vols, London, 1872), Vol. 3, p. 107.
43 Patrick Faulkner, 'Haddon Hall and Bolsover Castle', *Archaeological Journal*, 118 (1961), 180–7, p. 189.

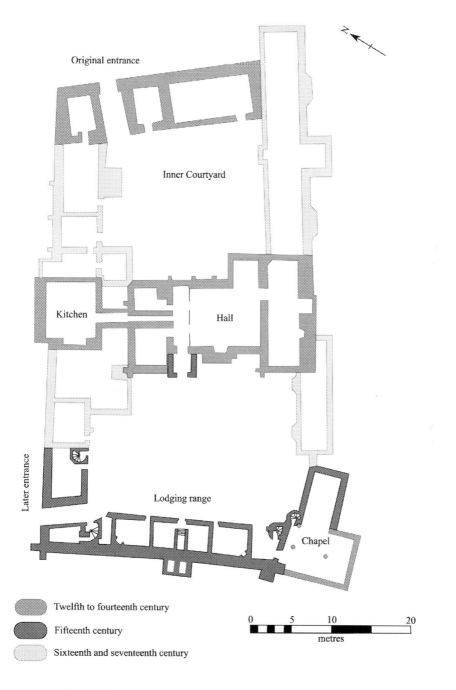

FIG. 11 PLAN OF HADDON HALL, SHOWING THE SEQUENCE OF CONSTRUCTION THAT ENVELOPED THE EARLY CHAPEL.

Nether Haddon, located in the outer courtyard, retains a twelfth-century nave and south aisle, and a thirteenth-century south aisle extension.

The archaeological remains at Haddon represent a family's rise and fall. Richard Vernon IV (d. 1400) commenced a considerable building scheme at Haddon Hall before he travelled to the Holy Land in 1357. His work can therefore be dated to the second quarter of the fourteenth century.[44] He built the hall with two-light, low-transomed windows, and the parlour was to the south of the hall, with the buttery, pantry, detached kitchen and bakery to the north. The screens passage separating the hall from the services is one of the best preserved in England.

Throughout the fifteenth century the Vernon family were among the wealthiest members of the gentry in Derbyshire.[45] Richard Vernon VI was a member of parliament for Staffordshire in 1419, justice of the peace for Derbyshire from 1423, and Derbyshire's Member of Parliament in 1426. He instigated a building plan to incorporate the early church within the great house through the construction of the outer courtyard. This transformed Richard IV's hall range into the cross-range of a double-courtyard house (Figure 11). Richard VI added a new entrance via the north-west tower, utilising a natural outcrop. The configuration of the north-west tower created an uneven ground-floor level; it increased steeply once inside the courtyard, rendering vehicular or mounted access impossible. This also affected the floor levels between the western lodging range and the tower, the result being an intriguing mix of squinches viewable from the courtyard (Figure 12).

Richard Vernon VI continued to rise through the ranks, gaining huge wealth in 1442 when he was appointed to the treasurership of Calais for life. After his death in 1451, however, the family's wealth declined when the house, role in parliament, and treasurership of Calais passed to his son, William (d. 1467), whose pro-Lancastrian stance caused local conflict, loss of his parliamentary position, and exclusion from government after the Yorkist victory. The family regained their standing when Henry Vernon married Anne Talbot, daughter of the second earl of Shrewsbury, and was appointed by Henry VIII to the position of High Steward of the King's Forest in the Peak.[46] After his death in 1515, Henry's son George continued the role, with a lifestyle earning him the nickname 'The King of the Peak'.[47] He reconstructed the private apartments in the south range of the inner courtyard to include a splendid gallery.

---

44   Faulkner, 'Haddon', p. 189.
45   Emery, *Greater Medieval Houses*, Vol. 2, p. 386.
46   Joseph Nigota, 'Vernon family' (2004), *Oxford DNB*. <https://doi.org/10.1093/ref:odnb/52800> [accessed 10th August 2021]; Timbs and Gunn, *Castles*, Vol. 3, p. 108.
47   Nigota, *Vernon*; Timbs and Gunn, *Castles*, Vol. 3, p. 108.

FIG. 12   PHOTOGRAPH SHOWING THE WEST RANGE OF THE OUTER COURTYARD AT HADDON HALL, INCLUDING THE LODGING RANGE IN THE CENTRE WITH SQUINCHES WHERE IT MEETS THE GATEHOUSE AT THE NORTHERN (RIGHT) END. AT THE SOUTHERN EXTENT WAS A LOBBY LEADING INTO THE CHAPEL.

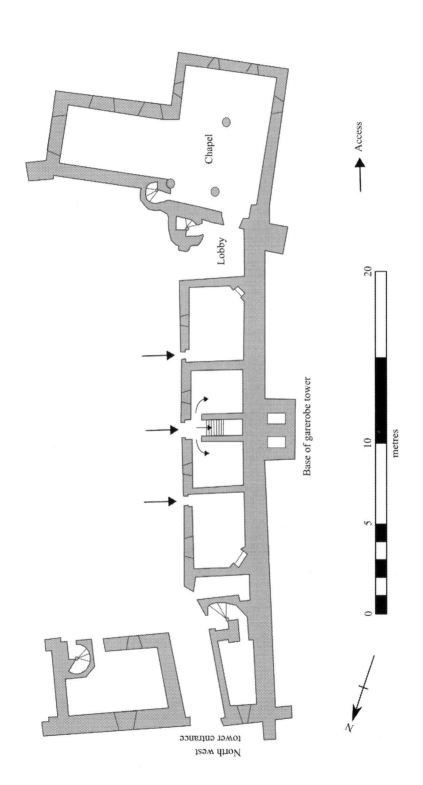

FIG. 13 GROUND-FLOOR PLAN OF HADDON HALL'S LODGING RANGE. THE THREE ENTRANCES FROM THE COURTYARD ARE SHOWN, WITH THE MIDDLE DOOR LEADING TO THE TWO CENTRAL ROOMS AND THE FIRST FLOOR.

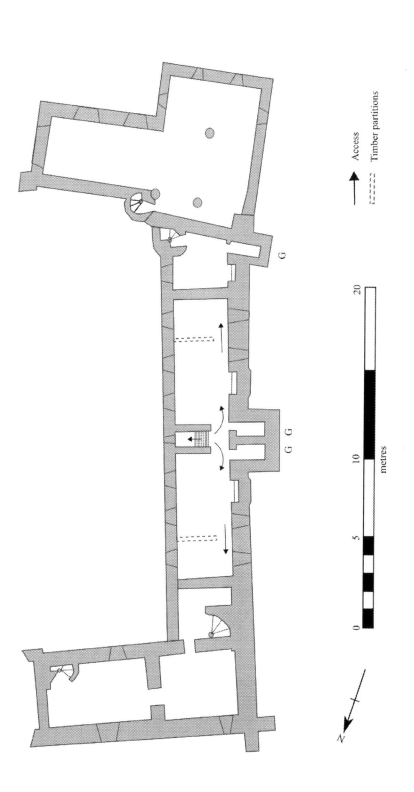

FIG. 14 FIRST-FLOOR PLAN OF HADDON HALL'S LODGING RANGE, SHOWING THE POSITION OF THE TIMBER SCREENS, ONE OF WHICH REMAINS PRESERVED IN THE NORTHERN (LEFT) ROOM, AND THE GARDEROBES (G) ON THE REAR WALL.

The lodging range was built by Henry Vernon, between 1470 and 1490, in the west range of the lower courtyard. Two of the four ground-floor rooms opened directly onto the courtyard (Figure 12). A central pair of rooms, each with an individual door, were accessible from the courtyard via a single door and lobby, which also contained the stairs to the first floor (Figure 13). These two central rooms were smaller than others on the ground floor and were not provided with a fireplace. All four ground-floor rooms had windows facing into the courtyard, contributing to a symmetrical façade, but no apertures on the exterior elevation, and no garderobes.

The door to the two central rooms and staircase was decorated with a hood moulding, a subtle differentiation to set it apart from the two other ground-floor doors (Figure 12). The staircase received light from a window above the door and terminated in a first-floor lobby which led to a room on each side (Figure 14). The two first-floor rooms provided greater comfort than those on the ground floor; each was the size of the two rooms below, with windows on both elevations, and garderobes. The garderobe tower extended from ground floor to first floor; however, it contained garderobes only on the first floor. As we have seen, in spite of what may be perceived as the convenience offered by building one garderobe above another, this indicates that this facility remained an exclusively high-status feature. There are two further first-floor rooms in the range, one at each end, which were slightly different. To the south, a room on the first floor was accessible by a newel at the chapel lobby; therefore it was not above a ground-floor room. The presence of a fireplace and single garderobe suggest that it housed the priest. At the north end of the range a room was accessible through the north-west tower; thus, almost the entire west range comprised accommodation.

Remarkably, two fifteenth-century timber screens were recorded by Patrick Faulkner when he surveyed Haddon; however, one had been removed when Anthony Emery visited some decades later.[48] That on the north-side of the lobby remains intact: it is the only *in situ* timber screen in a known lodging range. It was joined to the timber floor and ceiling, but not to the masonry walls. Its survival permits the first-floor plan to be identified. Each of the central rooms on the first floor contained one timber screen; that is, the two rooms accessible via the stairs and lobby which appeared to be of higher status than those on the ground floor due to their garderobes, windows and fireplaces (Figure 14). Each room measured 21m^2, with the timber screen separating the space into two unequal sections. The lobby at the top of the stairs led directly into the larger space. This 'outer' space was 4.5 metres wide. It contained the garderobe, fireplace and three

---

48   Faulkner, 'Haddon', p. 196; Emery, *Greater Medieval Houses*, Vol. 2, p. 389.

windows, and may be interpreted as an office space. It led into the smaller, 'inner' space. This was slightly more than 2 metres wide, with a window on each elevation. As this inner space was accessible only from the outer space, it could be interpreted as a bedchamber.

USE OF INNER AND OUTER SPACES

Haddon Hall provides a tantalising glimpse into how the rooms within lodging ranges were used, and extrapolating this knowledge across known examples is tempting. However, this is the only known instance of a timber screen surviving within a lodging range to divide a room into distinct spaces. We turn, therefore, to the variety of other collective-living buildings constructed in the late medieval period, such as vicarial and collegiate accommodation, to assist our interpretation. There are architectural similarities between these and lodging ranges, as shown in the compilation of plans below (Figure 15), such as the uniform façades, and the use of timber within to divide the range into rooms and then further into inner and outer chambers. The inner/outer nomenclature used here is borrowed from the accepted vocabulary pertinent in a number of medieval contexts, such as the inner/outer courtyards, inner/outer chambers in a lord's suite, and inner/outer rooms in townhouses.[49] These terms are imbued with status differentiation. The inner denotes a higher status and greater sense of privacy, through separation, than the outer. In none of these examples was there a public–private dichotomy; rather, the gradation was set within the context of the wider house. At Haddon, the outer space was larger and accessible directly from the stairs, and therefore a more 'public' space, through which one walked to get to the smaller, inner, more 'private' room. There are two central threads, therefore, which inform our understanding of Haddon: the architectural similarities with other collective-living ranges and the meaning of inner/outer spaces elsewhere in the great house. From this basis, the use of each space within the lodging range rooms will be considered.

Vicarial ranges also contained rooms with inner/outer spaces, demonstrating that the private–public continuum extended from courtyards and lords' suites throughout medieval buildings. As discussed in the previous chapter, vicarial ranges were built for vicars choral, the most senior members of the cathedral hierarchy, and provide a comparison for the use of rooms within lodging ranges. At Vicars' Close, Wells, two ranges were constructed by Bishop Beckington (1443–65), comprising

---

49 Jane Grenville, *Medieval Housing* (London, 1997), p. 103; Cooper, *Gentry*, p. 141; Woolgar, *Household*; Alcock and Laithwaite, 'Houses'.

twenty houses on the west side opposite twenty-two on the east.[50] As part of a medieval close (an enclosure within the cathedral precinct), Vicars' Close appears to be proto-terraces rather than true courtyard ranges, but it was similar in plan to lodging ranges in the great houses. Both types of range were long and divided into rooms which, in turn, contained features suggesting high-status, comfortable accommodation. As with lodging ranges, the vicarial range demonstrated a degree of privacy through separation from others and a sense of authority over the space through the individual door. Likewise, the internal configuration provides scope for comparison.

At Vicars' Close, each two-storeyed, stone-built house was separate from its neighbour. That is, there was no internal connection, much like the rooms within lodging ranges. Each floor within the houses consisted of one room measuring 3.9m by 6m (23.4m²), which is only slightly larger than the rooms on the first floor at Haddon or in Dartington's east range (Table 2; Figure 15). An individual door (one per house) led into the ground-floor room, which in turn led to the first-floor room. The latter was only accessible from the ground floor; therefore we can consider it the inner space, in contrast to the outer space on the ground floor. Both rooms had fireplaces and windows, some two-light, others narrow and single-light.[51] There is no evidence of timber screens; seemingly the use of two floors to create inner/outer spaces rendered them unnecessary. These two-room houses are very similar to the two-room suites in Gainsborough, which allows an assessment of the social identity of the people who lived within, as discussed in Chapter 2. In terms of how these spaces were used, William Pantin describes the ground-floor room at Vicars' Close as 'a kind of hall', suggesting that one might entertain, engage with visitors, and discuss business there: it was essentially an outer, more public, room.[52] The first floor comprised the inner chamber, a separate, or even private, room, which Pantin suggests served as a 'combined bed-chamber and study'.[53]

Like vicarial ranges, collegiate ranges were also divided into rooms with inner and outer spaces (Figure 15). These ranges, usually in a courtyard plan, were occupied by students and fellows of the academic college. The ranges were divided into rooms, or communal 'sittingroom[s]', which were then divided further with timber screens into 'study closets'.[54] The accommodation at New College (1380–86) and All Souls (1438–42),

50 William Pantin, 'Chantry Priests' Houses and Other Medieval Lodgings', *Medieval Archaeology*, 3 (1959), 216–58, p. 248.
51 Pantin, 'Lodgings', p. 248.
52 Pantin, 'Lodgings', p. 248.
53 Pantin, 'Lodgings', p. 248; Sarah Kerr, 'Collective Living and Individual Identities in Late Medieval England,' *Archaeological Journal*, 177 (2020), 83–98.
54 Wood, *House*, p. 183; Kerr, 'Collective'.

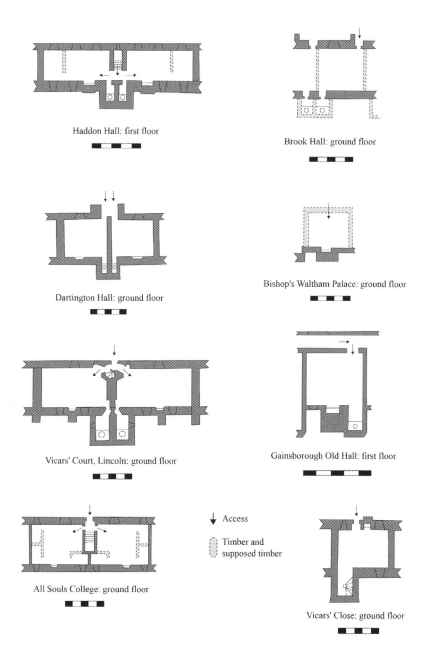

FIG. 15 A SELECTION OF ROOMS FROM LODGING, VICARIAL AND COLLEGIATE RANGES, SHOWING THE CLEAR SIMILARITIES IN FORM, ACCESS, AND PROVISIONS. FOR EASE, EACH HAS BEEN CONFIGURED SO THAT THE INNER, COURTYARD ELEVATION IS TO THE TOP OF THE IMAGE AND THE REAR, EXTERNAL ELEVATION TO THE BOTTOM. EACH SCALE BAR IS 0–5 METRES.

both at Oxford, consisted of several rooms, each with three study closets radiating from the central space. This central space, which appears to have contained the garderobes and fireplace, can be considered the 'outer' to the inner study closets, as it was accessible from the courtyard and was the only route to the study closets. There were windows of varying size, rather like those at Vicars' Close. In terms of the use of these spaces, Wood suggests that, based on the smaller windows, the study closets were for both rest and study.

Outer Spaces

The correlations between vicarial, collegiate and lodging ranges can be only tentatively drawn due to the different roles and social positions of the occupants and the different contexts of the wider estates in which they lived. When we focus on their outer spaces, however, there are similarities which unite them without denying each their unique context. Each outer space was accessed directly from either a courtyard or a lobby; each contained at least one window, fireplace and often a garderobe; and each provided the only access to the inner space. We can suggest, based on the architecture, that the outer spaces on Haddon's first floor were more socially and physically accessible and more public, and had a use separate to that of the inner space. This is supported when we view the similarities between the outer spaces of the lodging range and the outer spaces elsewhere in the great house. For example, the outer courtyard was more public compared to the inner; in later houses the hall was the outer space while parlours were added to serve as an inner, more secluded space; and a lord's or lady's suite of chambers often included an outer space more accessible than its inner counterpart.

Can this help assign a use to the outer spaces of Haddon? As a more accessible, public and well-lit space it may have been an office and meeting place, in which the retainers might conduct business with other members of the household or guests.[55] This would correlate to Pantin's description of the outer space at Vicars' Close and its use as something like a hall.[56] Suggestions that several people congregated here are supported by the communal 'sittingrooms' described at colleges.[57] Returning to the great house, the inventories of Caister Castle, Norfolk, appear to support the designation of office use. A chamber within the lodging range assigned to Cole and Watkin Shipdam, both auditors for John Fastolf, contained

55   Woolgar, *Household*, p. 65.
56   Pantin, 'Lodgings', p. 248.
57   Wood, *House*, p. 183.

beds and a chair, together with a piece of cloth for an accounting board.[58] Woolgar states that business was mainly conducted away from sleeping areas,[59] offering a contradiction to this interpretation, yet, looking elsewhere in the house, we see that this spatial immediacy was typical. Sleeping close to one's work was particularly true of servants and slaves, who slept in the kitchen, stables, hall or corridors.[60] Status influenced this. Greater status provided one with access to more spaces and more freedom of movement. For example, the kitchen clerk, who prepared and cooked food, and the hall marshal were prominent members of the household. They were, therefore, more likely to sleep in spaces close to but distinct from the kitchen. Kitchen children, however, who may have crouched beside the fires to turn meat on the spit, probably slept in the kitchen itself.[61] Dartington's lower residential block, directly above the services, may have provided accommodation for higher-status service staff such as the hall marshal and kitchen clerk, allowing them access to the kitchen, services and hall from their accommodation (Figure 6), whereas the kitchen children would have been restricted to the ground floor of the service range. This hints at a degree of freedom for the clerk and marshal, but it is only true in relation to servants of a lower status. This example reminds us once again that status was relational as, under the presiding power of the lord and the wider household hierarchy, they would have been restricted to this department.

Despite differing levels of freedom of movement throughout the household, there was a close association between sleeping arrangements and role, even with the lord and family. In the Paston letters, Margaret Paston (d. 1484) described to her husband, John, the arrival of four dormant tables. She informed him that one would go into his suite of rooms, although the bed would have to be moved to make room.[62] She also mentioned the presence in his suite of his '*cowntewery*', an accounting board.[63] This placement within the chamber of the tools that facilitated the running of the house further supports the idea that lodging ranges may have contained an office space. It is likely, as Leonie Hicks asserts,

---

58 Woolgar, *Household*, p. 67; MCO Fastolf paper 43; Thomas Amyot, 'Transcript of two rolls, containing an inventory of the effects formerly belonging to Sir John Fastolfe', *Archaeologia* 21 (1827), pp. 232–80.
59 Woolgar, *Household*, p. 65.
60 Woolgar, *Household*, p. 79.
61 Thorstad, *Culture*, p. 99.
62 Norman Davis, *Paston Letters and Papers of the Fifteenth Century*, 2nd edn (Oxford, 2004), p. 253; Additional MS 39848, BL; Additional MS 39849, BL; James Gairdner, *The Paston Letters 1422-1509* (4 vols, Westminster, 1901).
63 Davis, *Paston*, p. 253; Additional MS 39848, BL; Additional MS 39849, BL; Gairdner, *Paston*.

that the nature of business would affect the choice of the space in which it was carried out.[64] Paston had the choice to conduct business within his chambers, or in the parlour, or indeed in the hall, as he had authority over all of those spaces. The retainers, however, were unlikely to conduct their work or meet with guests or other household members (other than the lord) in the hall, as they may not have had jurisdiction over this space. Just as the clerk and marshal were restricted to their department, so too were the retainers. Their role as auditors, lawyers or gentle servants – discussed in the following chapter – did not necessarily provide them with authority over spaces outside their room. Moreover, the lord may have met guests less frequently in the hall as the medieval period continued.[65] Rather, the parlour, a more separated space, may have been increasingly preferred. As the use of the hall shifted towards less-frequent ceremonial events, the use of offices for everyday activities may have been routine. By the sixteenth century, Edward Stafford was updating his Thornbury and Bletchingly houses. The latter was equipped with 'many good lodgings and houses of offices' for his staff, suggesting specific places for carrying out work pertaining to the running of his estates.[66] We can surmise that, for the retainers to undertake their jobs, they required something like an office space that was physically close to where they slept. This is supported by Faulkner's description of the outer space at Haddon. He defines it as the 'main chamber' and describes it as 'almost of the nature of a hall'.[67]

Inner Spaces

If we consider that the outer space at Haddon was used as an office, what does this mean for the inner space? 'Inner' is used in medieval discourse to denote a level of privacy distinct from the comparatively more public and 'outer' space. At Haddon, like the inner spaces in vicarial and collegiate rooms, the inner space was accessible only from the outer space. Faulkner's description is significant: in describing the movement through the outer space to the inner, he defines an 'inner and more private chamber' as 'a form of minor chamber block'.[68] We can, therefore, explore the possibility that the inner space was the retainer's bedchamber.

---

64 Leonie Hicks, 'Magnificent Entrances and Undignified Exits', *Journal of Medieval History*, 35 (2009), 52–69.
65 Christopher Woolgar, *The Senses in Late Medieval England* (New Haven, 2006), p. 248; Amanda Richardson, 'Corridors of Power: A Case Study in Access Analysis from Medieval England', *Antiquity*, 77:296 (2003), 373–84, p. 377.
66 Carole Rawcliffe, *The Staffords, Earls of Stafford and Dukes of Buckingham: 1394–1521* (Cambridge, 1978), p. 87.
67 Faulkner, 'Haddon Hall', p. 195.
68 Faulkner, 'Haddon Hall', pp. 194–5.

The inner, smaller space at Haddon contained no garderobe or fireplace, drawing further comparisons with the collegiate 'study closets'. In their 1973 publication, Alcock and Laithwaite describe inner rooms, possibly bedchambers, beyond the high end of the hall in town, farm and priests' houses. They argue that half of these were unheated, since the timbers were un-blackened.[69] While unheated bedchambers seem unlikely, it would not be unprecedented in medieval accommodation. Edwards Roberts's survey of The Angel inn at Andover, Hampshire, reveals that each one-bay room was 'unheated and relatively cramped'.[70] Alcock and Laithwaite identify that only when the bedchambers were developed into parlours, in the eighteenth or nineteenth centuries, were fireplaces added.[71] It is something of a stretch to compare the inner rooms they describe with the inner space at Haddon; however, they all demonstrate a division of space into a more public outer and a more private inner through the addition of a timber screen. In addition, at Haddon, the collegiate ranges, and the houses described by Alcock and Laithwaite, the inner spaces were the termination points: that is, they did not lead to another room, and they all appear to have been unheated.

This interpretation of the smaller, inner bedchamber without a fireplace to some extent contradicts our understanding of medieval chambers, as they are more often than not identified principally by the presence of fireplaces and garderobes.[72] Indeed, the lodging ranges' perceived use is based on this accepted architectural language. However, the evidence from Haddon and comparable ranges suggests that, within the room, these provisions were in the office, not the bedchamber. The bedchamber may have been heated with a brazier, as was conventional in many medieval spaces.[73] Alternatively, the timber partition may not have fully isolated one section from the other, allowing the fireplace in the office to heat the entire room.

It was argued earlier in this chapter that the architectural similarities between the lord's accommodation and lodging ranges are marked, with high-status provisions creating comfortable living spaces; therefore some comparison of room use is beneficial here. Caister Castle's inventories of the mid-fifteenth century provide an insight into Fastolf's chambers and how they were divided (Figure 16). Fastolf built a suite of three rooms, including a bedchamber containing two beds, a folding table, and two chairs. Two rooms were accessible from the bedchamber: a stewhouse, for

---

69 Alcock and Laithwaite, 'Houses', p. 101.
70 Edward Roberts, 'A Fifteenth-century Inn at Andover', *Proceedings of the Hampshire Field Club and Archaeological Society*, 47 (1991), 153–70, p. 160.
71 Alcock and Laithwaite, 'Houses', p. 102.
72 For example, Dempsey, 'Hall', p. 381; Woolgar, *Household*, p. 170.
73 Wood, *House*, p. 261.

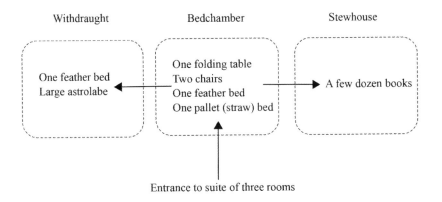

FIG. 16 ILLUSTRATION SIMPLIFYING THE POSSIBLE LAYOUT OF FASTOLF'S CHAMBERS AT CAISTER CASTLE.

bathing, which also contained a collection of books; and a withdraught, a withdrawing chamber. The description of Fastolf's withdraught and bedchamber can be interpreted as an inner and outer chamber, respectively, and aids the understanding of space utilisation within lodging ranges. The withdraught is often considered to be where most business was undertaken; essentially, it was utilised as an office.[74] However, Fastolf's withdraught contained a solitary feather bed and a large astrolabe, indicating a more separate space: a room for relaxing and enjoying hobbies rather distinct from the running of the house. The single bed, as opposed to the two beds in the bedchamber, suggests that the withdraught was Fastolf's principal room for sleeping and relaxing.[75] The two further beds in the bedchamber may have been used by his chamber servants, whose proximity to their lord was indicative of their importance in the household and their social status within and beyond.[76] This room may have doubled as an office when needed, since, as well as the two beds, there were a table and chairs, which would allow meetings to be conducted away from the remainder of the household. This is further supported when we consider the spatial configuration of the rooms; the withdraught was one of the most 'hidden' spaces in the great house, accessed via the bedchamber from the high end of the hall. Therefore the innermost space in Fastolf's suite and the inner space in Haddon's lodging range may have been primarily for sleeping rather than working.

74 Woolgar, *Household*, p. 65.
75 *Contra*. Woolgar, *Household*.
76 Thorstad, *Culture*, p. 106; Hollie Morgan, *Beds and Chambers in Late Medieval England. Readings, Representations and Realities* (York, 2017).

Henceforth, the outer space in the lodging ranges rooms will be referred to as the office and the inner space as the bedchamber. This demarcation of spaces for specific activities is supported by the compartmentalisation of space which was occurring as the medieval period progressed; however, I assign these terms only to suggest potential uses that may have existed alongside others. While the terms help us visualise the use of space, they imply a rigidity that was unlikely; therefore this is not to say that each space was exclusively one thing or another. This flexibility is shown through another excerpt from the Paston Letters. In *c*.1466, a declaration by Agnes Paston described dealing with the last will and testament of her husband William Paston.[77] She wrote that John Paston 'walkyd vp and down in the chamer' while she and John Dam 'knelled at the beddys fete'. The identification of the bed demonstrates that this incident took place in a bedchamber and even suggests, as Thorstad argues, that the will had been stored in this room prior to William's death.[78]

The terminology of the bedchamber requires some deconstruction. 'Chamber' derives from the Old French *chambre*, meaning a private room, especially a bedchamber;[79] therefore it is appropriate for the inner space, rather than the entire room including the office space. In the thirteenth century, *camera* or *chaumbra* had a variety of meanings, from a set of hangings for a bed, a room or suite of rooms, to the activities that were associated with them or, more generally, the area in which those activities took place.[80] Similarly, the term lodging could be used for sleeping spaces and rooms, including the principal chamber, as reported in Thornbury's inventories after Stafford's execution. This means that we cannot always detect the rooms for sleeping from the medieval description of a space, even when references are made to a chamber, as indicated by Fastolf's suite of rooms above. Although imperfect, this study will use the term chamber to indicate a room which provided space for sleeping amongst its other uses.

Size of Rooms

It is clear that there are terminological limitations in the discussion of the use of medieval space. What is more illustrative than assigning contradictory and overlapping terms is the architectural interpretation. Therefore we return to an examination of the fabric of lodging ranges, and a closer look at the size of rooms in other examples is illuminating

---

77 Davis, *Paston*, p. 33; Additional MS 39848, BL; Additional MS 39849, BL; Gairdner, *Paston*.
78 Thorstad, *Culture*, p. 158.
79 OED, 'chamber' (2021) <https://www.oed.com/> [accessed 10 August 2021].
80 Woolgar, *Household*, pp. 49–50.

(Table 2). The first-floor rooms at Haddon were 21m², an area that was subdivided into two unequal spaces. Similar sized rooms can be found throughout other lodging ranges: six of the rooms at Gainsborough measured 18m²; four of the rooms at Brook Hall measured 25m², while the east range at Dartington and the lodging range at Bishop's Waltham contained rooms of 20m². This allows a tentative projection of Haddon's division onto these comparable plans. If we apply the same configuration of partitions and organisation of features, we can postulate a similar division at Bishop's Waltham; that is, an individual door leading directly into a larger space with a fireplace, separated by timber from a smaller space. Similarly, at Brook, the larger outer space may have included the garderobe and window overlooking the courtyard, with the smaller inner space leading from it.

Across known lodging ranges, there are many examples of rooms larger than those of Haddon's first floor: in Dartington's west range the rooms were 30m², a little larger than some at Cotehele House, Cornwall, which measured 27.5m². Both examples were smaller than those at Thornbury and Old Newham, which were each c.38.5m². At Middleham and Amberley the rooms were 40m², while at Wingfield they were 42m². These were probably divided in some way or used by a small group of people, possibly in a manner similar to the contemporary collegiate ranges. The relative scarcity of the smaller rooms, those around 18–25m², compared to the larger rooms may suggest that they were the higher-status spaces reserved for elites within the lodging ranges. We could extend this to suggest that these smaller rooms were for fewer people, possibly even individuals, than the larger versions at, among other places, Dartington, Cotehele and so on.

Individual rooms were rare in the medieval period. The household was a dynamic environment, with guests frequent and travelling commonplace, particularly up to the later medieval period: one person per room was simply not a practical consideration. Nevertheless, in the period examined here, the peripatetic household had begun to decline and the household stayed for longer periods in fewer houses or one house, depending on the family's wealth and holdings. Guests were a major part of household life and the household itself had grown considerably, even to 'monstrous dimensions'.[81] This suggests that one person per room was highly unlikely, even in the sprawling great houses at Thornbury or Dartington. Furthermore, privacy was simply not desired in the way it is today; as such, sharing accommodation was not the concession it seems to modern sensibilities. Thorstad argues that there is a continuum from

---

81 Kate Mertes, *The English Noble Household 1250–1600* (Oxford, 1988), p. 185.

the past's lack of desire for privacy to today's constant need for it, with late medieval households falling somewhere within this;[82] but a growing desire for privacy does not mean it was afforded. There is some documentary evidence, however, that hints at individually-occupied rooms at Caister. The mid-fifteenth century inventories list twenty-eight rooms with thirty-nine beds; eighteen of the rooms were assigned to named individuals, but contained twenty-two beds between them. Fastolf's room had three beds, as discussed above, as did the lady's chamber, and her son from her first marriage was provided with two beds.[83] Woolgar and Cooper suggest that assigning rooms to individuals, and even naming the rooms after an occupant, was becoming more common precisely at the time under consideration here;[84] indeed, the desire for assigned rooms contributed to the compartmentalisation of space in the great house. While lodging ranges were built to comprise small rooms from their inception, Cooper notes that the desire for smaller rooms led to the divisions of existing larger spaces. At both Little Moreton Hall, Cheshire, and Blackmore Farm, Somerset, the spaces above the services were divided in the mid-sixteenth century to create two separate rooms with individual doors.[85] Therefore, individually occupied rooms were becoming desired during the late medieval period, and lodging ranges were both the product of this and part of the development towards the single-occupancy rooms of the post-medieval period.

The size of the rooms within lodging ranges suggests that they were low-occupancy spaces with high-status features shared among a small group or, in some instances, occupied by individuals. When we compare lodging ranges with other collective-living accommodation, particularly the single-occupancy vicars' choral rooms, we see the emerging notion of individual space in late medieval society. It may be the case that lodging ranges were sometimes occupied by individuals but, considering the flexibility inherent in the house, guests, colleagues, and/or servants also occupied them when needed. This further demonstrates their elevated status suggested by their provisions.

---

82 Thorstad, *Culture*, p. 154.
83 Woolgar, *Household*, p. 63.
84 Woolgar, *Household*, p. 61; Cooper, *Gentry*.
85 Cooper, *Gentry*, p. 296.

TABLE 2   APPROXIMATE SIZES OF ROOMS RECORDED WITHIN LODGING RANGES, SHOWING VARIETY ACROSS THE TYPE AND WITHIN EXAMPLES. SELECT VICARIAL AND COLLEGIATE RANGES HAVE BEEN ADDED FOR COMPARISON.

		Number of rooms	Area of each room (m2)
Secular ranges	Ince Manor	Four	50
	Amberley Castle	Four	40
	Dartington Hall	Sixteen in west range	30
		Two in west range	75
		~ Twenty-eight in east range	20
	Middleham Castle	Eight	40
	Brympton d'Evercy	Four	Varying 44–63
	Bishop's Waltham Palace	Twenty-two	20
	Wingfield Manor	Twelve	42
	Haddon Hall	Two on ground floor	13.5
		Two on ground floor	7.5
		Two on first floor	21
	Gainsborough Hall	Two two-room suites	60*
		One dormitory	45
		Six rooms	18
	Brook Hall	Four	25
		Two	55
	Thornbury Castle	Ten	24.5–52.5 with six measuring ~ 38.5
	Cotehele House	One two-room suite	80*
		Two rooms	27.5
		Two dormitories	61.75
	Old Newnham	Four	38
Vicarial ranges	Vicars' Close, Wells	Forty-four houses	46*
	Vicars' Court, Lincoln	Six	44–54
Collegiate ranges	All Souls College, Oxford	Sixteen	40 inclusive of studies

~ Approximate; * Combination of two floors

CONCLUSION

Discerning use is the principal step in understanding a building: it is the foundation from which more comprehensive queries can be explored. Examples of lodging ranges consistently demonstrate the following features: garderobes, fireplaces, windows and individual doors. This architectural language suggests that they were used as accommodation. We are able to piece together an impression of a warm, well-lit room, a comfortable space. By comparing this degree of comfort with other types of accommodation, both within and without the great house, we can be confident that these rooms were considered to have relatively high status. The scarcity of the provisions elsewhere, particularly the garderobes and individual doors, support this interpretation of status, as the level of comfort they provided was not afforded for all household members. They were reserved for those whose status demanded the comfort they offered.

Our understanding of lodging ranges is furthered when we explore the evidence for timber screens. While only Haddon Hall has archaeological evidence of this poorly preserved feature, we can suggest their presence in other lodging ranges based on the organisation of provisions. This allows some comparison with collegiate and vicarial ranges, whereby rooms were subdivided into what can be considered inner and outer spaces – the nomenclature chosen deliberately to evoke inner and outer courtyards and spaces in both the lord's chambers and other secular houses. The outer was the more public space, possibly similar to a 'hall' in the vicarial houses at Wells, and a communal space in the colleges. The inner was the smaller space, a separate and innermost space for sleeping, described as a minor chamber block at Vicars' Close. We see the division of rooms for the uses of sleeping, and working or studying, even possibly for entertaining or socialising. Translating this to lodging ranges and assigning one of these uses to the inner and another to the outer is tricky, particularly due to the flexible use of space in the medieval period. However, the period of lodging range construction, 1350–1550, was a period of reduced uses per space and reduced people per space. This is exemplified through the development from dormitories to *cubiculi* to individual rooms in contemporaneous vicarial ranges. It could be suggested that the inner, smaller, darker space was primarily for sleeping – that is, a bedchamber – while the outer space, benefiting from more space, heat and light, was a space for meetings and work – an office. These uses provide further evidence for classification as high-status spaces, as the work and entertainment may have been related to the running of the house and would therefore have been undertaken by the principal staff. While this greatly helps our understanding of the lived experience of lodging ranges, we must remember to allow a degree of flexibility in this interpretation. Each activity may have taken place in either space, depending on how many people were assigned to a room, the time of day, the status and gender of the occupant, the presence of guests, and individual agency.[86] Even offices and bedrooms today are not solely for one use. Therefore we can consider the inner and outer spaces as bedchambers and offices, while accepting that this may not always have been the case for each example or for any example over the course of its use.

The detected status of lodging ranges comprises a number of elements, including the comfort described above. When describing comparable ranges, Pantin defines Vicars' Close as a 'superior kind of accommodation', while Stocker states that the vicarial houses were 'sumptuous'.[87] This was a reflection not only of the comfortable living space created through heat and light but of the separation from others. Lodging ranges, and their counterparts in colleges and cathedrals, are indicative of considerable societal change in notions of separation. This change occurred throughout society, with greater emphasis placed on separated spaces, as demonstrated in the development of York's vicars choral accommodation, and seen in other urban situations such as inns. The architecture reveals a shift divergent from the public living familiar to medieval society towards a degree of privacy. This was epitomised by the individual door: the status it bestowed should not be underestimated. It created a physical barrier to access, a tangible representation of the ease of movement that some people – but not all – had when accessing the space. It hints at authority over the space beyond the door, even a notion of independence. Therefore the individual door encapsulates many of the threads discussed throughout this chapter: privacy, authority and status. So far, the emphasis has been on detecting these attributes in a space – the lodging ranges – but this cannot be fully separated from the people who occupied the spaces. The next chapter will extend this understanding of high-status space to the residents. In doing so we address this attribute as a facet of a person's identity.

---

86 Felicity Riddy, '"Burgeis" Domesticity in Late-medieval England', in Maryanne Kowaleski and P. J. P. Goldberg (eds), *Medieval Domesticity: Home, Housing and Household in Medieval England* (Cambridge, 2008), pp. 14–36, at p. 24.
87 Pantin, 'Lodgings', p. 248; Stocker, 'Quest', p. 21.

2

EXPRESSIONS OF INDIVIDUALITY AND COLLECTIVITY

IDENTITY AND ARCHITECTURE

In the previous chapter it was discussed how the architecture of lodging ranges indicated their use as high-status accommodation. The provisions such as garderobes and fireplaces made each room distinctly comfortable and grand. The individual door had a crucial role in creating a sense of privacy and allowing authority over the space within the room beyond. While lodging ranges were clearly high-status spaces, this chapter will extend this concept from place to person. That is, lodging ranges were not only high-status spaces, but were built to *reflect* status. In the last chapter we defined status as the social and professional position of each person, and, in this way, it was integral to a person's identity. Identity can be considered as the multi-threaded composition of qualities that creates a notion of self. These threads are what make us unique, and what bind us to other people. There is a literal component, the fact of being who you are, but this should be considered a thread within identity rather than the total sum. An incomplete list of other threads within one's identity would include gender, ethnicity, religion and occupation. Therefore, when discussing identity, I refer to the sum of these threads, although some are more evident in the architectural record than others. Those detectable through building remains, and discussed in this chapter and the next, include occupation, status, kinship, authority and independence. As we discuss the interrelationship of lodging ranges and identity it will become clear that these threads are not always evidential at the same time. We see hints of one identity being projected while another identity might be imposed. Therefore, like status and privacy in Chapter 1, we consider identity as relational. Identities were not static but shifted as an individual did, and they were impacted by – and impacted on – other people's identities. They were created, performed and practised by the identity holder, yet could be imposed from afar even if the identities were in contrast with one another.

Each facet of a person's identity was shaped by their social, cultural and physical surroundings. This is an important element of identity studies, particularly at a time when DNA testing and categorising people into percentages of a nationality are on the rise. It is absurd to consider identity as quantifiable. The reality is that identity is messy. While our past shapes us, so does our present. The surroundings into which we are born and in which we grow up, sleep, eat and learn influence our sense of self and view of the world. Identity is integral to the lived experience, be it modern or medieval. While the study of identities and their social and cultural surroundings emerged from social sciences, it is studied through and applied in a variety of disciplines. The fundamental idea is that people derive part of their identity from the social and cultural groups to which they belong.[1] For most people, there are numerous such groups: family, colleagues, teachers, friends, acquaintances, co-participators in hobbies, fellow students. These social and cultural surroundings are considerable forces in shaping identity, but by their nature they are fluid and flexible. Therefore it is accepted that they differ in strength and content, and do not override individual agency, particularly as the individual must perform their identity for it to exist. For the early medieval context, William Frazer argues that there are vast differences in identities between people who are ostensibly from similar social and cultural groups.[2] For the high medieval period, Katherine Weikert demonstrates how identities were affected by both social expectations at a collective level and the individual agency within set social and cultural structures.[3]

In reality, it is impossible, or erroneous, to separate cultural, social and spatial surroundings. The former two have a spatial dimension, in that they are enveloped by space, and, as such, space is imbued with social and cultural meanings. However, studies tend to explore identity

---

1 J. Turner, M. Hogg, P. Oaks, S. Reicher, and M. Wetherell, *Rediscovering the Social Group: A Self-categorization Theory* (Cambridge, 1987).
2 William Frazer, 'Identities in Early Medieval Britain', in William Frazer and Andrew Tyrell (eds), *Social Identity in Early Medieval Britain* (Leicester, 2000), pp. 1–22, at p. 5.
3 Katherine Weikert, *Authority, Gender and Space in the Anglo-Norman World, 900–1200* (Woodbridge, 2020), p. 8.

from one of the cultural, social or spatial viewpoints depending on their disciplinary focus. Spatial surroundings and identity have been explored in a wide variety of temporal contexts. In the medieval period, space and identity have been examined from literary perspectives, as for example in medieval Swansea, and within landscapes, such as the English fenlands.[4] Space, as fabricated by buildings, and identities have been explored in a number of medieval contexts, all of which stress the ways in which buildings represented identity. This has been discussed at length with regard to royalty and the upper nobility in the late medieval period. In some instances, as Christopher King notes, the works end at the simplistic conclusion that a building was a representation of economic prosperity;[5] however, more and more studies are diving into the complexities and pluralities of identities. Anthony Emery explores how various elements of the house represented status, political aspirations and new money.[6] In addition, his statement that 'a household ... was a male society'[7] asserts, without saying so directly, that architecture reflected another thread of identity: gender. However, this was a simplified and androcentric view echoing a wider problem in studies of the past more broadly. As Margaret Conkey and Janet Spector point out, the so-called invisibility of women in the past is the result of a false notion of objectivity rather than an inherent absence of such data.[8] In the context of medieval buildings, there has been considerable push-back against seeing the architecture of great houses as representations of male identity only. For example, Karen Dempsey's work on castles in Ireland, Britain and France addresses elite female agency.[9] She builds on Roberta Gilchrist's work, which recognises the relationship between buildings and aspects of identity such as sexuality and multiple genders.[10] Amanda Richardson also looks at gender identity in medieval

---

4   Catherine Clark, 'Place, Identity and Performance: Spatial Practices and Social Proxies in Medieval Swansea', *Journal of Medieval History*, 41:3 (2015), 256–72; Susan Oosthuizen, 'Culture and Identity in the Early Medieval Fenland Landscape', *Landscape History*, 37:1 (2016), 5–24.
5   Christopher King, 'The Interpretation of Urban Buildings: Power, Memory and Appropriation in Norwich Merchants' Houses, c. 1400–1660', *World Archaeology*, 41:3 (2009), 471–88, p. 472.
6   Anthony Emery, 'Late-medieval Houses as an Expression of Social Status', *Historical Research*, 78 (2005), 140–61.
7   Emery, 'Status', p. 144.
8   Margaret W. Conkey and Janet D. Spector, 'Archaeology and the Study of Gender', *Archaeological Method and Theory*, 7 (1984), 1–38.
9   Karen Dempsey, 'Gender and Medieval Archaeology: Storming the Castle', *Antiquity*, 93:369 (2019), 772–88.
10 Roberta Gilchrist, *Gender and Material Archaeology: The Archaeology of Religious Women* (Abingdon, 1994); Roberta Gilchrist, *Gender and Archaeology: Contesting the Past* (Abingdon, 1999).

buildings, particularly in terms of the space in and between rooms. She explores the apartments of queens in English high to late medieval palaces to consider how they reproduced gender ideologies in comparison to the kings' apartments. She concludes that, while personality and preference had a role in the performance of a queen's identity, facets such as power and influence were shaped and restricted through the architecture.[11]

Several other studies have looked at architecture in the construction and performance of identities: that is, the idea that buildings shape identities. Aidan O'Sullivan argues that early medieval houses in Ireland created and continually shaped identities and the ways in which they were enacted and performed.[12] Therefore, while identities were flexible, this was only the case within the set configurations of the building. King discusses the ways in which late to post-medieval urban buildings were used to construct both collective and individual identities. He argues that certain architectural features, such as large halls, were constructed to maintain the performance of an identity of legitimacy. He concludes that the ways in which houses were remodelled indicate the desire to create symbols of traditional value and political authority.[13] Across studies of medieval buildings there is an increasing desire to better understand the identities of the occupants. Weikert sets out that buildings were indicators of the life within them, while Emery extends this to state that houses represented 'almost the soul' of those who lived there.[14]

There was, therefore, a reciprocal relationship between architecture and identities. People constructed buildings to reflect their identity or the identity they wished to portray; this, in turn, shaped the identities they were able to perform. In this study, the examination of architecture reveals a number of identities. Primarily, we see the identity of the lords. Lodging ranges, and all of the great house, were physical testaments to the lord's status, wealth, authority and power, and how they wanted these things to be perceived by others. This will be touched upon here and discussed fully in Chapter 3. This chapter, however, will focus on the other identities portrayed through lodging ranges. Explorations of the great house are often restricted in their focus on the lord and family, or on the upper ranks only. I want to actively shift the focus onto the middle-

---

11   Amanda Richardson, 'Corridors of Power: A Case Study in Access Analysis from Medieval England', *Antiquity*, 77:296 (2003), 373–84; Amanda Richardson, 'Gender and Space in English Royal Palaces c.1160–c.1547: A Study in Access Analysis and Imagery', *Medieval Archaeology*, 47 (2003), 131–65.
12   Aidan O'Sullivan, 'Early Medieval Houses In Ireland: Social Identity and Dwelling Spaces', *Peritia*, 20 (2008), 225–56.
13   King, 'Urban', p. 485.
14   Weikert, *Authority*, p. 6; Emery, 'Status', p. 160.

ranking members of the household: those 'troublesome to define'.[15] These identities were also a consideration in the construction of lodging ranges and this provides an understanding of the occupants, their identities and their lived experience.

Displays of Identity

Identities were displayed in numerous ways beyond architecture, and these displays could be tangible or intangible. For the late medieval lord it was important to ensure that the correct identity was displayed. This was a period of increased social mobility among the upper echelons of society and, as such, the importance of displaying identity outwardly, in as many ways as possible, increased. One way in which a lord expressed their identity, from c.1300, was by maintaining a large retinue. Doing so ensured that one was not mistaken for another rank: posing as a noble when in fact a member of the gentry was illegal, and no member of the nobility wanted to be mistaken for gentry. Margaret Wood argues that this went beyond social appearance; indeed, it could be politically unwise for a lord not to display a desirable reputation.[16] She argues that displaying identity was not only an advertisement but a method of protection. We can see, therefore, the threads of identity the lord wished to demonstrate: status, social rank, prestige and permanence.

Buildings and retinues, in terms of both size and impact, were significant displays of these threads of identity, but were bolstered by a variety of other displays. Family crests were added on keystones and stained glass windows, suggesting an unfailing and perpetual identity as well as one's personal status. For example, the insignia of Richard II was added to a central boss at Dartington Hall, indicating his half-brother John Holland's political identity. Over the course of the late medieval period, the great house became an elaborate stage for such displays of status. As the household became less peripatetic, there was more time and money spent in and on singular residences, allowing a concentration of decoration, comfort and order within the house and household. This seeped out into the landscape of the estate. Audrey Thorstad, in her study of Tudor houses, stresses the role of landscape in displaying the lord's privilege.[17] Just as a building was a deliberate and meaningful construction, the landscape too was modified

---

15 Kate Mertes, *The English Noble Household 1250–1600* (Oxford, 1988), p. 55.
16 Margaret Wood, *The English Medieval House* (New York, 1965), p. 179; Jill Campbell, 'Architectural design and exterior display in gentry houses in 14th- and 15th-century England' (unpublished Ph.D. dissertation, Queen's University Belfast, 2012).
17 Audrey Thorstad, *The Culture of Castles in Tudor England and Wales* (Woodbridge, 2019), p. 55.

to ensure that a correct identity was displayed. This was not unique to the Tudor period; as Oliver Creighton shows, designed landscapes emerged much earlier in the medieval period.[18] This went beyond ensuring that the route to the house was aesthetically pleasing; lakes, ponds, walkways and deer parks were created, with certain animals displayed, such as peacocks, swans and rabbits, to ensure that an elite identity was communicated to the viewer.

Identity was performed in an ongoing and often intangible display. Felicity Heal shows that hospitality was central to displaying identity in the late medieval period.[19] It was an opportunity for a person to demonstrate their authority and power, but it was also considered a social virtue, even equivalent to honesty or honour. Henry Wotton described the great house as a 'theatre of hospitality', suggesting that the house was a stage upon which hospitality was performed.[20] Therefore each element of hosting guests in the house was an opportunity to display one's identity, from greeting a guest to offering them board and extravagances of generosity. Indeed, it could be embarrassing for the lord and household if they did not perform hospitality in the ways deemed appropriate by society.[21]

Being a generous host involved providing food and accommodation, and as such was another opportunity for displaying status. Christopher Woolgar argues that there were distinctive elements in what was consumed by medieval people.[22] For example, game and prestigious birds were elements of a high-status meal, and venison, in particular, represented wealth and land ownership when it was supplied from one's own park.[23] Food as a representation of identity was not restricted to the uppermost classes; Woolgar shows that it was the main form of gift-giving among medieval villagers and between tenants and their lord. These transactional performances of identity, as Ilana Krausman Ben-Amos argues, indicated the status of both the giver and the receiver; likewise, host and guest.[24] While lords wanted to display their identity by providing a lavish meal for guests, the guest in return expected their identity to be respected. Where they sat within the hall, when they were served meals, and the

---

18   Oliver Creighton, *Designs upon the Land, Elite Landscapes of the Middle Ages* (Woodbridge, 2009); Oliver Creighton, 'Overview: Castles and Elite Landscapes', in Christopher Gerrard and Alejandra Gutiérrez (eds), *The Oxford Handbook of Later Medieval Archaeology in Britain* (Oxford, 2018), pp. 355–70.
19   Felicity Heal, *Hospitality in Early Modern England* (Oxford, 1990).
20   Henry Wotton, *The Elements of Architecture* (London, 1624).
21   Thorstad, *Culture*, p. 126; Heal, *Hospitality*.
22   Christopher Woolgar, *The Great Household in Late Medieval England* (New Haven, 1999).
23   Woolgar, *Household*, p. 11.
24   Ilana Krausman Ben-Amos, *The Culture of Giving* (Cambridge, 2008).

comforts of their accommodation were expected to be appropriate to their status, rank and authority. Heal's study of hospitality in the sixteenth and seventeenth centuries makes clear that the performance of hospitality was based on common understandings, reciprocal expectations and, indeed, mutual benefits.[25]

The desire to display identity permeated all aspects of medieval life: some displays were set in stone and others were intangible and performative. This gives the impression that displays of identity were thus both explicit and subtle. While this is likely to be the case, what was once explicit may appear subtle to today's viewer. We must be careful not to underestimate the impact of such displays, even when they seem ephemeral to our modern eyes. Landscapes, hospitality and gift-giving, as well as architecture, were so inextricably linked to identity that people strove to display them conspicuously.[26] As such, both explicit and seemingly subtle displays should be considered equally impactful and significant contributions to the medieval lived experience, and the same is true of those presented through lodging ranges.

FUNCTION AND USE

This chapter will attempt to add a layer of humanisation to our understanding of lodging ranges by exploring two case studies: Gainsborough Hall, Lincolnshire, and Caister Castle, Norfolk. While we know that they were used as accommodation, they also had a role in constructing identities. While these factors overlap, a distinction must be made between function and use in order to fully comprehend the complexity of medieval buildings. Function and use are not dichotomous; rather, each is a layer of meaning that is deciphered from the fabric. Graham Fairclough's 'Meaningful Constructions' extends Amos Rapoport's ideas by describing a building's different meanings as facets of function: indicating that they co-exist, yet are not necessarily of equal importance.[27] He argues that meaning was the main function of a building, and in the case of a lodging range this can be visualised through their individual doors. The door, as all doors, provided and restricted access: this was its *use*. The architectural language of use was read by the medieval audience with the same clarity as the *function* of the door: epitomising the difference between those who could enter and those who could not. It further communicated a sense of ownership of, or

---

25 Heal, *Hospitality*.
26 Krausman Ben-Amos, *Giving*; Thorstad, *Culture*.
27 Amos Rapoport, *The Meaning of the Built Environment* (Tucson, 1990), p. 187; Graham Fairclough, 'Meaningful Constructions – Spatial and Functional Analysis of Medieval Buildings', *Antiquity*, 66:251 (1992), 348–66, p. 351.

rights over, the rooms on the other side. Therefore there is a distinction, at least to us in the present translating the past, between its use, as a point of entrance, and its function, of communicating its meanings in terms of access and ownership. In this chapter I will give priority to meaning over use. What was the meaning of a lodging range? Through exploring the architecture of the case studies, alongside the inventories of Caister, I will explore how their meaning was communicating to the medieval audience the identities of the individual occupant and collective retinue.

It was established in the previous chapter that reading the architectural language of a medieval building communicates its former use, and we can extend this translation between building and the modern viewer to the medieval audience. There is a difference, however, between how modern and contemporary audiences viewed a medieval building. In the process of studying, there is an active consciousness, while in daily life the surrounding world is experienced subconsciously. Thomas Markus argues that we experience the world through a detailed prism encompassing comprehensive social, cultural and political contexts, built from all of our past experiences and our understanding of society.[28] This allows an ease to the communication between building and viewer, although we may not be aware at the time of this communication taking place. This is true for people in the past too, as discussed more thoroughly in Chapter 3. The medieval audience viewed their architectural and spatial surroundings and subconsciously arrived at an informed interpretation based on their stored knowledge and life experiences.[29] Therefore the meaning of lodging ranges was detected and understood by those who viewed them.

It was stated above that lodging ranges displayed the lord's identity; therefore this was one of the building's meanings perceived by the medieval audience. They may have perceived both the lord's wealth, due to the number of retainers supported, and the lord's social reputation, evidenced by their ability to attract and command a following. However, when viewing the lodging range, the medieval audience may have viewed other identities than the lord's: the identities of the occupants. The variety of accommodation types provided in the great house suggests strongly that they reflected the occupant's identity. In Chapter 1, the spatial immediacy between sleeping and working spaces is discussed in relation to the kitchen marshal and service children. The latter slept within the kitchen and service rooms, which demonstrated

---

28 Thomas Markus, *Buildings and Power: Freedom and Control in the Origin of Modern Building Types* (Abingdon, 1993).
29 C. Pamela Graves, *The Form and Fabric of Belief* (York, 2000); Kate Giles, 'Seeing and Believing: Visuality and Space in Pre-modern England', *World Archaeology*, 39 (2007), 105–21; Simon Roffey, 'Constructing a Vision of Salvation', *Archaeological Journal*,163 (2006), 122–46; Weikert, *Authority*.

FIG. 17 PHOTOGRAPH SHOWING THE INNER FACE OF THE LODGING RANGE AT AMBERLEY CASTLE. THERE WERE CLEAR DISTINCTIONS IN THE PROVISIONS ON THE GROUND AND FIRST FLOORS IN TERMS NOT ONLY OF SIZE BUT OF DECORATION. THESE WINDOWS WERE OVERLOOKING A SEVERE DROP CREATED THROUGH THE CASTLE'S POSITION ON A MODIFIED OUTCROP; AS SUCH, DEFENCE WAS NOT A CONSIDERATION.

their low status and their job. The marshal's room may have been above the services in a more comfortable and separate space, indicating their greater authority and status, and higher-profile job. This connection between accommodation and identity can also be detected in lodging ranges. Based on the argument that lodging ranges were used as high-status accommodation, we can surmise that those within were considered of high status in the great house. Of course, this was relational: the retainers in the lodging range would be considered to be of a higher status than those who slept in dormitories, yet of a lower status than those who slept within the lord's chambers. Therefore a hierarchy of identities was represented in the architecture of the great house.

The architectural language of lodging ranges described in Chapter 1 reveals varying subtleties in their elevations and provisions. This intimates that the household's hierarchy percolated into the lodging ranges. The disparity of provisions is perhaps most clearly indicated by the differences between the first and ground floors, as for example at Amberley Castle,

Sussex (Figure 17). The rooms on the ground floor of the lodging range had flat, undecorated lintels over the fireplaces, in contrast to the arched and architraved versions on the first floor. More strikingly, the ground floor had small, cruciform windows with wide splays on the outer wall, striving to spread the little light coming in. The first-floor rooms were adorned with trefoil-cusped, two-light windows with open quatrefoil spandrels which allowed light to flood into the room. The ground-floor cruciform windows were not built in this shape to provide privacy to the occupant, often an argument used for disparities in window sizes, as they were on the external wall of the range, and the window was several metres from the base of the wall, meaning prying eyes were not a concern. Likewise, defence was not the reason for the small window. The monolithic-appearing edifice of the external wall may suggest defence, but in reality the wall could easily have been scaled due to the protruding kitchen located directly beside the lodging range. Therefore the architectural differences within the lodging range were physical representations of the different identities living there, and it is clear that the facet of identity portrayed was related to individual status. A common architectural principle in medieval accommodation was the housing of those of higher status on the first floor and those of lower status on the ground floor; indeed, the lord's chamber was frequently located on the first floor, above the parlour at the high end of the hall.[30] The embedding of the social hierarchy in the architecture is a good indication that the common organisation was socially and widely accepted. As such, the higher-status retainers may have expected rooms on the first floor and lodging ranges were built to satisfy this requirement. In the case study of Gainsborough Hall the architectural representation of hierarchical identities will be explained further.

GAINSBOROUGH HALL, LINCOLNSHIRE

Gainsborough Hall is located near the River Trent in Lincolnshire. It was built almost entirely in the third quarter of the fifteenth century by Thomas Burgh, the son of Elizabeth Percy, a co-heiress to a junior branch of the earls of Northumberland, and Thomas Burgh, who fought during

---

30 Jane Grenville, *Medieval Housing* (London, 1997), pp. 116–17; William Pantin, 'Medieval English Town-House Plans', *Medieval Archaeology*, 6:1 (1962), 202–39; John Blair, 'Hall and Chamber: English Domestic Planning 1000–1250', in Gwyn Meirion-Jones and Michael Jones (eds), *Manorial Domestic Buildings in England and Northern France*, Society of Antiquaries Occasional Papers 15, (London, 1993), pp. 1–21; Jane Grenville, 'Urban and Rural Houses and Households in the Late Middle Ages', in Maryanne Kowaleski and P. J. P. Goldberg (eds), *Medieval Domesticity: Home, Housing and Household in Medieval England* (Cambridge, 2008).

FIG. 18 PHOTOGRAPH LOOKING NORTH TOWARDS THE THREE-SIDED COURTYARD OF GAINSBOROUGH HALL. THE LODGING RANGE WAS ON THE WEST (LEFT) AND THE HALL WAS IN THE CROSS RANGE. THE BRICKWORK SEEN POST-DATES THE ORIGINAL CONSTRUCTION DATE.

the Hundred Years War under Clarence the Bastard. Burgh inherited the estate from his mother in 1455, aged twenty-four. He gained massive wealth and standing, and became a leading magnate in the country, having served four kings of Lancastrian, York and Tudor houses.[31] As a supporter of Henry VI, Burgh was granted land, and when he changed his allegiance to the Yorkists in 1460, he was appointed sheriff of Lincolnshire. It appears he was a favourite of Edward IV: he was appointed constable of Lincoln and Bolingbroke castles in 1461, an esquire of the king's body and knight of the king's chamber in 1463, and master of the king's horse in 1465. In 1471 Burgh helped Edward IV escape from Middleham Castle before joining him at the Battle of Barnet that April. Burgh managed to retain his power during the accession of Richard III; he was appointed knight of the garter and entertained the king at Gainsborough Hall in 1483. Under Henry VII he was made Lord Burgh.[32]

The fifteenth-century great house filled three sides of a courtyard (Figure 18), with a six-bay, timber-framed hall in the cross-range. Two tiers of wind braces and heavily moulded arch-braces adorn the hall's roof and, although built as late as the 1460s, there was a central hearth. A stone-built bay window was added to the north elevation of the hall, illuminating the dais. Perpendicular in style and noticeably asymmetrical, it may have been brought from a dissolved monastery by Thomas, fifth Lord Burgh, at the end of the sixteenth century.[33] The house was built within a small inland port with the estate stretching to a market place in the south, the parish church in the north-east and the river Trent in the west. In the late nineteenth century warehouses were built along the waterside and houses were later built surrounding the Hall, drastically changing its environment. The current approach is from the south, although the original access may have been from the north.

The west range of the open courtyard was a four-bay, three-storey lodging range, built c.1480. The north end of the lodging range abuts the low end of the cross-range, although the internal doorway connecting the two is a modern insertion. The low end of the cross-range contained the buttery, pantry and a central passage leading to the substantial kitchen (Figure 19), originally separate from the other service rooms. A fine example of a late medieval kitchen, it retains its fireplaces and bread oven. A newel from beside the servery hatches led to a parlour-type room on the first floor, with garderobe and fireplace. It was connected to a larger room

---

31   Anthony Emery, *Greater Medieval Houses of England and Wales 1300–1500* (3 vols, Cambridge, 2000; 2000; 2006), Vol. 2, p. 242.

32   S. J. Gunn, 'The Rise of the Burgh Family, c. 1431–1550', in Philip Lindley (ed.), *Gainsborough Old Hall* (Lincoln, 1991), pp. 8–13, at pp. 8, 9.

33   Philip Lindley (ed.), *Gainsborough Old Hall* (Lincoln, 1991), p. 24.

EXPRESSIONS OF INDIVIDUALITY AND COLLECTIVITY

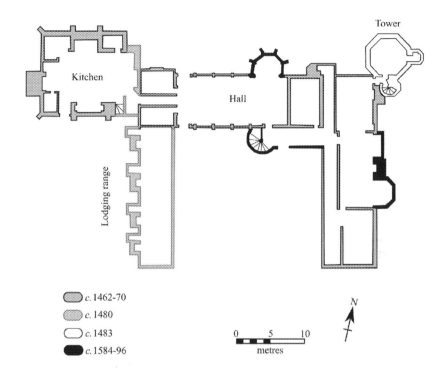

FIG. 19 PLAN OF GAINSBOROUGH HALL SHOWING THE PHASES OF CONSTRUCTION, WITH THE EAST RANGE, HALL, AND KITCHEN PREDATING THE LODGING RANGE. THE TOWER WAS ADDED TO ENHANCE THE FAMILY APARTMENTS AND LATER ADDITIONS INCLUDED THE BAY WINDOW.

over the services and cross-passage. These rooms may have been steward's chambers; alternatively, the larger room may have been a mess hall for the retainers accommodated in the lodging range. The failure to integrate the lodging range and low end of the cross-range, with neither a doorway nor common floor levels, may be the result of the later construction date of the lodging range, or it may have kept the function of the two clearly distinct. Dendrochronology has provided a reasonable sequence of construction for the ranges of Gainsborough, with the upper cross-wing, east range and great hall having felling dates within the 1460s, while the west range was dated to c.1479.[34] This provides a reasonable sequence of construction whereby the east range, containing the family apartments, and the cross-

---

34 Emery, *Greater Medieval Houses*, Vol. 2, p. 243.

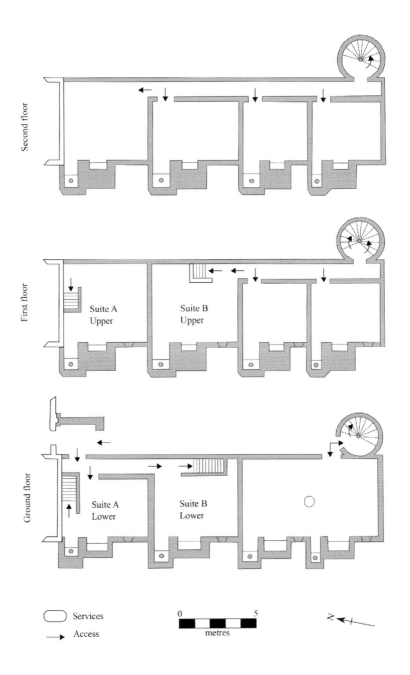

FIG. 20 GROUND, FIRST, AND SECOND FLOOR PLANS OF THE LODGING RANGE AT GAINSBOROUGH HALL. SUITE A AND B EACH COMPRISED TWO ROOMS, ACCESSIBLE INITIALLY VIA A PORCH THEN A CORRIDOR. EACH GROUND-FLOOR ROOM LED TO A FIRST-FLOOR ROOM WITH THE SAME PROVISIONS. THE FIRST FLOOR OF SUITE B HAD A SUPPLEMENTARY DOOR. THE SECOND FLOOR COMPRISED FOUR ESSENTIALLY IDENTICAL ROOMS, ALL ACCESSIBLE VIA A NEWEL THEN A CORRIDOR.

range were built first, then the western lodging range later. Despite the later construction date of the west range, it was probably planned from the house's inception. It demonstrated Burgh's ascension through the social ranks and his ability to afford a retinue, and was thus a crucial addition to his great house.

The lodging range was almost entirely timber-framed, with only the garderobes and fireplaces on the west elevation constructed of brick. In the late sixteenth century the south-facing gable was restored in English-bond brickwork by Thomas, fifth Lord Burgh. In the eighteenth century, the ground floor of the east elevation was underbuilt with brick to support the deteriorating timber frame.[35] Nevertheless, considerable tilting can be seen, particularly on the east façade.

There were three types of rooms within the lodging range, with evidence for corridors and a mixture of newel and straight staircases. There were two two-room suites, one dormitory, and six one-bay rooms. The suites are so-called as each comprised two rooms, one per floor, connected by an internal staircase (Figure 20). The result is strong architectural similarity to the two-storeyed houses at Vicars' Close, Wells. The suites at Gainsborough were located at the north end of the lodging range, with access granted through a porch. The porch was positioned in the corner where the lodging range and cross-range met, and it led from the courtyard into the lodging range and into the lower end of the hall.[36] In the lodging range, the porch opened into a corridor which contained two doors, each of which led to one of the suite's ground-floor rooms. In the northernmost room (Figure 20: suite A lower), the staircase to the first floor ascended from the west to the east, and in the other room (Figure 20: suite B lower), it climbed north–south. Within each room, ground floor and first floor, there was a garderobe and fireplace on the west wall. These were constructed in brick, with the northernmost garderobe's exterior rebuilt in the Victorian period. Windows were provided in the west elevation while one window on the east appears to be later.

The southern end of the ground floor comprised a two-bay dormitory (Figure 20). The west elevation contained two garderobes, two windows and two fireplaces, hinting that the space may have been divided into two rooms following the bays; however, the central post shows that there was no permanent partitioning. Unlike the other cross-frames in the range, the beam terminated in a wide octagonal head and joined a tie-beam which has no evidence of studs, indicating that the cross-frame was open at

---

35 Lindley, *Gainsborough*, p. 22.
36 N. Field, 'Excavations and the West Range', in Philip Lindley (ed.), *Gainsborough Old Hall* (Lincoln, 1991), pp. 34–42.

ground-floor level. The door was probably on the east elevation, although the brick underbuilding has rendered its location unknown.

There were a further six rooms within the range. Two were on the first floor and four on the second, all measuring approximately the same size and granted access from outside via a polygonal, external newel at the southern end of the east elevation. Evidence for the newel derived from excavations, which also suggest that it was removed in the seventeenth century.[37] It opened onto corridors running along the inside of the eastern elevation. On the first floor, the corridor occupied only the southern extent, as the northern end comprised the upper rooms of the suites. The corridor terminated at a door leading into the upper floor of one of the suites. Therefore suite B had access from the porch and corridor on the ground floor, and via the newel and corridor on the first floor (Figure 20). The first-floor corridor also gave access to the two one-bay rooms. The extant timber framing has preserved mortices demonstrating the position of the doors. It is clear there was one door per room. Within, the rooms each contained a garderobe, fireplace and window on the west elevation.

The external newel continued to the second floor, and again opened into a corridor that extended almost the full length of the range (Figure 20). It terminated at the entrance to the room at the northernmost end. While there are no floorboards on the second floor, meaning the mortices cannot be viewed, the position of the doors was noted during restoration. All but one of the entrances were at the northern end of each bay, thus reflecting the position of the entrances to the two rooms on the first floor. As before, each room contained a fireplace, garderobe and window on the west elevation, although the ceiling height was lower than on the first floor.[38] There are a number of windows of dubious date on the east and south elevations. The small windows on the east elevation may be original, as they were between the studs. On the south wall there were two windows, which again may respect the position of earlier versions, as the internal splays appear original.

The inclusion of a garderobe, fireplace and window in each bay on each floor created a strikingly uniform west façade. The brick-built fireplaces and garderobes were spaced equally in the otherwise timber range. The visual effect was heightened by crow-stepped gablets, evoking crenellations, on the garderobe towers which rose beyond the roof-line. Likewise, the chimney stacks displayed crow-stepped gables that stretched higher still beyond the pitch of the roof, creating a remarkable display of brickwork (Figure 21). This overwhelming uniformity belies the combination of

---

37 M. V. Clark, 'The West Range', in Philip Lindley (ed.), *Gainsborough Old Hall* (Lincoln, 1991), pp. 43–56; Lindley, *Gainsborough*, p. 26.
38 Clark, 'Range', p. 46.

FIG. 21 PHOTOGRAPH OF THE LODGING RANGE AT GAINSBOROUGH HALL. THE EXTERNAL ELEVATION, FACING AWAY FROM THE COURTYARD, DISPLAYED A STRIKINGLY UNIFORM ELEVATION COMPRISING BRICK-BUILT CHIMNEYS AND GARDEROBE TOWERS AGAINST A TIMBER-FRAMED RANGE. EACH WAS UNIQUELY DECORATED WITH GABLETS EVOKING CRENULATIONS.

rooms within: there was a juxtaposition between the uniform façade and the mixture of rooms. Gainsborough was one of only a few known lodging ranges to utilise internal corridors. It seems that this allowed the creation of a variety of rooms without their reflection on the façades.

The east range contained the private apartments of the Burgh family, and has been much altered over the centuries. The original plan consisted of two unequally sized rooms on each floor. Both floors were served with a corridor along the western side of the range; that is, the side overlooking the courtyard. In the 1480s, an octagonal residential tower was added at the north-eastern corner of the east range. It was constructed of brick and stone, possibly in time for Richard III's visit in 1483, and may therefore post-date the west range. The tower provided further rooms and a stairway to connect the smaller rooms of the east range's ground and first floors. The first-floor room of the tower also contained a newel to the tower's second floor. This was the only second-floor room to the east of the hall, until William Hickman squeezed second-floor rooms into the roof bays in the sixteenth century.[39]

---

39 Emery, *Greater Medieval Houses*, Vol. 2, p. 246.

By turning his support throughout the Wars of the Roses and after, Burgh died a very wealthy man in 1496. He left the seat of the Burgh family and its great wealth to his son Edward, who, in 1477, married the widow, Anne Cobham, thus bringing Scarborough Castle into Burgh ownership. He followed in his father's footsteps in his early years, increasing his wealth, gaining a knighthood at the battlefield of Stoke in 1487, and joining parliament for Lincoln in 1492, but seemed to lack his father's skill in staying on the right side of the monarchy. This resulted in huge debts and imprisonment in Fleet Prison; he was later declared mentally ill and, having never regained full mental capacity, died in 1528.

When Thomas, fifth Lord Burgh, took a seat at the House of Lords in 1584, the family returned to national prominence. As well as the bay window on the north-facing elevation of the hall, he added the substantial newel staircase and first-floor gallery on its southern elevation (Figures 18 and 19). This has been attributed to the nineteenth century, when the ground floor was underbuilt in brick; however, the central pendant is carved with a Burgh emblem, dating the addition to 1584–96.[40] When Burgh was Governor of Brill in the Netherlands, *c*.1595, he wrote several letters mentioning his failing health.[41] He sold Gainsborough in 1596 and died one year later.

Hickman bought the house in 1596 and made the aforementioned changes to the second floor of the east range. He instantly exploited his manorial rights over the town, which had been all but neglected while Burgh was abroad.[42] He faced considerable opposition, resulting in court cases; however, with no local government or borough status at the time, Hickman was able to exploit the town with ease. The turbulent period ended with Hickman's death in 1625. The Hickman family's ownership of the house ceased when Frances Hickman died in 1826 with no heirs, and it passed to her cousin Henry Hickman Bacon. It had been scarcely used as a home for a century; the east range was leased as a house, while the west range was used as tenements, alongside workshops and a public house. The hall became a public hall, then a successful theatre.[43] In 1949 the Friends of the Old Hall Association was established and they set about repairing the neglected areas, including elements of the hall's roof, west range and kitchen, including replacing the louvre.[44]

---

40 Lindley, *Gainsborough*, p. 24.
41 J. Vernon, 'A Fine Wreck of the Feudal Age', in Philip Lindley (ed.), *Gainsborough Old Hall* (Lincoln, 1991), pp. 27–33.
42 Vernon, 'Feudal', p. 29.
43 Vernon, 'Feudal', p. 32.
44 Vernon, 'Feudal', p. 33.

JUXTAPOSED IDENTITIES

Gainsborough Hall provides an intriguing insight to the juxtaposition of identities embedded in one building type. The lodging range, on one side of the three-sided courtyard, comprised three distinctly different types of accommodation. When we accept that buildings reflect identities, we can see that the lodging range accommodated a variety of people, rather than one homogeneous group. We see a number of threads of identity represented here, primarily different social status. Gainsborough's lodging range appears to be ranked accommodation, suggesting that it was planned with an awareness of the social stratification among the household, and the requirements or demands of each stratum.

The six small rooms each measured just 18m^2, suggesting that they were low occupancy or for individuals. Therefore we see a further thread of identity: the ability to command privacy or social separation. When compared with the two-bay dormitory on the ground floor, we see a distinction between those who had authority over space and those who shared their space with many others. The six small rooms and the two two-room suites were accessed via corridors. These led, for most of the rooms, to an individual door; that is, one door per room. This suggests that the occupants had a level of ownership over the rooms. Of the two two-room suites, suite B had one entrance on the ground floor and a possible second entrance on the first floor. This makes this space more open and accessible, both physically and socially. As such, our perception of the occupants' identity here does not quite include ownership to the same degree as for the neighbouring suite (Figure 20).

Another thread of identity detected is individualism. Rather than one homogeneous retinue, its identity was segmented, suggesting that there was some independence from the group. This is implied by the individual doors. The occupants of each small room, unlike those of the dormitory, had some control over their door: who could enter and who could not, when the door was open and when not, relied on an individual's decision, unlike the dormitory's door. Even if the rooms were occupied by pairs, or possibly by three individuals, there was still a greater independence in the decision-making regarding when that door was opened. This suggests a level of individual responsibility, possibly seen most clearly when comparing the two suites (Figure 20). The occupants of suite B do not appear to have had the same degree of authority and responsibility over the space and who could enter, because of its two entrances. Their control was dispersed over these entrances, whereas the occupants of suite A could focus their attention and control on only one door.

The two-room suites at Gainsborough are architecturally similar to the houses of Vicars' Close, Wells, built over a century before. We can extend the supposed uses of the vicarial range to Gainsborough and suggest that the ground-floor room, or 'outer' space, was an office: a miniature hall and meeting place.[45] The upper, inner space may have been the bedchamber. These uses, as well as the architecture, suggest that these were some of the most comfortable and prestigious rooms in the house, probably reserved for the highest-status retainers. The frequency of accommodation with distinct spaces in comparison to undivided spaces is low. At Haddon Hall, the lodging range comprised six rooms, of which only two were divided into an office and bedchamber. At Gainsborough there were two suites and six other rooms plus a dormitory in the range. This scarcity of suites and divided rooms in each case suggests that they accommodated occupants of considerable social standing.

While we can detect occupants' identities in the fabric of the lodging range, they were not static like the building. Rather, identities had to be performed to be maintained. For example, if the ground floor of the suite at Gainsborough was an office or meeting space, the occupant's authority and responsibility was performed when they invited other household members or guests in to discuss matters pertaining to the house. For those living in the dormitory, their relative lower status was reinforced through the lived experience of the space, such as sharing provisions or occupying shared spaces. The practice of opening and closing the only entrance to the space, allowing in some and not others, was another performance of one's status, authority and individualism. While the architecture shaped how these identities were performed, individual agency contributed.[46] There was a uniqueness, therefore, to how each person used their surroundings to portray their identity, heightening the sense of individualism in lodging ranges. This notion of individualism requires further examination, which will be conducted through the case study of Caister Castle, below. While Caister has lost the majority of its fabric, two household inventories provide an insight into those who may have lived within its lodging ranges.

CAISTER CASTLE, NORFOLK

Caister Castle was built in c.1431–45 by John Fastolf, an English knight who fought in the Hundred Years War, serving in France on numerous occasions during the reigns of Henry V and Henry VI. Fastolf was born into a minor gentry family but gained wealth through his marriage to

---

45   William Pantin, 'Chantry Priests' Houses and Other Medieval Lodgings', *Medieval Archaeology*, 3 (1959), 216–58, p. 248; Wood, *House*; David Stocker, 'The Quest for One's Own Front Door: Housing the Vicars' Choral at the English Cathedrals', *Vernacular Architecture*, 36 (2005), 15–31.
46   Weikert, *Authority*, p. 9; Frazer, 'Identities', p. 5.

Millicent, daughter of Lord Tiptoft, in 1409.[47] He was made a knight-banneret in 1424 and knight of the garter in 1426. In the following decade he purchased land in England, mainly in Norfolk, with his profits from war, constructing Caister upon his return from France.[48] He is immortalised through the remains of his castle, his contribution to military theory and literature, with which his stepson Scrope assisted, and the less-than-favourable association with John Falstaff from Shakespeare's Henriad. A more accurate and less Shakespearean account of his life reveals a knight who survived the Battle of Patay; he was wealthy, honoured and well connected, which allowed him to retain a large household in his fashionable house at Caister. It was certainly this latter impression that Fastolf hoped would endure beyond him.

The castle, situated near Great Yarmouth in Norfolk, is one of the oldest brick edifices in England, with parts of its exceptional brickwork preserved in a circular tower.[49] The house had a double-courtyard plan (Figure 22) and was surrounded by a moat which also separated the two courtyards, although this central arm of the moat has since been filled in. Practically all of the inner walls are gone, but parts of the exterior elevations and the circular tower, which possibly contained some of Fastolf's private rooms, remain.[50]

The inventories of Caister are dated 1448, with notes up to 1455, and 1462.[51] They therefore straddle the death of Fastolf in 1459 and the castle's transfer to the Paston family in the same year. Caution is required when using the inventories. They describe about fifty different spaces in both the outer and inner courtyards, allowing some to be located within the current ruins: the caveat, however, is that we can only guess at the route taken by the surveyor. They include details of rooms' furnishings and in some instances the names of those who occupied them. Once again, however, we do not know what was ignored or considered unimportant. They list

---

47 G. L. Harriss, 'Fastolf, Sir John', (2004), *Oxford DNB*. < https://doi.org/10.1093/ref:odnb/9199> [accessed 23rd August 2021].
48 Harriss, 'Fastolf'; Emery, *Greater Medieval Houses*, Vol. 2, p. 56.
49 Colin Platt, *The Architecture of Medieval Britain: A Social History* (New Haven, 1990); Alasdair Hawkyard, 'Sir John Fastolf's "Gret mansion By Me Late Edified": Caister Castle, Norfolk', in Linda Clark (ed.), *The Fifteenth Century V: 'Of Mice and Men': Image, Belief and Regulation in Late Medieval England* (Woodbridge, 2005), pp. 39–68; Historic England, *Caister Castle*, List Entry Number: 1287573 (2014) Available online: <https://historicengland.org.uk/listing/the-list/list-entry/1287573> [accessed 23rd August 2021].
50 Emery, *Greater Medieval Houses*, Vol. 2, p. 56.
51 Woolgar, *Household*, p. 67; Norman Davis, *Paston Letters and Papers of the Fifteenth Century*, 2nd edn (Oxford, 2004); MCO Fastolf paper 43; Thomas Amyot, 'Transcript of two rolls, containing an inventory of the effects formerly belonging to Sir John Fastolfe', *Archaeologia* 21 (1827), pp. 232–80.

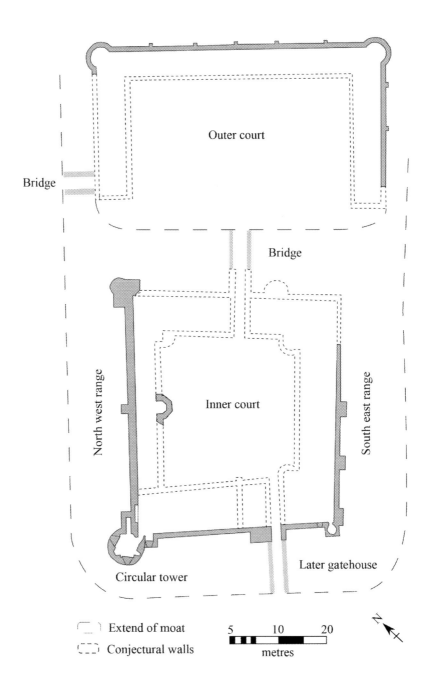

FIG. 22 PLAN OF CAISTER CASTLE, SHOWING THE EXTENT OF THE REMAINS AND THE CONJECTURAL WALLS. THE CASTLE COMPRISED TWO COURTYARDS ONCE SEPARATED BY A MOAT. THE MAIN ACCESS DURING FASTOLF'S OWNERSHIP WAS VIA THE BRIDGE IN THE OUTER COURTYARD AND DURING THE PASTON OCCUPATION A GATEHOUSE IN THE INNER COURTYARD WAS ADDED.

twenty-eight rooms with thirty-nine beds, indicating a concentration on the higher-status elements of the house. Spaces of relative lower status were not overlooked; for example, the gardener's chamber was listed as containing two mattresses and further sheets and coverlets,[52] but the inventories focused on the inner and outer courtyards, which were of high status in the context of the wider estate. Despite the limitations of using inventories and the paucity of archaeological remains, their combined use allows the tentative placement of two lodging ranges, one in the outer courtyard and one in the inner, in a manner similar to the contemporaneous Wingfield Manor.

The three-ranged outer courtyard was situated to the north-east of the inner courtyard (Figure 22). Its south-west side was open and faced the inner courtyard, to which it was previously connected by a bridge, while its entrance was via a further bridge and opening through the north-west range. Little of the north-west range has survived, although the exterior walls of the north-east and south-east ranges are extant. They were constructed of brick in varying hues and the quality of the brickwork appears to be poorer than that of the inner courtyard. The walls included two-storey rounded corner towers at the north and east, of the same material, and brick buttresses to the exterior. The elevation was interrupted by a series of arrow slits with splays and timber lintels; otherwise, as it remains, it is essentially featureless. The inventories help to illuminate the use of the outer courtyard: they list accommodation for Bokking (lawyer), Fitzrauf (gentle servant), Thomas Fastolf, and the cook. Each room is described as containing one bed and furnishings such as testers and celures (bed canopies). The listing of individual rooms, with high-status furnishings, allows a tentative conclusion that this accommodation was in the form of a lodging range. In the context of the house's hierarchy, and evidence for a further lodging range in the inner courtyard, the occupants here may have been of a slightly lower rank, despite their apparent abilities. The range in which these rooms were located is unknown.

The inner courtyard was slightly smaller than the outer and is similarly ruinous. Its truncated state is dominated by the six-storey circular tower at the junction of the north-west and south-west ranges (Figure 23), which reached approximately 29 metres and connected to a polygonal stair-turret on the south side that was higher than the circular tower itself. The lower four storeys of the stair turret were small, square rooms lit by rectangular windows. The ground floor of the south-west range was illuminated by a two-light Perpendicular window with deep splays, suggesting that this was the dais end of a hall (Figure 24). Above the window at first-floor level there were seven two-light windows. These may have lit the hall, if the

---

52   Woolgar, *Household*, p. 63; MCO Fastolf paper 43; Amyot, 'Transcript'.

FIG. 23 PHOTOGRAPH OF THE SOUTH-WEST RANGE OF THE INNER COURTYARD AT CAISTER CASTLE, WITH THE SUBSTANTIAL CIRCULAR TOWER AT ITS JUNCTURE WITH THE NORTH-WEST RANGE. THE PERPENDICULAR WINDOW AND FORMER FIREPLACE CAN BE SEEN ON THE RIGHT AND THE LATER GATEHOUSE IS CENTRE-LEFT.

hall was open to the first-floor ceiling, which seems reasonable (Figure 24). The presence of a fireplace located perpendicular to the large window supports the location of a dais here. Furthermore, between the window and fireplace there was a door, decorated with a four-centred arch that led directly into the circular tower. The elaboration of the tower suggests that this was a high-status area within the house; as such, the rooms within may have been part of Fastolf's suite of rooms. These may have continued from the tower along the north-west range.

If the south-west range had contained the hall, one would expect services at the low end. There is no evidence of such; rather, there appears to be accommodation related to the gatehouse. The gatehouse, which bisects the south-west range, was adorned with a machicolated parapet, matching the curtain wall (Figure 23). However, there is considerable evidence to indicate that the gatehouse was built at least two decades after the remainder of the range. The external elevation of the gatehouse was built upon an earlier buttress with the later brickwork almost concealing a stone gargoyle resembling those on extant buttresses elsewhere. It appears that the gatehouse was added after an attack on the curtain wall when the house was in the possession of John Paston, to whom it passed after Fastolf's death. In 1469 Caister was attacked by the Duke of Norfolk, who succeeded in taking the castle by force; and when he died shortly after it returned to Paston ownership.[53] The later date of the gatehouse allows the tentative suggestion that it replaced a part of the range which had contained the services. H. D. Barnes and W. D. Simpson suggest that this area also contained a postern prior to the gatehouse's construction.[54]

The most convincing evidence for the hall is the cluster of features at the potential high end (Figure 23): however, we cannot determine their relative status without comparison to other features which do not survive. Consequently, we must consider other locations for the hall. Henry Swindon's 1760 plan of Caister indicated that the south-west range contained a dining room, with the main hall located in the south-east range. Barnes and Simpson used this and the inventories to suggest that the 'dining room' was in fact a winter, or nether, hall, thus explaining the features indicative of a hall, while the summer, or upper, hall was, as depicted by Swindon, in the south-east range.[55] This dual-hall plan is, as Alasdair Hawkyard says, 'most unusual',[56] although not entirely unheard of: a large vaulted undercroft at Wingfield Manor may have served as a

---

53 H. D. Barnes and W. D. Simpson, 'Caister Castle', *Antiquaries Journal*, 32:1–2 (1952), 35–51, p. 35.
54 Barnes and Simpson, 'Caister', p. 42.
55 Barnes and Simpson, 'Caister', p. 43.
56 Hawkyard, 'Fastolf', p. 57.

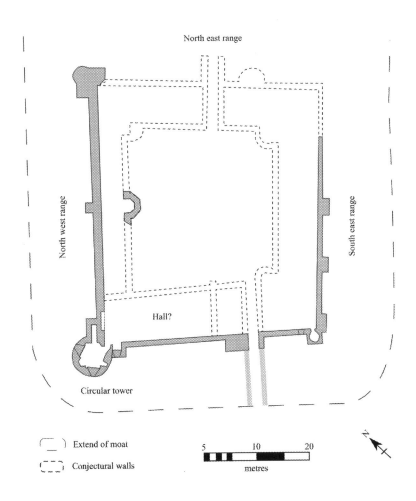

FIG. 24 PLAN OF CAISTER CASTLE'S INNER COURTYARD WITH SUGGESTED LOCATION OF THE HALL IN THE SOUTH-WEST RANGE. THE FOOTPRINT OF A CENTRAL STAIR TURRET ON THE NORTH-WEST RANGE IS INDICATED.

winter hall, with the summer version directly above, as suggested by its four doors and decorative bosses.

With distance from the circular tower, the ruin's fabric becomes more and more sparse. The south-east range may have contained the summer hall as well as the chapel, as suggested by Barnes and Simpson;[57] however, this is almost entirely conjecture. Directly opposite the south-east range,

---

57 Barnes and Simpson, 'Caister', p. 43.

the north-west range retains evidence for a vaulted ground floor, above which there may have been accommodation. Architectural evidence draws from two large windows at first-floor level and a square-plan tower, which contained garderobes, connecting the north-west range to the circular tower. What is clear from the architectural remains is that there is not enough fabric to determine with certainty the position of even typical features from which others could be identified through common spatial ordering. However, the little evidence there is in the western corner of the inner courtyard does allow some very tentative suggestions, when combined with the information from the inventories. Based on these, there may have been a lodging range in the north-west or south-east range of the inner courtyard (Figure 24).

The inventories list an individual room provided for the steward of Caister, John Rafman, within the inner courtyard, beside a room for Stephen Scrope, Fastolf's stepson.[58] There were further rooms for Cole and Watkyn Shipdam, both auditors; Geoffory, who was the chaplain; and William Lynde, whose role is unknown.[59] This collection of rooms suggests the presence of a lodging range somewhere within the inner courtyard. The roles of the occupants were pertinent to the running of the house, suggesting that the inner courtyard lodging range was of a higher status than its counterpart in the outer courtyard. The location of Fastolf's room helps determine the lodging range's whereabouts.

Fastolf had a suite of three rooms in the inner courtyard: one for his personal use, a stewhouse for washing and bathing, and a chamber for his secretary, William Worcester, and his chamberlain, Ludovic Pole.[60] Next to Fastolf's personal chamber was the White Chamber, given to a principal officer, Henry Inglose. Woolgar suggests that these rooms were located above the summer hall in the south-east range, which would place the accommodation described above, potentially the lodging range for Rafman, Cole, Shipdam, and Scrope, in the opposite, north-west range.[61] The only extant architectural evidence to support this – albeit tentatively – is the footprint of a stair turret placed centrally in the north-west range (Figures 24 and 25). This hint of a uniform façade, typical in a lodging range, is reflected in Barnes and Simpson's depiction of four evenly spaced one-light windows on the ground floor.[62] However, considering the common spatial ordering of the medieval hall, the lodging range may equally have been in the south-east range (Figure 24). This seems more

---

58   Jonathan Hughes, 'Scrope, Stephen', (2015), *Oxford DNB*. <https://doi.org/10.1093/ref:odnb/66283> [accessed 23rd August 2021].
59   Woolgar, *Household*, p. 67; Davis, *Paston*.
60   Emery, *Greater Medieval Houses*, Vol. 2, p. 59.
61   Woolgar, *Household*, p. 67.
62   Barnes and Simpson, 'Caister', p. 39.

FIG. 25 PHOTOGRAPH OF THE NORTH-WEST RANGE AT CAISTER CASTLE. DESPITE THE FORMER PRESENCE OF A CENTRALLY PLACED STAIRCASE, WHICH HINTS AT UNIFORM ARCHITECTURE, THE POTENTIAL LOCATION OF THE HIGH END OF THE HALL ADJOINING THE CIRCULAR TOWER SUGGESTS THAT THIS RANGE WAS FASTOLF'S ACCOMMODATION.

likely, due to the grand and architecturally elaborate circular tower. Such a striking display may have been part of Fastolf's suite or part of his route from hall to suite. That would place the hall (with high-end Perpendicular window and fireplace) in the south-west range and Fastolf's suite in the north-west range, with the circular tower at their juncture (Figure 25). If this was the layout, the lodging range would have been in the south-east range, potentially beyond the low end of the hall, as at Wingfield Manor. A crucial point that either of these potential layouts demonstrates is the separation of Fastolf's accommodation (including that for his highest-ranking servants, Worcester, Pole and Inglose) from the lodging range.

Upon Fastolf's death the entirety of his lands in Norfolk and Suffolk passed to John Paston. Caister was sold in 1659 to William Crow and it subsequently passed to the Bedingfield family by marriage. A plan published in 1776 indicated that the majority of the buildings were still intact, including a bridge connecting the two courtyards.[63] The site was then subjected to considerable robbing of the fabric, including the removal of a 122-step stone newel from the circular tower by Parson David Collyer for his house at Wroxham.[64] The moat was altered in the late nineteenth century and in 1952 the castle was in the ownership of Charles Hamblen-Thomas.[65] The grounds to the south-west of the ruins host a motor museum.

THREADS OF PERSONHOOD

Caister Castle allows a greater understanding of the identities of those who lived within lodging ranges. Hawkyard writes of the Caister inventories: 'the inconsistencies and contradictions with each are so extensive as effectively to prevent a plausible reconstruction of the entire layout'.[66] While, indeed, a detailed layout may be beyond us, I am somewhat more optimistic. Using the inventories alongside common architectural principles, we can locate two potential lodging ranges: one in the inner courtyard and one in the outer. The inventories describe four individual rooms in the outer courtyard, for Bokking, Thomas Fastolf, Fitzrauf and the cook. The Bokking room has been attributed to John Bokking, Fastolf's lawyer, while Fitzrauf was a gentle servant.[67] Thomas Fastolf was not John Fastolf's son, as the latter died without an heir, although Thomas

---

63 Historic England, 'Caister'.
64 C. R. B. Barrett, 'Caister Castle and Sir John Fastolfe', *Journal of the British Archaeological Association*, 2 (1896), 37–47.
65 Historic England, 'Caister'.
66 Hawkyard, 'Fastolf', p. 56.
67 Woolgar, *Household*, p. 63.

Fastolf's room contained a tester of red say with the Fastolf arms.[68] Each person had their own room, and these were perhaps similar to some of the rooms at Gainsborough. Therefore the display of individualism through ownership and authority over space can also be detected here. Rather than the group members occupying a dormitory, they were granted a degree of independence from one another. Each of the four rooms contained one bed and a variety of comforts, such as testers, celures and decorated coverlets. The similarities between the rooms suggest that they may have been within a lodging range, which is supported by the relative high status implied by the mention of the occupants' roles in the inventories. Furthermore, three of the four occupants were named, while those in other spaces for sleeping were not; for example, there were mattresses in the great stables and the gardeners' chamber. The naming of the occupants in the inventories implies something akin to a social bond between retainer and lord. The inclusion of their name alongside or instead of their role appears to prioritise social or familial elements of their identity over professional or military aspects. This allows us to revise our understanding of the retainer–lord relationship while diminishing the overly militarised interpretation discussed previously.

The inventories suggest a further lodging range in the inner courtyard. There are numerous individual rooms listed for the inner courtyard, including for John Bossherde and Robert Carpenter, although their jobs are not given.[69] In addition, there are individual rooms listed for the porter and the rector, although their names are not given. This variance in how individuals were recorded in the inventories once again demonstrates how certain identities were prioritised or deemed prominent over others. We gain a sense of the individual identities within Caister, which is enhanced when the location of this lodging range in the inner courtyard is considered. This suggests that there was a demarcation of status within the lord's followers represented by their physical position within the house. As discussed above, this follows the accepted architectural principle of the courtyards which is partly based on the 'inner' and 'outer' continuum.[70] Inner and outer are imbued with status differentiation. The inner denotes a higher status and greater sense of privacy, through separation, than the outer. Therefore those retainers in the inner courtyard can be considered higher-status household members than those in the outer. This division of a homogeneous retinue into smaller groups was also detected at Gainsborough, as the status of different retainers was reflected in the

---

68   Woolgar, *Household*, p. 67.
69   Although surnames could be used to suggest an occupation.
70   For example, Wood, *House*; Matthew Johnson, *Behind the Castle Gate: From Medieval to Renaissance* (London, 2002).

different types of rooms. Caister's inventories, too, suggest that the inner courtyard rooms were certainly of the same or higher comfort as those in the outer courtyard. As well as at least one bed per room (Scrope's room had two), some had wall hangings, chairs and tables. If the occupants of the inner courtyard's lodging range were of a higher social status than those in the outer, it generates two insights into the individuals' identities: first, that a continuum of social status was physically represented within the great house, with spatial distance from the lord's chambers representing social distance from his rank; second, the hierarchy of the wider medieval society was represented, and possibly reinforced further, within the great house. This suggests that status was a thread of identity which needed to be displayed centrally in the individuals' lived experience. As such, it is not surprising that it appears prominently in our understanding of the individual's identity. We can extend this, however, to explore precedence: that is, who could approach whom, when, and how frequently. The separation of the courtyards, connected by a bridge spanning the moat, suggests that those in the outer courtyard interacted with other staff in the outer courtyard more frequently than they would have interacted with those in the inner, including Fastolf. It is evident that adherence to the architectural principle of inner and outer spaces representing higher and lower status is representative of the ways in which the ordered domestic world was described in the courtesy books: that is, social norms influenced the architecture and the architecture reinforced these practices. As such, the ways in which status was performed may have been different for the retainers in the outer and inner courtyards.

Our understanding of individualism can be strengthened through the instances in Caister's inventories which list both a name and a job for the occupant of a room. It is important to make clear that a name is not someone's identity; as stated earlier, one's identity is made up of multiple threads. A job is not an identity either. However, the combination of name, job, status and the lived experience of these allows a deeper sense of each individual. Stephen Scrope (1397–1472) was the son of Millicent Fastolf from her first marriage, and thus became Fastolf's stepson in 1409. His room, in the inner courtyard, contained two beds, one of which was folding, plus hanging cloths. The flexible use of space, discussed in Chapter 1, can help understand his room. It was discussed how the architecture and spatial dimensions suggest that rooms within lodging ranges were low-occupancy or even housed individuals, but were flexible, changing as and when required. The presence of a folding bed in Scope's rooms supports this, as it implies that a second person may have occupied the room on only a temporary basis, rather than being the norm. Scrope spent his adolescence in secretarial service for Fastolf in Normandy, and subsequently provided his stepfather with a compilation of the wisdom of ancient philosophers. The strength of this personal relationship is suggested by the inclusion of his name in the inventories, while servants such as the cook and the rector go unnamed. In later life Scrope worked as an author and translator, and Woolgar suggests that four other household members were also authors.[71] We get a sense of a handful of high-ranking staff who were keenly interested in literature.

As well as Scrope's room in the inner courtyard, there was a room for the steward of the household, John Rafman. Rafman was responsible for the day-to-day running of the manor, and supported Fastolf in the manorial court or replaced him in his absence. He may have welcomed guests, and arranged their food and board. He held a prestigious position in the household and, alongside his bouche de court, was paid 66s. 8d. by Fastolf in 1430–31.[72] He would have managed a number of staff, possibly including coadjutors who would act in his absence, and had authority over many other members of the household.[73] There was also accommodation for Cole and Watkyn Shipdam, both auditors; and William Lynde, whose role is unknown.[74] They were probably senior financial officials who worked on the accounts of the estate, managing financial records and providing advice to Fastolf.[75] There was another room for Geoffory, who was the chaplain and may have kept accounts, written letters when needed, and managed the religious activities of the manor. This gives a sense of the people in Fastolf's employ as being more than merely retained staff: they were people he worked with rather closely and probably regularly. He would have sought his retainers' council and company, creating something akin to partnership.[76] An awareness of this partnership, albeit unequal, is important in understanding the retainers' identity. The language of indentures defines a retainer's role as being to serve their lord 'in times of war and peace'; however, it is clear that they additionally kept their lord company, provided advice when required, played him at dice, and shared in the chase.[77] Retainers – at least those of appropriate rank – were named individuals to their lord, indicating a social relationship: they were not merely servitors or soldiers.

Occupants of lodging ranges appear to have had roles such as lawyer and auditor, or high-ranking service positions such as steward and cook. This supports the discussion in Chapter 1, where I argued that within the

---

71   Hughes, 'Scrope'; Woolgar, *Household*, p. 180.
72   Woolgar, *Household*, p. 137.
73   Woolgar, *Household*, p. 17; Wood, *House*, p. 177; Mertes, *Household*, p. 17.
74   Woolgar, *Household*, p. 67.
75   Woolgar, *Household*, p. 18; Davis, *Paston*.
76   Andrew Spencer, *Nobility and Kingship in Medieval England: The Earls and Edward I, 1272–1307* (Cambridge, 2014), p. 259.
77   Michael Hicks, *Bastard Feudalism* (London, 1995), p. 46.

lodging ranges' rooms there was space used for office work. Here, we see what sort of work may have been carried out. These roles required a place to work and meet other household members and guests. They were crucial to the running of the house and management of the estate, implying that the occupants were there on a fairly permanent basis. Those in the inner courtyard in particular would have lived in the house when Fastolf was in residence, which was probably for months at a time. Some, such as Rafman and the cook, may have continued to live there to support the household even when Fastolf himself was absent.

COLLECTIVE IDENTITIES

The identities of Caister's occupants were performed as they were at Gainsborough. The nature of each job allowed the individuals' identities as high-ranking, learned men to be performed. It was not the case, however, that repetitive and daily performance cemented one's identity; rather, it was the dynamic and relational nature that endured. Therefore, when one of Fastolf's retainers travelled from his room to the hall, the aspects of his identity related to ownership and independence gave way to servitude, control by his lord and membership of the retinue. Likewise this subservient identity was performed. For example, for John Bokking, the lawyer, his identity as a member of the household was displayed through his seating position in the hall and the food provided to him. It was further reinforced through intangible performances such as precedence: would he interact with those retainers who lived in the inner courtyard or was he restricted to mingling with relatively lower-ranking household members? His identity as an individual and as a member of the wider collective existed in unison, bobbing to the surface at different times.

This multi-compositional aspect of identities was also demonstrated in the architecture of Gainsborough's lodging range. While the rooms within the range appear to hint at an element of individualism, the range itself portrays a strong sense of collective identity. The architecture of the west elevation was extremely uniform (Figure 21). Each brick-built garderobe was paired with a brick-built chimney, with four sets of each equally spaced along the elevation. Between each pair were small windows, one per room. The repetitive architecture was a striking, impressive and captivating display of *sameness*. This uniform architecture served a function. It communicated this notion of sameness to the viewer, even that the sameness seeped inwards to the range's occupants. However, the internal layout shows that the regularity ended with the thickness of the wall. The architecture, therefore, was a concealment. There was a juxtaposition between external uniformity and internal variety, with each reflecting different identities: the collective and the individual.

When we compare this to other examples, we can suggest that displaying a collective identity was a function of lodging ranges. At Haddon Hall, the differences within the rooms were barely perceptible from outside the range. The garderobe tower appears at first glance to host a number of latrines; it only becomes clear through closer inspection within the range that the first-floor rooms were provided with garderobes while the ground floor of the tower was a cesspit (see Figure 3). Likewise, at Dartington Hall the west range presented one of the most strikingly uniform elevations, with repeated groups of doors and equally spaced windows. The north end of the range displayed a slight change in the pattern: one door per floor rather than two (see Figures 9 and 10). This subtle change does not distract from the overwhelming sameness detected throughout the courtyard, which was probably heightened further by the now much-altered east range. Despite being a persistent feature across lodging ranges, uniform architecture such as this was rare in the medieval period. There were some allusions to uniformity within medieval spaces, such as strict axial symmetry in the hall, frequently furthered by blind arcading behind the dais, which reflected the service doors at the opposing low end. The function of this architectural order was to replicate the desired social order and imply a socially proper household.[78] This extended from the hall over the following centuries; social order was realised architecturally in the double-courtyard 'perfect house' of the late medieval period.[79] Displays of uniformity on façades, however, were infrequent and as such they are much more associated with Elizabethan houses. From the mid-sixteenth century, great houses, or prodigy houses, displayed uniform façades that concealed the variety of rooms within. Kirby Hall, Northamptonshire, built c.1570, had chimney stacks ordered at regular intervals, which John Alfred Gotch described as giving 'dignity and rhythm' to the rear façade.[80] As at Gainsborough, they stretched beyond where the roof line would have been. Defiantly uniform elevations remained central to architectural design in Jacobean and Georgian buildings, but other than in lodging ranges (and collegiate and vicarial accommodation) they were exceptional in the medieval period. This suggests that the uniformity had a function specific to this building type, which, arguably, was to display a collective identity.

When discussing the representations of individual identity in architecture we see threads of status, authority and ownership. But what

---

78 Mark Gardiner, 'Conceptions of Domestic Space in the Long Term – the Example of the English Medieval Hall', in Mette Svart Kristiansen, Else Roesdahl, and James Graham-Campbell (eds), *Medieval Archaeology in Scandinavia and Beyond: History, Trends and Tomorrow* (Aarhus, 2015), pp. 313–33.
79 Woolgar, *Household*, p. 69.
80 John Alfred Gotch, *Early Renaissance Architecture in England* (London, 1901).

of the collective identity? The inventories from Caister show that lodging ranges were constructed to house retainers with various names, jobs, titles and backgrounds, from different places and families. Retainers were individuals, yet they were united as a retinue under their lord's banner. They were connected to one another legally through indentures, and symbolically through livery and retainer badges: this created a horizontal collective identity, unifying them as retainers.[81] This *collectivity* was performed through the acts of dressing in livery and sitting, eating and socialising with other retainers. The first-floor parlour-type room above the services at Gainsborough may have been the retainers' mess hall. If so, convening for meals and socialising separately from the remainder of the household, including the lord, was a performance of their unity as a group and demonstrated their shared distinction from all others. This was further performed when travelling with the lord as a retinue, or living in the same range, and was reinforced by the uniform architecture of their accommodation. Each retainer was, therefore, physically and visually bound to the others, in a horizontal collective identity.

This allows a consideration of the emergence of a wider horizontal identity, extending beyond the great house into medieval society. There were strong architectural similarities between lodging ranges and collegiate and vicarial ranges, hence the designation of these as collective-living buildings, and of particular note is their composition: of low-occupancy, high-status rooms within the courtyard of a wider institution. In this chapter the architecture of lodging ranges has been connected to the retainers' identities and this analysis can be extended to academic fellows and vicars choral. The sense of individual authority and privacy is most evident in the vicars choral accommodation, such as Vicars' Close, Wells, where it is epitomised by the individual door leading to each vicar's own two-floor house. The importance of the door to the vicars' identities was evident in its development from the earlier *cubiculi*, discussed earlier. The academic fellows lived in small groups of three or four, yet there were indications of social separation through the creation of study closets, probably individual, radiating from a shared central space. There were clear representations of individual identity in these comparable ranges, yet, as with the retainers, the fellows and vicars were under the presiding control of the senior canon or college master respectively. The dual, juxtaposed identities existed, akin to those described for lodging ranges, and were represented in architecture in similar ways as to the way they were shown in the great house. Therefore, in all three building types, despite their

---

81   Simon Walker, *The Lancastrian Affinity, 1361–99* (Oxford, 1990); Gordon McKelvie, *Bastard Feudalism, English Society and the Law: the Statutes of Livery 1390–1520* (Woodbridge, 2020).

uniqueness, the uniform architecture and comparable displays of both individual and collective identities were paralleled. None of these buildings existed or developed towards this plan in a vacuum: they responded to roughly contemporaneous social norms and individuals' decisions. So we can suggest a further thread to the collective identity, one that connected the occupants across the ranges: the emergence of the middling sort.[82]

The term 'middling sort' was adopted in the seventeenth century to describe people (rather than things, as it had been used from at least two centuries before).[83] It is an only slightly less contentious synonym for the middle class and is rarely applied to the medieval period. Part of this contention stems from a wariness of uncritical conflation with the anachronistic 'middle class', which is a nineteenth-century term, and of imposing our modern ideas of the middle class upon earlier societies. Historian Jack Hexter's 'myth of the middle class' argument stemmed from this and it was reasonable to argue for caution for the Tudor period he examined.[84] Hexter also argued, however, that those in the middle of the social hierarchy during the Tudor period were concerned primarily with emulating their social superiors and that there was no 'middling identity' distinct from that of the landed elite until the Industrial Revolution. There has been considerable rethinking of these ideas, with suggestions that by the seventeenth century those of the middle social ranks had similar values and mentality to the Victorian middle class and indeed were an antecedent to the middle class of today.[85]

Once again, I must define the parameters of a term before using it in this discussion. 'Middling sort' is used here to describe those in the middle ranks of late medieval society, with no suggestion that the people to which it refers were identical to today's middle class. The middling sort were those who were neither comfortably within the social elites, such as the lords of the great houses discussed here, nor were they lower-status servants, peasants or slaves. They were within the many middle ranks. Research on the middling sort has been primarily undertaken by historians – in other words, from the presence of the term in known written sources; as such, there is little discussion on the medieval period.[86] Arguing that the

---

82 For a detailed discussion see: Jonathon Barry and Christopher Brooks (eds), *The Middling Sort of People* (Basingstoke, 1994).
83 Keith Wrightson, '"Sorts of People" in Tudor and Stuart England', in Jonathon Barry and Christopher Brooks (eds), *The Middling Sort of People* (Basingstoke, 1994), pp. 28–51, at p. 43; Sarah Kerr, 'Collective Living and Individual Identities in Late Medieval England,' *Archaeological Journal*, 177 (2020), 83–98.
84 Jack H. Hexter, *Reappraisals in History* (London, 1961).
85 Peter Earle, 'The Middling Sort in London', in Jonathon Barry and Christopher Brooks (eds), *The Middling Sort of People* (Basingstoke, 1994), pp. 141–58, at p. 158.
86 Barry and Brooks, *Middling*; Earle, 'Middling'; H. R French, *The Middle Sort of*

middling sort emerged at the same time as the appearance of the term has obvious limitations, and I suggest it is a useful term for the earlier period. Middling sort is relevant for the discussion on lodging ranges, because the buildings were definitely not low-status spaces yet, equally, were not quite the most grand. Similarly, retainers were not menial servants, but neither were they at the level of society's uppermost. This middle-social placement is true, too, for the occupants in other types of ranges: the vicars choral in the vicarial ranges were neither junior clergy nor were they canons; and fellows in collegiate ranges were of a higher status than the undergraduates but not as high-status as the prebendary or college master. Just as with lodging ranges, this middle rank was reflected in the architecture.

Although *middling* is an adjective, we could also consider it a verb to suggest that these sorts of people were performing their identity and place within the middle social ranks. This is reasonable when we consider this chapter's focus: that identities were performed, in fact they required *doing* to exist. The middling sort, therefore, is impressionistic and relational, as it only makes sense in the context of those in the upper and lower social ranks. Middling, I suggest, is a useful term as a reminder that stringent and dichotomous categories of people are deceptive and do little to assist our understanding of society.

The development from communal to collective-living buildings, particularly from dormitories to low-occupancy rooms with individual doors, indicates that the occupants were no longer considered low-status servants. Their identity was no longer appropriately reflected in lower-status spaces. Essentially, the development of the architecture paralleled the development of a new social group. This indicates that their identity was recognised by those who built their accommodation: those of society's uppermost ranks. This recognition, even agreement, demonstrated through the undertaking of the ranges' construction, allows the supposition that the occupants too saw themselves in this way. We can trace lines of likeness between the retainers, vicars choral, and fellows due to the identities and lived experience embedded in the architecture of their accommodation. This contradicts Hexter's earlier notion that there was not a distinct identity within society's middle ranks; in fact, this was clearly emerging before the Tudor period. Indeed, there is now greater awareness that non-elites, including peasants,[87] created horizontal identities among those socially similar to distinguish themselves, and even

---

People in Provincial England, 1600-1750 (Oxford, 2007); H. R. French, 'The Search for the "Middle Sort of People" in England, 1600–1800', *The Historical Journal*, 43:1 (2000), 277–93.

87 Sally Smith, 'Materializing Resistant Identities among the Medieval Peasantry', *Journal of Material Culture*, 14:3 (2009), 309–32, p. 326.

to resist the imposition of other identities. This implies a contentment within the middle ranks rather than a constant desire for social ascension through emulation. The medieval middling sort set their own standards for their middling identity, within what was socially acceptable, and this included low-occupancy, high-status accommodation.[88]

The previous scholarship defines the seventeenth-century middling sort as those who worked for their income, so were not landed elite, but their jobs were not those held by the poor, servants or slaves. Jonathon Barry presents their roles in society as divided into two general types: those who traded in the products of their hands, such as yeomen or artisans, and those providing business or professional expertise, such as merchants and lawyers. He suggests that, in the seventeenth century at least, a central part of the display of their identity was their place of work. Their trading spaces, such as an office or shop, allowed economic and social independence and a place through which to define themselves.[89] Collective-living ranges were similarly cornerstones of the occupants' identities, including their professional identity. Lodging ranges were part of the retainers' payment for their service; likewise, the vicars choral were granted accommodation for their role in the cathedral, and fellows' accommodation was provided for the duration of their academic development. Collective-living ranges were clearly intertwined with professional, economic and social identities within the middle part of the social hierarchy.

A balance between vertical and horizontal associations should be emphasised. The clear horizontal association between the occupants of collective-living ranges demonstrates that they had a distinct identity separate from the other rungs of the social hierarchy, including the head of the institution, and from lower-status servants. While this indicates again that social emulation was not at the forefront of shaping their identities, it demonstrates that the vertical associations were ever-present. In addition to representing society-wide identity, the emergence of collective-living buildings indicates architectural fashion, and social trends, such as early signs of the development towards privacy, compartmentalisation of the house, and specialisation of space.

Returning to the great house, the collective identity perceived is one of kinship and sameness. This may have produced a sense of group loyalty, unity, and even camaraderie, and may even have extended to a degree of herd mentality, not necessarily viewed favourably by contemporaries, nor by Charles Plummer or other proponents of bastard feudalism. Plummer

---

88 David A. Hinton, '"Closing" and the Later Middle Ages', *Medieval Archaeology*, 43:1 (1999), 172–82.
89 Jonathon Barry, 'Introduction', in Jonathon Barry and Christopher Brooks (eds), *The Middling Sort of People* (Basingstoke, 1994), pp. 1–27.

argued that, as well as full-scale war, including the Wars of the Roses, retainers were to blame for many minor skirmishes between rivalling retinues. He suggested that retinue-led violence and other turbulent activities such as forcible entry were 'everyday occurrences'.[90] While it is tempting to consider this the reason for individual doors, since, after all, if one door were breached the other rooms remained secure, it is unlikely, as great houses featured few defensive features. While defence was thus not a priority, Gainsborough was in fact attacked by a rival retinue in 1470. The Warkworth chronicles described how Lancastrian enemies of Thomas Burgh travelled to Gainsborough and then 'pullede down his place and toke alle his goodes and cataylle that their myghte fynde'.[91] The later construction date of the lodging range, as indicated through tree-felling dates, could support this narrative. It may be that the Lancastrians focused their attack on the retinue's accommodation, causing its destruction and the need for it to be rebuilt. This hints at rival groups, each acting as a unit, protected by a group identity, and bolstered by the bravado of a collective.

As discussed in the introductory chapter, Plummer and Stubbs's interpretation of bastard feudalism as unruly and overly violent was misjudged.[92] The system in reality was not vastly more corrupt and immoral than that which preceded it.[93] Rather, disorder often attributed to bastard feudalism was probably the product of pressure for land and the opportunities created through political instability.[94] Gordon McKelvie argues that a more precise interpretation of bastard feudalism includes its use to create cohesion.[95] Whether this cohesion was desired as a means of protecting against, as Chief Justice Fortescue described, 'ovur mighti subgiettes' or more simply to administer control and order, we cannot know for certain, although a combination is likely.[96] Indeed, there is evidence of retainers who were not violent but simply a poorly behaved group whose manners fell short of what was expected. When Margery Kempe and her

---

90 Charles Plummer (ed.), *The Governance of England* (Oxford, 1885), p. 21.
91 J. O. Halliwell (ed.), *A Chronicle of the First Thirteen Years of the Reign of King Edward the Fourth by John Warkworth*, The Camden Series, 10:1 (London, 1839) ; Emery, *Greater Medieval Houses*, Vol. 2, p. 244.
92 William Stubbs, *The Constitutional History of England in Its Origin and Development*, Vol. 1, (Oxford, 1903).
93 Hicks, *Bastard*; McKelvie, *Bastard*.
94 Simon Walker, *Political Culture in Later Medieval England: Essays*, edited by. Michael Braddick, (Manchester, 2006).
95 McKelvie, *Bastard*, p. 162.
96 Quoted in: Plummer, *Governance*; Michael Hicks, 'Bastard Feudalism, Overmighty Subjects and Idols of the Multitude during the Wars of the Roses', *The Journal of the Historical Association*, 85:279 (2000), 386–403.

husband arrived at the hall of Archbishop Arundel at Lambeth in 1413, she described 'rekles [reckless] men bothe swyers [esquires] & yemen which sworyn many gret othis & spokyn many reckless wordys'.[97] Regardless of the motive for cohesion, a collective identity was imposed upon the group through architecture, livery and retainer badges and performative acts. This indicates that the lord was trying to enforce the group's identities. The construction of a lodging range with such overwhelming sameness, such as Gainsborough's, implies a desire to set their retainers' identity, literally, in stone.

CONCLUSION

The architecture of lodging ranges indicates that the rooms within were of high status and, in this chapter, this has been extended to those who occupied them. I have attempted to present this status not in a transactional way but to explore the lived experience of those whom Mertes described as 'troublesome to define'.[98] This allows an understanding of one central facet of retainers' identity – status – alongside a variety of other threads. Through features preserved at Gainsborough Hall we can surmise the independence and authority over space permitted to the retainers. Coupled with the Caister inventories, we get a sense from these that the occupants were learned men with responsibilities within the household. The agency involved in performing these identities suggests a degree of individualism: a perceptible difference from a homogeneous retinue. This identity is not to be considered in isolation from the collective identity also perceived; rather, the culmination of physical, symbolic, and visual representations of the collective identities appears almost robust, hinting at a permanence to the horizontal collectivity. The indentured relationship was intended to be service to the lord for life, and while in reality the retainer could leave a lord's service, this adds an important dimension to the horizonal collectivity; it was crafted entirely through vertical association. Livery denoted the lord's name and status, the retainer badges were the family emblem, and the ranges were within the lord's house. Rather than an accurate demonstration of a uniform identity, these things represented a uniform identity being *imposed* on a group of individuals. It appears that the individuals in the retinue were branded as the lord's follower, each aspect of their lived experience was shaped by their vertical association. As such, it appears that the lord may have wanted, perhaps, to generate a collective identity to administer control and order by overriding the individual identities. However, the architecture of Gainsborough's lodging

97   S. B. Meech and H. E. Allen (eds), *The Book of Margery Kempe* (London, 1940).
98   Mertes, *Household*, p. 55.

range demonstrates a desire to construct a collective identity while allowing some sense of individualism. Therefore there was something of a coexistence between the lord's control and the independence of the retainer. By placing emphasis on meaning, and function over use, we gain a better understanding of the lived experience and the multitude of identities on display.

3

THE THEATRE OF DISPLAY

THE POWER PLAY

The focus of Chapter 2 stresses the ways in which medieval buildings reflected and were part of the construction and performance of identities. By looking closely at the architecture of lodging ranges we were able to consider their role in constructing and maintaining the identity of retainers, as individuals and as a collective, through features such as individual doors. This chapter now turns to the lord and scrutinises how his or her identity was displayed and received through lodging ranges in the great house. It will once again touch on the construction of identity; however, this time the identity is one actually created by the individual, rather than imposed upon them by someone else, as with the retainers. Constructing one's own identity does not mean it is any less contested, inaccurate, or even propagandistic.

This chapter retains the focus on the *function* of the building rather than the *use*; that is, the reason beyond the utilitarian for which it was created. As before, the function is considered to have been to communicate meaning to the medieval audience. Therefore it adds another layer of meaning to what we know about lodging ranges. With each chapter we understand further why they were built in such a way.

Here it will be argued that the meaning communicated to the medieval audience, in this case, was the lord's idea of their own identity. This might seem an incredibly obvious thing to point out; after all, the entirety of the great house represented the identity of the lord, from the size and style to the decoration and heraldry. There is a considerable amount of literature on how lords displayed their identity through their buildings;[1] however, there is an overwhelming focus on status, rather than the more complex, more messy identity. This focus has helped to determine that status was a crucial consideration in the medieval and late medieval houses, with all elements therein constructed deliberately to portray the correct type of status. Norman Pounds argues that a lord's house was, in essence, 'a status symbol. It suggested power and rank and it implied that its owner was well able to look after himself. It suggested, further, that its contents were worth protecting.'[2]

While this is an accurate summation, the focus on status in the previous scholarship has led to a consideration that the identity of a lord is synonymous with status only. We have the tools to see beyond such a one-dimensional analysis. Through looking closely at the great house we are able to deconstruct an all-encompassing 'status symbol' into something with more depth. We can consider, then, the size and grandeur of the house as an impression of the lord's wealth; the use of space as a representation of gender ideologies; heraldry as a reflection of political and familial rise; and architectural styles as a portrayal of permanence and ambition. While these overlap with status, it is important to add this nuance, even humanisation, to our understanding of a lord's identity. The retainers' identity included, among other aspects, individualism, collectivity, authority and ownership; the lord's identity was equally as complex.

Focusing on lodging ranges reveals this complexification of the lord's identity. The lord's social rank, status, wealth, and so on, are visible as explicit displays. However, more interestingly, there are also abstruse displays in the form of illusory architecture and of manipulation of the senses. Translating these from the ruins hints at an identity with threads of instilling fear, intimidation and imposing control. It is these indistinct identities and their representation in the architecture on which this chapter will focus. These may be harder to detect, but when we consider the medieval lived experience, particularly that of a visitor, it appears that these displays were extremely impactful. It may seem contradictory to describe displays as explicit or implicit and then suggest they were as impactful as each other, but we must remember how meaning is understood, through both context and stored information. Think, for example, of viewing a glass skyscraper in central London and how we would

1   Anthony Emery, 'Late-medieval Houses as an Expression of Social Status', *Historical Research*, 78 (2005), 140–61; Philip Dixon and Beryl Lott, 'The Courtyard and the Tower', *Journal of the British Archaeological Association*, 146 (1993), 93–101; M. D. Nevell, R. Nevell, and B. H. Grimsditch, 'Power, Status and War', in B. H. Grimsditch, M. D. Nevell and R. Nevell, *Buckton Castle and the Castles of North West England* (Salford, 2012), pp. 1–35.
2   Norman Pounds, *The Medieval Castle in England and Wales: A Social and Political History* (Cambridge, 1990), p. 276.

understand its meaning. We may assume its function as the headquarters of a finance or technology company. The meaning we perceive may be a mixture of wealth, capitalism, globalisation, even architectural monotony. *Habitus*, Pierre Bourdieu's term for our taken-for-granted understanding of our surroundings,[3] suggests that an implicit understanding of the built environment allows us to perceive these meanings through the implicit display; that is, we understand the building's meaning without reading an explicit sign above a door.

Visitors and Visuality

In the same way, the medieval audience viewed buildings and understood meaning from implicit and explicit displays with ease. The approach to Wingfield Manor utilised both methods to represent Lord Cromwell's identity. It comes into view from almost 2 kilometres away, due to its placement on top of a knoll, and almost appears to erupt from the surrounding landscape (Figure 26). During the approach, the chimney stacks of the house became visible. They once reached far above the roof-line and, along with the garderobe towers, created a chaos of display, jabbing at the sky. Even at a distance, physically from the house and temporally from its construction, Cromwell's identity is latently communicated. For the medieval visitor, the approach would have been slower, allowing more time to view the entire presentation. Once within the house, heraldic panels displayed both the crossed purses of the Lord Treasurer's office, and Cromwell's family arms. It was long before seeing these crests, however, that Cromwell's identity was communicated, and the display did not end at chimneys and heraldic panels. Exploring the full architectural demonstration allows consideration of the visual relationship between medieval viewers and the buildings. This is not without its limitations; as Kate Giles argues, we must be careful to not impose normative and modern ways of thinking onto past visual relationships. In 'Seeing and Believing',[4] she builds on discourse from art and architectural history to demonstrate that medieval seeing was much closer to a tangible form of feeling than we consider it today: that it was affective.[5] Therefore, in her exploration of seeing and experiencing medieval space, which focuses on medieval wall paintings, she argues that

3   Pierre Bourdieu, *Outline of a Theory of Practice* (Cambridge, 1977).
4   Kate Giles, 'Seeing and Believing: Visuality and Space in Pre-modern England', *World Archaeology*, 39 (2007), 105–21.
5   Including: Hal Foster, *Vision and Visuality* (Seattle, 1988); Suzannah Biernoff, *Sight and Embodiment in the Middle Ages* (Basingstoke, 2002); Robert Nelson, *Visuality Before and Beyond the Renaissance* (Cambridge, 2000); Tim Ingold, *The Perception of the Environment* (London, 2000).

FIG. 26 PHOTOGRAPH LOOKING SOUTH-EAST TOWARDS WINGFIELD MANOR. ITS POSITION ATOP A KNOLL, PLUS THE HEIGHT OF THE CHIMNEY STACKS, MEANS IT CAN BE VIEWED FROM ALMOST TWO KILOMETRES AWAY. AS SUCH, THE DISPLAY OF CROMWELL'S IDENTITY COMMENCES FROM THIS POINT.

we follow Hal Foster's distinction between vision and visuality.[6] Vision should be considered the physical operation of sight, and visuality as the social and cultural constructedness of vision. They are not opposites, but neither are they the same; rather, both were parts of a culturally constituted visual experience.[7] Therefore we should look differently at familiar and tangible things and explore buildings through the lens of visuality. We will look contextually at the architecture and space and the interrelationships between these and the viewer, by considering the view and movement of a male visitor to the house.

A visitor's visuality experience has been considered for houses throughout the medieval period and it is clear that access and doors were important components of this experience. In the last chapter we discussed the lodging ranges' individual doors – their meaning as a representation of separation and use as an entrance – and it appears access to the great house was even more multifarious. Matthew Johnson argues that access was graded and manipulated: how someone entered depended on their identity, particularly their political affiliation and social status, as well as the

6   Foster, *Vision*.
7   Alexa Sand, 'Visuality', *Studies in Iconography*, 33 (2012), 89–95.

occasion.[8] Furthermore, a late medieval house had a number of entrances. The gateway's great door may have been opened for some visitors, but others may have entered through the wicket gate – the smaller door within the main door. Otherwise they may have used a postern gate, such as that at Caister Castle which was replaced by a secondary gateway when the house changed hands in the late fifteenth century. Postern gates were intended for the servants, and Caister's was possibly beyond the low end of a hall in the inner courtyard. The way in which one entered the great house, therefore, created different visuality experiences, which imposed an identity onto the guest. Identities are relational and performative: it will be seen that the lord's identity was constructed in relation to the guests' and, to a degree, was even performed through the movement of the visitors.

The experience of a guest entering the great house has been explored by Johnson. He describes how passing through a gatehouse meant being embedded in the dark tunnel between the doorways. He proposes that either one or both doors could be closed and the visitor would be 'trapped like a rat'.[9] Often gateways were tall and decorated, sometimes with heraldic panels as at Wingfield Manor. This was a display of the lord's familial identity implying legacy and permanence. However, a tall gateway also allowed an intimidating identity to be displayed; it drew the visitor's eye upwards, imparting a sense of minusculariy. The desire to make visitors look up is clear in a number of areas within the great house. Thornbury Castle, Gainsborough Hall and Wingfield all contained towering, elaborately decorated chimneys. The adornment of Thornbury's decorated chimneys requires a pause to really see the level of detail: doing so gives a sense of the lord's upward aspirations.

The study of what the medieval audience could see and when, and how it was manipulated and controlled, has been explored in archaeological discourse. One approach is viewshed analysis, which is an exploration of visual relationships between people and things. It has predominately been used in the context of prehistoric landscapes,[10] although Thomas Markus applies Hillier and Hanson's concepts of access analysis to line-of-sight within modern buildings.[11] For medieval buildings, C. Pamela

---

8   Matthew Johnson, *Behind the Castle Gate: From Medieval to Renaissance* (London, 2002).
9   Johnson, *Castle*, p. 72.
10 Peter Fisher, Chris Farrelly, Adrian Maddocks and Clive Ruggles, 'Spatial Analysis of Visible Areas from the Bronze Age Cairns of Mull', *Journal of Archaeological Science*, 24 (1997), 581–92; M. W. Lake, P. E. Woodman and S. J. Mithen, 'Tailoring GIS software for archaeological applications', *Journal of Archaeological Science*, 25 (1998), 27–38; J. Pollard and A. Reynolds, *Avebury: The Biography of a Landscape* (Cheltenham, 2002).
11 Thomas Markus, *Buildings and Power: Freedom and Control in the Origin of*

Graves explores the architectural fabric of late medieval churches, and the fixtures such as statues and altars, to determine the scope of visual relationships and their impact on the laity's experience of Christianity.[12] She also argues that distinct social identities were constructed through the spatial arrangement of the late medieval parish. Similarly, Simon Roffey examines how space, light and, particularly, vision can be used to illustrate a wider social dimension of chantry chapels.[13] He argues that vision was integral to religious experience and practice, with squints (hagioscopes or 'leper windows') being added to create clear lines of sight between specific areas within the church.

In the secular space, Katherine Weikert argues that viewability was important in the high medieval house. She demonstrates this through the permeability of the hall and chamber in early manorial houses. In some of her case studies, in contrast to what we find in the late medieval period, the hall and chamber were at equal depths in access analysis plans: that is, they were equally accessible.[14] This suggests that lords wanted to be viewed in these spaces and that viewability was a representation of their social status and authority over that space. She draws the discussion down to the viewability of smaller, movable objects of the great house. These, like the immovable gateway, also represented the identity of the lord. She describes how lords may have performed their identity with objects in front of guests, such as the act of locking a casket or withdrawing precious objects from view. Therefore what could not be seen, as well as what could, contributed to the display. In relation to screens and wall hangings, she notes that 'particular impressions had to be made at particular times for particular audiences'.[15] Returning to lodging ranges, as built elements of the great house they were a constant part of the display. We can therefore consider the buildings and their spaces as the stage upon which other displays of identity took place.

It appears that each and every element of the great house contributed to displaying the lord's identity. From the immovable buildings to the movable items, everything was staged deliberately, with identity then performed

---

Modern Building Types (Abingdon, 1993); Bill Hillier and Julienne Hanson, *The Social Logic of Space* (Cambridge, 1984).

12   C. Pamela Graves, *The Form and Fabric of Belief* (York, 2000); C. Pamela Graves, 'Social Space in the English Medieval Parish Church', *Economy and Society*, 18 (1989), 297–322.

13   Simon Roffey, 'Constructing a Vision of Salvation', *Archaeological Journal*, 163 (2006), 122–46.

14   Kate Weikert, *Authority, Gender and Space in the Anglo-Norman World, 900–1200* (Woodbridge, 2020), pp. 90–1.

15   Weikert, *Authority*, p. 90.

in and around them. Indeed, Weikert describes the elite 'setting a scene, curating a space for a particular meaning'.[16] Similarly, Charles Coulson describes Edward I's Caernarfon Castle as 'theatre', while Dover's austere elegance was 'classical drama'.[17] The allegory percolates from the house as the theatre to each element therein as a key prop; indeed, Johnson refers to the gatehouse as part of this 'stage-setting'.[18] Philip Dixon focuses on the royal castle of Knaresborough to demonstrate how this stage was set for a medieval visitor. He describes how, within Knaresborough's donjon (central tower), the approach to first-floor rooms involved 'theatrical propaganda' to enhance the visitor's impression.[19] What Dixon describes was a quite different visitors' experience than that described by Johnson. Dixon provides a description of entering a gracefully vaulted passageway, ascending gentle steps into a waiting room which was warm and well-lit.[20] The visitor was afforded time to admire the vaulting, the tracery and the twin doors ahead. Providing a comfortable experience such as this for a guest was paramount to good hospitality, which was central to the lord's identity and the running of the great house. The food and accommodation offered to guests was an opportunity for lords to display their identity, and hospitality included the ease and comfort of moving through the house. This was described by Henry Wotton, in *Elements of Architecture*, an adaptation of *De Architectura* by Marcus Vitruvius Pollio.[21] Wotton described how a house was the lord's 'theatre of hospitality', implying that each person, space and thing had its role in ensuring the correct performance of hospitality. However, providing comfort to visitors was not in opposition to the intimidating experience described by Johnson, and indeed Knaresborough displayed spurious defensive features alongside its comforts. To stretch the metaphor, comfort and intimidation could be thought of as plots within the great house's play.

We can extend Wotton's words to consider the house in its entirety as a theatre of display for a lord and suggest that each and every element was created deliberately to display a certain facet of identity, and even that it was a physical manifestation of how they saw themselves. Coulson implies that the castle was imbued with the personality of the lord who

---

16   Weikert, *Authority*, p. 90.
17   Charles Coulson, 'Fourteenth-century Castles in Context: Apotheosis or Decline?', in Robert Liddiard (ed.), *Late Medieval Castles* (Woodbridge, 2016), pp. 19–40, at p. 23.
18   Johnson, *Castle*, p. 71.
19   Philip Dixon, 'The Donjon of Knaresborough: The Castle as Theatre', in Robert Liddiard (ed.), *Late Medieval Castles* (Woodbridge, 2016), pp. 333–48, at p. 333.
20   Dixon, 'Knaresborough', p. 346.
21   Henry Wotton, *The Elements of Architecture* (London, 1624).

built it, with architectural elements as 'pure propaganda'.[22] He continues that the 'ego-trip was so widespread' that what we see at Dover was 'self-indulgence'.[23] He may have been building on Wotton's ideas of the house and home as 'the seat of self-fruition'.[24] We can take this further and include ideas of visuality to consider the view of the house as an embodiment of the lord, and that, through the construction of a house, the owner constructed an impression of themselves. Weikert contemplates 'how to construct yourself as a social elite' and, by focusing on performative acts, she implies that this impression was not only constructed from the tangible architecture but curated through movement in and around it.[25] Coulson may have been hinting at this when he said that 'showmanship was an original as well as a later feature' of the castles in his studies.[26] Therefore, by combining visuality and the theatre of display, we can consider how the medieval audience experienced the lord's identities. When we look more closely at Thornbury and Wingfield it becomes clear that guests' movement through the house was part of the theatrics and that lodging ranges were a supporting character. What is evident from both examples is that it was not only the physical lodging ranges themselves, but also their role in movement and visuality, which displayed the identity of the lord.

WINGFIELD MANOR, DERBYSHIRE

Ralph, Lord Cromwell, treasurer of England between 1433 and 1443, acquired Wingfield not without difficulty. The manor of Wingfield was held by the Heriz family between the early twelfth and mid-fourteenth centuries, then passed to the families of Belers and Swyllington.[27] When John Swyllington died in 1418 his estate passed to his sister, who subsequently died without a direct heir, and Cromwell was deemed her nearest heir. He acquired the estate in 1428, leading to a ten-year dispute with other claimants which was only resolved by a compromise which allowed the Heriz family to keep the majority of the estate, with Cromwell keeping the manor. Almost immediately, in the autumn of 1439 or more probably the spring of 1440, Cromwell cleared the site of the twelfth century house and began building his great house. At the time of writing,

22 Coulson, 'Apotheosis', p. 22.
23 Coulson, 'Apotheosis', pp. 22–3.
24 Wotton, *Elements*, p. 82.
25 Weikert, *Authority*, p. 90.
26 Coulson, 'Apotheosis', p. 39.
27 Anthony Emery, *Greater Medieval Houses of England and Wales 1300–1500* (3 vols, Cambridge, 2000; 2000; 2006), Vol. 2, p. 450.

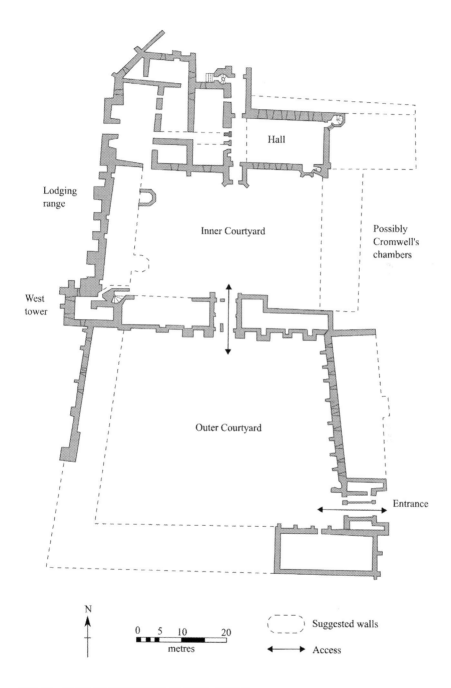

FIG. 27   PLAN OF WINGFIELD MANOR, SHOWING THE INNER AND OUTER COURTYARDS, THE POSITION OF THE HALL AND THE PROBABLE POSITION OF CROMWELL'S ROOMS.

the house was owned by English Heritage, except the eighteenth-century farmhouse built within the ruins, which was occupied.

Cromwell's multi-courtyard house was constructed in approximately sixteen years with no discernible phases. The current entrance is via a ruinous section of the outer courtyard's west range, while the medieval entrance provided both vehicular and pedestrian access through the south-east corner (Figure 27). The gateway into the outer courtyard was flanked by a lodging on each side, whose protruding walls almost enclose the gateway, commencing an intimidating impression which is carried throughout the great house. Although partly ruinous and partly occupied, the outer courtyard appears to comprise a possible lodging range or lower-status accommodation in its eastern range, with the remaining ranges probably administrative, storage and household accommodation.

The east range of the outer courtyard had an exterior, buttressed wall. In between the evenly-spaced buttresses were small, one-light windows on the ground floor creating a façade with alternating features. On the first floor, fragments of stone tracery indicate there were windows of two lights, each with cinquefoil-cusp and open spandrels. It appears that the first-floor rooms benefited from larger windows, a standard feature in medieval accommodation. Previous surveys suggested that the ground floor of the range comprised two rooms, each approximately 15 metres in length, with a garderobe tower on the east wall.[28] No evidence of a garderobe remains, but this suggests accommodation. Anthony Emery stated that there were narrow rebates around 1.2m above ground level for beds, which suggests a plan similar to a monastic dormitory.[29] The first floor was accessible via a stone newel at one end of the range and a timber version at the opposing end, neither of which remain.

Opposite the east range lie fragments of the west range's exterior wall; the inner wall is lost. Variably-spaced windows and buttresses can be seen on the surviving façade; this irregularity suggests an assortment of functions within the range. Some accommodation was probably provided here, as there is evidence of a solitary garderobe. The south range of the outer courtyard contained a five-bay, stone-built building with a timber roof. Directly opposite was the cross-range and access to the inner courtyard. As with the outer gateway, the cross-range provided both vehicular and pedestrian passageways. This was elaborately decorated with a heraldic panel displaying the crossed purses of the Lord Treasurer's office and Cromwell's family arms, dominated by flanking turrets and substantial chimney stacks. These were in view from the main entrance to the outer courtyard; that is, once through the gateway in the south-east corner, one

---

28 Emery, *Greater Medieval Houses*, Vol. 2, p. 451.
29 Emery, *Greater Medieval Houses*, Vol. 2, p. 450.

THE THEATRE OF DISPLAY

FIG. 28   PHOTOGRAPH OF THE REMAINS OF THE LODGING RANGE AT WINGFIELD MANOR. THE BOTTOM LEFT OF THE IMAGE SHOWS THE ENTRANCE TO THE SEMI-OCTAGONAL TURRET. THIS LED TO STAIRS, ASCENDING AND DESCENDING, TO EACH FLOOR WITHIN.

turned to the right to face the cross-range separating the inner and outer courtyards (Figure 27).

The inner courtyard occupied the northern extent of the great house with the hall range opposite the cross-range. The hall range followed the standard medieval plan with the services to the west of the cross-passage and the hall to the east. A substantial two-storey porch with buttresses at the angles gave access to the cross-passage and contributed to an imposing south-facing façade. The eastern dais end of the hall was illuminated by a traceried bay window with side splays and an upwards slant, allowing in further light from the inner courtyard. There was a narrow newel beneath the bay window at the south-eastern corner of the hall, giving access to a rib-vaulted undercroft, which occupied the space created by the slope of the hill. The undercroft had just three windows on the north wall, but an entrance at every corner. There were highly decorative bosses, and its use is unknown; undercrofts were often storage places in the great house, and the multiple entrances may support this, but the access from the dais suggests a higher-status use. The dais end would also have connected to Cromwell's apartments; however, the exact position of these is unknown. Nothing remains of the east range of the inner courtyard, perpendicular

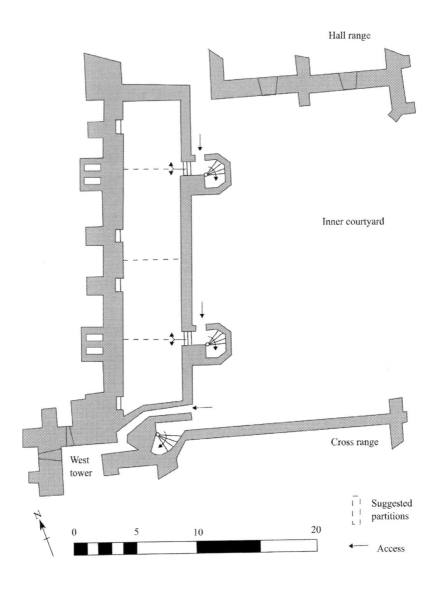

FIG. 29 GROUND-FLOOR PLAN OF THE LODGING RANGE AT WINGFIELD MANOR, SHOWING ACCESS THROUGH THE STAIR TURRET. THE LACK OF PROVISIONS IS EVIDENT WHEN COMPARING THIS WITH THE FIRST-FLOOR PLAN (FIGURE 31).

FIG. 30   PHOTO OF THE INNER FACE OF THE LODGING RANGE'S EXTERIOR WALL AT WINGFIELD MANOR. AT THE SOUTH END, ABUTTING THE WEST TOWER, FIREPLACES, WINDOWS, AND PAIRED GARDEROBE DOORS CAN BE SEEN ON THE FIRST AND SECOND FLOORS (FROM LEFT TO RIGHT). ONLY A FIREPLACE WAS INCLUDED ON THE GROUND FLOOR.

to the hall, but this seems a likely position for the lord's apartments. Otherwise they may have extended east from the hall, or occupied both of these spaces (Figure 27). Wingfield was a richly decorated and spacious house; therefore we can assume Cromwell's apartments were considerable in size and had many high-status features.

The natural slope of the outcrop allowed a basement level at the low end of the hall too, west of the vaulted undercroft. At basement-level there was a small service courtyard comprising storage rooms. A bridge spanned from the cross-passage over the basement-level services, connecting the hall to the kitchen and a number of chambers for staff. North of the small service courtyard was a chamber tower, rectangular in plan. The rooms appear to have increased in status with height: the basement-level room, which was accessible from the service courtyard, contained a fireplace noticeably less decorated than its equivalent at ground level. The two uppermost floors, the first and second floors, were of a higher status again. The second floor could only be reached from the first; this lack of access suggests a more restricted space or possibly an inner chamber to an outer chamber below. Each floor in the chamber tower had a corresponding smaller, triangular-shaped room to the west. The smaller room may have provided accommodation for staff serving those in the larger rooms. The wall separating the chamber tower from the triangular-shaped rooms supported a belvedere, suggesting a high-status resident within the chamber block. The tower's position beyond the low end of the hall draws comparison with Dartington Hall, Devon, where high-status rooms on the floors above the services may have been provided for staff or guests. The latter may have been the case at Wingfield (it is worth noting that Mary Queen of Scots was a resident there in the sixteenth century).

The lodging range was located in the west range of the inner courtyard, opposite what was probably Cromwell's accommodation in the east range. The western, exterior façade indicates the lodging range's plan while the eastern, courtyard-facing elevation remains as intermittent footings beneath an enormous, mature apple tree. There were three floors, with the ground floor at half-basement level, in a similar plan to Thornbury. The spacing of the provisions indicates that each floor was divided into four rooms although no timber partitions remain. Access to all of the floors appears to have been via two semi-octagonal stair turrets on the eastern elevation, the low footings of which remain *in situ*. The stone courses show that one entered the turret via a door on the north side, that is, the side facing the hall range (Figure 28). This led to three steps down to the half-basement rooms. Each room at this level had a fireplace but no garderobe, suggesting lower-status occupants; furthermore, there is no evidence for windows (Figure 29), though there may have been downward-pointing

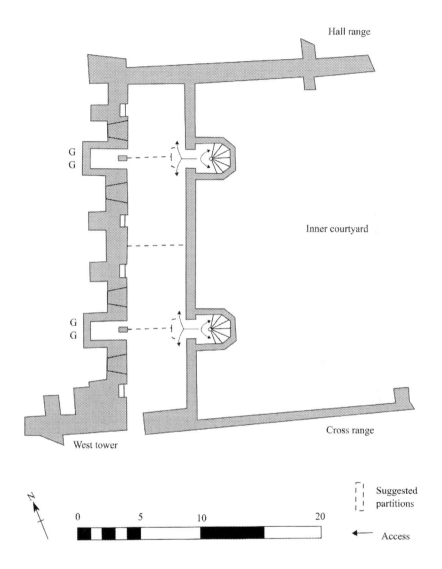

FIG. 31 FIRST-FLOOR PLAN OF THE LODGING RANGE AT WINGFIELD MANOR. ALL FOUR ROOMS ON THIS FLOOR CONTAINED A WINDOW, FIREPLACE, AND GARDEROBE (G), A PLAN THAT WAS REPEATED ON THE SECOND FLOOR. THIS CREATED A DISTINCTLY UNIFORM EXTERNAL ELEVATION.

splayed windows on the inner wall, as at the comparable lodging range at Thornbury.

The first and second floors of the lodging range were probably accessed by the stair turret; however, nothing remains of the ascending stairs. Both floors followed the same plan, with the provisions repeated along the west elevation (Figures 28 and 30). It appears that each floor was divided into four rooms, so each turret led into two rooms per floor. However, the size of the turret suggests it connected to the range via one door rather than two; therefore there may have been a lobby between the rooms, with the doors to each room leading from this, as with the first floor of Haddon Hall, Derbyshire. Each of the eight rooms contained a fireplace, window and door to a shared garderobe tower (Figure 31). There is no discernible difference in provisions or status between the first and second floors; all the fireplaces have flat arches and the garderobe entrances are lightly decorated with a chamfered edge along the quoins and lintel. All windows comprised two trefoil-cusped lights with closed spandrels.

The first- and second-floor rooms at the southernmost end of the lodging range were connected to the substantial tower at the western extent of the cross-range. A further door on the north face of the west tower indicates the presence of a wall walk on top of the lodging range. There is no evidence to suggest the west tower connected to the west range of the outer courtyard, which lay to the south, as it did the west range of the inner courtyard (that is, the lodging range).[30] There was a door from the lodging range to the west tower at half-basement level, but this appears to have connected the west tower to the courtyard, utilising a narrow, curvilinear corridor (Figure 29). The ground floor of the west tower contained a battery of garderobes, with the access corridor from the courtyard imparting a sense of public use – at least for those people whose relative status permitted them access to the inner courtyard. The upper rooms of the west tower may have contained rooms and offices; there appears to be some gradation of status with evidence of a number of garderobes and fireplaces. The remains of a two-light, cinquefoil-cusped, open spandrel window can be seen on the east façade along with two-light, trefoil-cusped windows on the stair turret, reflecting those of the lodging range.

COMPARABLE THEATRES

Wingfield Manor provides an insight into the variety of displays Cromwell utilised to portray his identity. The expansive double courtyard, with its smaller ancillary courtyard, provided the opportunity to embellish

---

30 *Contra.* Emery, *Greater Medieval Houses*, Vol. 2, p. 450.

gateways with heraldic panels, create dominating porches, and install long repetitive ranges for retainers. As will be shown below, Cromwell's great house was strikingly similar to Thornbury Castle, rebuilt by Edward Stafford, the third Duke of Buckingham, in the early sixteenth century. The similarities across the two examples allow a deeper insight into the implicit displays, particularly in terms of what can be seen, when, and how, as the viewer passed through the house.

The houses were built by two of the most powerful men in the kingdom, although they were not contemporaries. Ralph, Lord Cromwell (1393–1456), was a descendant of a minor Lincolnshire family. While he spent his early years in the service of the Duke of Clarence and Henry V in the French wars, he rose to be one of the most powerful men of the mid-fifteenth century. As well as Wingfield Manor, he built Tattershall, began a new great house at Collyweston in Nottinghamshire, built a church and house at Lambley and had a London residence.[31] His gained his vast wealth, in part, from his administrative abilities which saw him appointed as Treasurer of England between 1433 and 1443. In addition, his marriage to the heiress Margaret Deincourt brought him properties worth £500 a year.

Unlike Cromwell, who endured a legal battle to acquire Wingfield, the Staffords had owned Thornbury for decades. Ralph Stafford, who was granted the title Earl of Stafford during the Hundred Years War, acquired it through his marriage to Margaret, daughter of Hugh de Audley, Earl of Gloucester. Upon her death in 1348, Stafford succeeded to her property, including Thornbury.[32] Edward Stafford, third Duke of Buckingham, was born in 1478 (d. 1521). His father, Henry Stafford, second Duke of Buckingham, was executed in 1483 for plotting with the Lancastrians against Richard III. When Henry VII ascended the throne, one of his first acts was to reverse Stafford's attainder and restore the jointure to Katherine Dowager Duchess of Buckingham.[33] Henry VII's mother, Lady Margaret Beaufort, acquired the remainder of the Stafford estates, plus the wardship of the young Edward and his brother. As with royal wards, Stafford's wealth and position were exploited, arguably even more so as he was one of the wealthiest and most serious potential threats to Henry VII. Indeed, in 1515 Stafford addressed a bill of complaint to the late King Henry's executors and argued that he had been unfairly treated.[34] He appears to have been in favour with Henry VIII for some time: he

---

31 Johnson, *Castle*, p. 55–65.
32 Carole Rawcliffe, *The Staffords, Earls of Stafford and Dukes of Buckingham: 1394–1521* (Cambridge, 1978), p. 9; Audrey Thorstad, *The Culture of Castles in Tudor England and Wales* (Woodbridge, 2019), p. 16.
33 Rawcliffe, *Staffords*, p. 35.
34 Rawcliffe, *Staffords*, p. 36.

rode through London with the king after his marriage to Catherine of Aragon in 1509, was appointed Lord High Steward, and journeyed with the king to meet Francis I at the Feast of the Cloth of Gold.[35] However, Carole Rawcliffe points out that his proximity to the throne and family history 'placed him under constant suspicion', and his position at court was always ambiguous.[36]

There are manifold similarities in the house-plans of Thornbury and Wingfield despite one being the product of a *nouveau riche* and the other of a long-standing noble family. Both were multi-courtyard houses with expansive outer courtyards. At Thornbury the outer courtyard was a vast 110 by 80 metres with at least one side comprising a lodging range. At Wingfield the outer courtyard measured 45 by 62 metres, with household accommodation in the eastern range. Neither courtyard was square; both tapered, drawing the eye to focus on different elements of display. Each cross-range was decorated elaborately; these were explicit displays of wealth in the form of towers and heraldry.

Where the plans diverged was in the position of the lodging ranges. In Thornbury, there was at least one lodging range in the outer courtyard, at the eastern end of the north range. At Wingfield, there was household accommodation in the outer courtyard (although its ruinous remains do not permit a full analysis) and a lodging range in the inner courtyard on the west range. Despite the locational variance, the internal layout was also similar at each lodging range: both were intended to have three levels, although Thornbury was incomplete, with the ground floor at Thornbury and half-basement at Wingfield clearly lower status than the floors above. Access to the lowest levels at both ranges was via turrets, either semi-octagonal or square, within the courtyard, followed by a small number of steps. The stair turrets appear to have led to the first and second floors at Wingfield, and at Thornbury led to the unfinished second floor (but not the first floor). This shows strong similarities between the lodging ranges, but where they were most similar was in their presentation of uniformity.

Uniformity, as introduced in Chapter 1, was a key element of the lodging ranges' architectural language. Part of its role, as discussed in Chapter 2, was to communicate to the medieval audience the individual and collective identities of the occupants. While uniformity could have been created through identically sized rooms within the range, it was the outward display of uniformity on the elevations which was comparable at Thornbury and Wingfield. Both retain uniform external elevations; that is, the façade facing away from the great house. In addition,

---

35   Thorstad, *Culture*, p. 32.
36   Rawcliffe, *Staffords*, p. 36.

Thornbury's inner elevation, that facing inwards to the courtyard, is extant and the uniformity displayed provides a hint as to what may have once been visible upon Wingfield's inner elevation, now lost. Uniformity on the elevations was created through consistency, repetition, symmetry and pairing. Pairing, or mirroring, was the placement of two identical features beside one another. At both Thornbury and Wingfield, the garderobes were built in pairs along the ranges. This allowed the creation of substantial garderobe towers on the exterior elevation, providing a feature to draw the eye upwards. Fireplaces were also paired together at Thornbury and Wingfield; therefore the view from outside the range showed a sequence of paired garderobes followed by paired chimneys. The repetition of the paired features created a uniform external elevation, which was striking in itself and was bolstered at Wingfield by the height of the features. Something similar may have been intended at Thornbury, which remains in an incomplete – and now ruinous – state. The uniformity of the repetition was heightened further by the consistent even spacing between the features seen on the elevations. At Thornbury the stair turrets were placed midway between the entrances to the first floor and the windows for both the ground and first floors. Therefore the view of the range from within the courtyard was as uniform as that of the external elevation. The inner elevation at Wingfield can only be surmised; however, the stair turrets were equally spaced, suggesting the remaining features were also uniform in their placement.

There were a number of practical reasons for employing uniformity, although practicality may not have been paramount. Placing two fireplaces beside one another meant the use of only one flue, and with garderobes the same chute could be utilised for one cess-pit rather than requiring individual cess-pits. With paired doors, there were often shared jambs in between. This meant fewer dressed stones, which in some cases may have been a non-local variety to articulate the doorway. While there were these practical, easier or cheaper elements to pairing features, it seems unlikely that they were a primary concern for the founders. Thornbury and Wingfield were spaciously grand, elaborately decorated great houses, built by wealthy lords. Pairing features was not a way to cut corners; rather, it appears no expense was spared when creating dramatic, contemporary, high-status, even palatial great houses.

We return to the visual effect of *sameness* across the elevation to consider why uniformity was employed. At Thornbury and Wingfield, the ranges comprised different types of rooms with the uniformity displayed on the elevation, concealing this variance. The difference between room and elevation was not quite as stark as at Gainsborough, as there was some consistency in room size at Thornbury and Wingfield. However, the rooms varied more than those at, for example, Dartington.

There seems to be a motivation to create a collective identity among the occupants, as discussed in Chapter 2, but the reason for employing the uniform elevation extends beyond the retinue. This architectural style appears to have been emerging as a desirable aesthetic in the late medieval period before becoming the dominant fashion during Elizabeth's reign. Invariably symmetrical, displaying repeated and paired features, consistently spaced along elevations, Elizabethan houses were emphatically uniform, and many of the methods of Elizabethan uniformity appear in lodging ranges. What unites the Elizabethan houses and lodging ranges particularly is the contrast between the uniform elevations and the complexity of rooms within. It is not the case that Elizabethan-era prodigy or country houses derived from the earlier use of uniformity; rather, uniformity was developing across the continent during the late medieval and Tudor periods and culminated in the façades of the late-sixteenth and early seventeenth centuries. It had simply become unfashionable to build in any other way: when Raby Castle, Durham, passed to the crown after Charles, sixth Earl of Westmoreland, fled into exile, royal commissioners noted that the 'marvellous huge house' had 'no order or proportion in the building thereof'.[37]

Similarly, uniformity was emerging as the preferred aesthetic beyond the great house. Prior Goldstone of Christ Church, in the mid-fifteenth century, constructed an inn with thirty-eight single rooms around a courtyard, at what is now the corner of Butter Market and Burgate, Canterbury. The street-facing elevation was fairly uniform with paired windows and within the courtyard individual staircases led to each room.[38] Urban terraces, such as those in London and York, similarly displayed uniform elevations from the early fourteenth century. Lady Row in York has been securely dated to the early fourteenth century;[39] 39 metres in length, it comprised five houses in ten bays with a jettied first floor, with a uniform elevation facing Goodramgate. The contemporary vicarial and collegiate ranges also exhibited similarly uniform architectural features, as discussed in previous chapters.

Mark Girouard suggests that the reason for building in this uniform way during the medieval period may have been more allegorical than practical. The ideals of structure and harmony were of such importance that they were projected onto objects, and indeed buildings. Girouard suggests that a particularly important harmonious relationship was that

---

37 After: Mark Girouard, *Life in the English Country House: A Social and Architectural History* (New Haven, 1978), p. 87.
38 Anthony Quiney, *Town Houses of Medieval Britain* (London, 2004), p. 204; see also Alan Everitt, 'The English Urban Inn 1560–1760', in A. Everitt (ed.), *Perspectives in English Urban History* (London, 1973), pp. 91–137.
39 Quiney, *Town*, p. 257.

between macrocosm and microcosm.[40] The macrocosm comprised the universe, with God at the pinnacle, ruling over the microcosm which was humans.[41] This was perceived to be the natural order: realised, recreated and repeated through the social organisation. As society was ruled by the king, the household was ruled by the lord. Uniform and harmonious architecture indicates that such beliefs were projected onto buildings in the late medieval period, before becoming a principal architectural development of the Elizabethan era.

But it is in the context of the lord's theatre of display that uniformity seems to be most crucial. This is not to say that the desire for uniformity was not underpinned by allegory, or that it did not also create a sense of sameness across a group of diverse people; however, within the lord's theatre, it is uniformity's illusory quality that dominates. When we consider the placement of lodging ranges we can see the impact of the illusion at both Thornbury and Wingfield. It appears that the illusion was to be seen by visitors to the house as they moved from gatehouse to hall, and in the case studies of Thornbury and Wingfield this contributed to representing the identities of Stafford and Cromwell.

THORNBURY CASTLE, GLOUCESTERSHIRE

In the early fourteenth century, Margaret Audley, daughter of Hugh and Margaret de Clare, was set to inherit from her mother's side of the family lands extending from Norfolk to the Welsh Marches. She was to be so wealthy, such a 'valuable prize' on the marriage market, that she was abducted by Ralph Stafford, trusted captain of Edward III, and they were married in 1340.[42] In 1343–47 Stafford acquired the vast estates, including Thornbury, which allowed him to support the earldom bestowed in 1351.[43]

There are no architectural remains from Audley's or Ralph Stafford's ownership of the estate. Financial accounts suggest a double-courtyard great house with a hall running north–south within the inner courtyard and a chapel to the east. It is likely that some features were incorporated into the major rebuilding during the early sixteenth century, and it is suggested that the earlier hall and chapel formed the east range of the later inner courtyard, based on descriptions from a late sixteenth century inventory and supported by archaeological investigation.[44] The east range

---

40 Girouard, *Country*, p. 87.
41 Girouard, *Country*, p. 87.
42 Rawcliffe, *Staffords*, p. 8.
43 Rawcliffe, *Staffords*, pp. 8–10.
44 Historic England, *Thornbury Castle*, List Entry Number: 1000569 (2021)

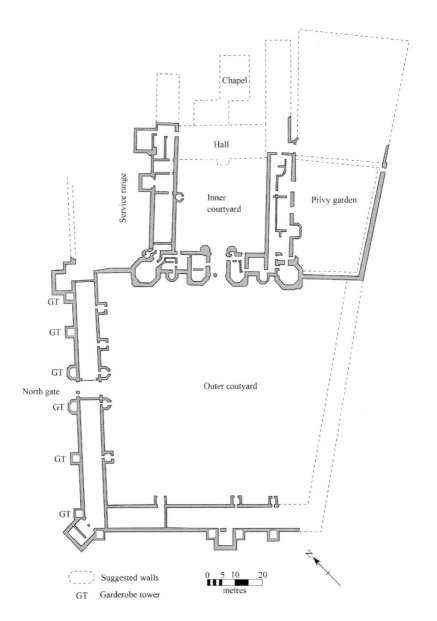

FIG. 32 PLAN OF THORNBURY CASTLE, SHOWING THE HUGE EXTENT OF THE OUTER COURTYARD AND THE NOW-LOST FEATURES OF THE INNER COURTYARD, INCLUDING THE HALL. THE UNIFORMITY CREATED, PARTICULARLY THROUGH THE REPEATED USE OF GARDEROBE TOWERS AND STAIR TURRETS, CAN BE PERCEIVED EVEN IN PLAN FORM.

of the inner courtyard was completely demolished sometime before the early eighteenth century.

The sixteenth-century rebuilding was undertaken by Ralph's descendant, Edward Stafford, third Duke of Buckingham (d. 1521). The work commenced c.1500 with the licence to crenellate granted in 1510.[45] Building ceased temporarily in 1519 due to other expenses, including a royal visit to Penshurst, his daughter's wedding, and his display at the Field of the Cloth of Gold. While building resumed in early 1521, with the aim of completing the gatehouse and outer court, Stafford's execution in May 1521 sealed the fate of Thornbury and it remained incomplete. The site was returned from the king's possession to the Stafford family in 1554 but no further construction occurred; in fact, a survey in 1583 indicated that sections were in decay. It is now in private ownership operating as a hotel.

Stafford's great house was intended to be an extensive multi-courtyard complex; however, the remains comprise only two ranges in the outer courtyard and three ranges in the inner (Figure 32). The cross-range was located in the west range of the inner courtyard and planned with a showy six towers across its length: today it allows access through a stunted central gatehouse (Figure 33). As only two of the six towers on this range were completed, the building sequence is easily identifiable. The south range of the inner court was completed, with construction radiating out from there and leaving the outer court incomplete.

The south range of the inner court comprised the Duke's and Duchess's apartments and culminated, where they met the cross-range at the western extent, in an octagonal tower with machicolated parapet (Figure 33). The tower gives no indication of the splendid southern façade of the south range, which was adorned with three full-height bay windows; the most elaborate of these contained 720 panes of curved glass in a cinquefoil plan. Despite the great height of the south range it comprised a series of parallel apartments across only two floors. The highly fenestrated façade overlooked a private garden enclosed by an embattled wall. This incorporated a ground-floor loggia and first-floor gallery; the latter was accessible from the Duke's apartments on the first floor.

The east range of the inner courtyard included the now-demolished great hall and chapel, probably those dating from the fourteenth or fifteenth century (Figure 32). The remaining three ranges of the inner courtyard were restored in the late nineteenth century by Anthony Salvin, commissioned by Henry Howard.[46] The north range comprised the

---

Available online: <https://historicengland.org.uk/listing/the-list/list-entry/1000569> [accessed 8th August 2021].
45 Thorstad, *Culture*, p. 16; Emery, *Greater Medieval Houses*, Vol. 3, p. 183.
46 Historic England, *Thornbury Castle*.

FIG. 33 PHOTOGRAPH OF THORNBURY CASTLE'S CROSS RANGE. TWO OF SIX PLANNED TOWERS WERE MOSTLY COMPLETED, LEAVING FOUR STUNTED ALONG THE RANGE. THE LARGE COMPLETE TOWER (FAR RIGHT) COMPRISED PART OF THE DUKE AND DUCHESSES' ROOMS, WHICH CONTINUED ALONG THE RANGE PERPENDICULAR.

services, beyond the low end of the hall range. These are immortalised with the 'bolying house' signage in the hotel; however, the interior is much altered from its medieval and Tudor plan.

The enormous outer courtyard contained the lodging ranges. The north range is the best-preserved within the courtyard and was bisected by the north gate, while the west range is occupied by mature trees but retains some useful architectural fabric *in situ*. The east range comprised the cross-range described above (Figure 32), and it is likely that the south range was never completed, and may never even have been started. The north gateway was decorated with a Tudor arch; the double arch on the external elevation retains the groove for a portcullis.

The section to the east of the gateway contains the best-preserved and least-altered part of the lodging range (Figure 34). There were three stair turrets on the courtyard-facing inner elevation and three garderobe towers at the rear. Incomplete, it comprised two storeys: one which appears to be at half-basement level and one which is halfway between ground and first floor at 75 centimetres above the current level of the courtyard. It is probable, however, that the ground level within the courtyard has been raised. An excavation in 1992 north of the inner courtyard revealed approximately one metre of accumulated soil above the Tudor garden

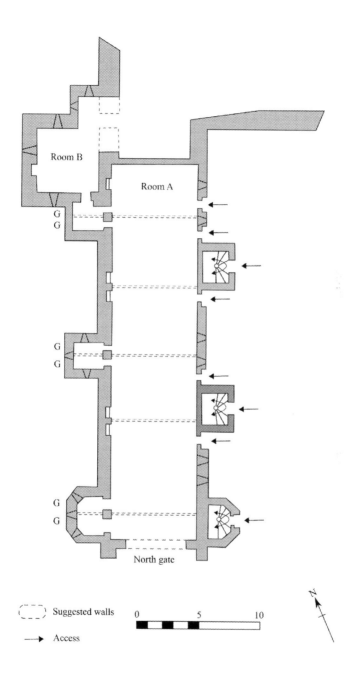

FIG. 34 FIRST-FLOOR PLAN OF THE LODGING RANGE AT THORNBURY CASTLE. THE ENTRANCES TO THESE ROOMS, DIRECTLY FROM THE COURTYARD, ARE INDICATED, AS ARE THE GARDEROBES (G) ON THE REAR WALL. IN ADDITION, THE STAIR TURRETS THAT PROVIDED ACCESS TO THE GROUND AND SECOND FLOOR CAN ALSO BE SEEN.

FIG. 35 PHOTOGRAPH SHOWING THE PROVISIONS WITHIN THORNBURY CASTLE'S LODGING RANGE. FIVE FIREPLACES CAN BE SEEN, EACH OF WHICH HEATED ONE ROOM (ONE IS JUST SEEN AT THE FURTHEST EXTENT OF THE WALL). IN BETWEEN THE FIREPLACES THE REMAINS OF TWO GARDEROBE TOWERS CAN BE DETECTED, EACH WITH TWO GARDEROBES. THE GARDEROBE DOORS IN THE MIDDLE OF THE IMAGE HAVE LOST THEIR CENTRAL SHARED JAMBS.

and the ruins of the hall.[47] This suggests that the half-basement floor was originally the ground floor and the upper floor was at first-floor level. As such, they are so-called here. A second floor to the lodging range was planned but never accomplished.

The first floor comprised five rooms with a sixth, very small, space abutting the north gate. Each of the five rooms contained a window, fireplace, garderobe and individual door opening directly from the courtyard (Figure 34). The doorways were articulated with large jambs and two-stone elliptical arches, all with chamfered edges. There must have been a series of steps ascending to the doors, almost certainly of wood, to allow access. Each door was located beside the corresponding window for the room, one of which retains two lights, each with a four-centred arch, recessed spandrels and hood moulding with square label stops. Garderobes, located in projecting towers on the exterior elevation of the range, received light from cruciform loops: a motif repeated throughout the great house including on the cross-range. Each garderobe tower served

47 Historic England, *Thornbury Castle*.

two rooms, with access through articulated doorways. Each room was equipped with a fireplace, most of which have kept their four-centred lintels with chamfer decoration and voussoirs above (Figure 35). Four of the fireplaces are paired together in twos and evenly spaced between the garderobe towers. This equally-spaced repetition presented a uniform architectural display which was perceptible from beyond the range. The rooms were approximately the same size. Room A was slightly smaller than the others and shared a garderobe with Room B, which was set to the north of the remainder of the range. Access to Room A was from the courtyard, while Room B was entered from the now demolished area to the east, likely to have been a kitchen or sevice courtyard (Figure 34).

The ground floor rooms were not granted the same provisions as the those on the first floor. Due to the change in the courtyard level, the ground-floor windows are now only 30 centimetres from the ground. They have downward splays to allow in as much light as possible; it is clear, however, that these rooms were considerably darker than those on the first floor. There were no fireplaces in these rooms, suggesting lower-status accommodation. Access to the ground floor was unusual and utilised a configuration not found in any other lodging range, apart from Wingfield Manor. There were three projecting stair turrets on the inner elevation, two of which were square in plan, while that closest to the north gate was semi-octagonal. Each contained a doorway accessible from the courtyard. Currently, the doors appear oddly close to ground level, but they were actually at first-floor level. Although all three of the doors have been partially blocked and the turrets altered internally, the medieval plan can be detected. Four rows of putlog holes within the turrets indicate the former presence of wooden stairs. These descended to a door below the level of the turret's doorway: that is, they led to the ground floor of the range. Therefore, to enter the ground-floor rooms from the courtyard, one had to ascend stairs to enter the turret, and then descend stairs to the room.

There are two indications that a second floor was planned for this range. The putlog holes within the turrets continue to the top of the first floor, indicating that the stairs would have continued to a second floor. This appears to have been the only planned access to these rooms. Furthermore, latrine chutes within the garderobe towers at the exterior of the range begin at what is now the top of the ruined first-floor wall, indicating they would have originated at garderobes on the second floor. Therefore the eastern extent of the north range was intended to have three floors: the ground and second accessible from the stair turrets, while the first floor was accessible directly from the courtyard and external staircases. The second-floor rooms would have had garderobes, probably individual doors, fireplaces and windows.

The range continued to the west of the north gate and this western section differed from the eastern section just described. The external elevation was broken by two garderobe towers, one semi-octagonal and one square, each with the cruciform loop windows as before. The courtyard-facing elevation had similar features to the eastern end of the range with two turrets providing access to the planned second floor, as before; access to the first floor was directly from the courtyard. There were only two doors into the first floor with each leading to a large room with a garderobe tower (Figure 32). This suggests that this end of the range comprised two dormitories on the first floor, rather than the smaller, low-occupancy rooms as in the eastern end.

A tripartite bastion connected the north range with the west, and the configuration changes again. What appears to be another projecting stair turret on the courtyard-facing elevation is actually a 2.4 metre-wide porch with a four-centred arch leading to another archway. This seems to be the only original entrance to this section of the range, although there are further apertures leading from the corner bastion into this range which appear to be later insertions. This section of the west range comprised a room on a grand scale with no discernible features other than one full-sized window, almost abutting the north range, now blocked. The function of this room has been debated: Emery and Thorstad both suggest a stable, probably based on the large entrance, while Historic England suggests an early indoor tennis court, with viewing gallery.[48] There are corbels high on the walls which may have supported a gallery, while numerous small rectangular holes, slightly larger than putlog holes, may have provided light. This section was reused and part of a nineteenth-century roof remains, as well as plaster on the walls, obscuring any other evidence relating to this unusual space.

The remainder of the west range is the most ruinous: it was probably incomplete at the time of Stafford's death and its form is now much obscured by mature trees and patches of rubble. Within the range there were fireplaces, suggesting it may have been a further lodging range; this is supported by garderobe towers on the exterior wall and stair turrets and doorways on the inner elevation. These projecting towers, some semi-octagonal and others square, were repeated across the inner and outer elevations across both extensive ranges in the outer courtyard. The uniformity this created can clearly be seen even from the plan (Figure 32), and the building is striking when viewed.

48 Emery, *Greater Medieval Houses*, Vol. 3, p. 185; Thorstad, *Culture*; Historic England, *The Outer Court of Thornbury Castle and Walls of Kitchen Court*, List Entry Number: 1321132 (2021) Available online: <https://historicengland.org.uk/listing/the-list/list-entry/1321132>. [accessed 8th August 2021].

HOMOGENEITY AND *HABITUS*

The case studies, and their similarities, allow an insight to the ways in which some lords created a theatre of display. The multitude of displays adopted by a lord were discussed earlier, including heraldry, a liveried retinue and the provision of comforts to guests. Here, it will be stressed that lodging ranges were also a character within these theatrics. Fundamentally, this is because all buildings displayed the identity of their builder. Lodging ranges, just as much as a hall or a barn, required financial wealth. Wealth was required to purchase materials such as stone, timber and dressed stone for articulation, as well as to hire the task force to complete it. Therefore the very existence of a lodging range was a display of the lord's financial wealth: a facet of their identity.

The use of the lodging range, to house a lord's retainers, bolstered the lord's identity further. As part of the bastard feudal system, those living in the range were paid in cash, livery, bouche of court, and in the accommodation itself. Therefore the larger the range, the more wealthy the lord appeared to the viewer. The reflection of financial wealth was important, certainly, but the lodging ranges also displayed a social identity. The lord possessed the character and social prestige to hire people into service, as indicated in their indenture, 'in times of war and peace'.[49] It demonstrated the lord's social ability to attract and hire retainers who were of middling to high status themselves. Some were certainly educated, possibly with some wealth and land of their own. Their accommodation within the great house indicated their subordination to the lord, their willingness to follow and to provide support. Whether this created an identity of social dominance or a more collegial identity for the lord is unknown. It was probably both, and variable. Therefore lodging ranges, in different ways to other buildings, represented further layers of the lord's identity.

In order for the lord's identities to be displayed as such, the medieval audience had to understand that the range housed retainers. While Pierre Bordieu's *habitus* suggests an implicit understanding of the built environment,[50] can we be sure how a lodging range was understood? The degree of homogeneity across all examples of lodging ranges indicates that there was a socially-accepted, standardised plan for retainer accommodation. The standardisation of certain constructions has been

---

49 Charles Plummer (ed.), *The Governance of England* (Oxford, 1885), p. 15; Michael Powicke, *Military Obligation in Medieval England* (Oxford, 1962), p. 168; K. B. McFarlane, *The Nobility of Later Medieval England* (Oxford, 1973), p. 104; Nigel Saul, *Knights and Esquires* (Oxford, 1981), p. 60; Michael Hicks, *Bastard Feudalism* (London, 1995), p. 63; Christopher Woolgar, *The Great Household in Late Medieval England* (New Haven, 1999), p. 8.
50 Pierre Bourdieu, *Outline of a Theory of Practice* (Cambridge, 1977).

detected elsewhere, such as the architectural principals of the courtyard house or the spatial ordering of the medieval hall. The consistency of halls, for example, allowed its meaning to be clearly understood by the medieval audience; as such, the hall both followed and enhanced social norms. Lords of great or minor wealth would build their halls with the same plan: a higher-status dais end with a cross-passage and services beyond the low end. A viewer understood the function, use and meaning of the building without even entering its space. Johnson calls this system of following or copying a certain, socially-accepted building form 'repetition',[51] but, as we have architectural repetition on the lodging ranges' elevations, we could call this 'typological homogeneity' to avoid confusion. We must consider, however, how this information was gathered. What if the visitor did not understand the architecture on display or if this was the first lodging range they had seen? Everyone who viewed a lodging range had to see one for the first time at some point; how did they understand the building without prior knowledge? Johnson suggests that there was partial understanding which required nurturing. He states that 'if the castle is theatre, some productions need narrators'.[52] Likewise, visual cues informed the viewer. It has been suggested that the individual doors of lodging ranges were included 'so that armed men could be mustered quickly'[53] and presented 'in the court in front of their dwelling'.[54] While these analyses were based on an overly militarised view of the retainers, the retainers might have been mustered in a display to welcome guests, particularly prestigious visitors. The visual cue would have been a message of a lord's authority over their retinue, as well as their social relationship with them, and it would have informed the viewer of the lodging range's use. Indeed, Giles argues that viewing was 'an essential part of understanding and remembering',[55] and, as such, the viewer may have understood its meaning for the next time a lodging range was encountered.

Aspects of lodging ranges were ubiquitous: length, high-status features, individual doors, low-occupancy rooms and overwhelmingly uniform façades. It is the last feature which may have been the most crucial for generating *habitus*, as it was so perceptible from outside. Furthermore, despite uniformity emerging as a trend, it was not yet a common architectural feature: as such, it was distinct from the remainder of the architecture on view. We can suggest, then, that visitors were likely to read the building and its architectural language, and infer its use as

51 Johnson, *Castle*, p. 82.
52 Johnson, *Castle*, p. 69.
53 Rawcliffe, *Staffords*, p. 86.
54 Margaret Wood, *The English Medieval House* (New York, 1965), p. 184.
55 Giles, 'Seeing', p. 107.

accommodation for retainers. This did not need to be explicitly stated each time it was viewed: the viewer combined what they saw with what they knew about society, what they had viewed elsewhere and visual cues. This understanding of architecture was inherent. So much so that, when Stafford was charged with building Thornbury in a way which was *too* splendid to be allowed, his accusers did not specify the ways in which it was too grand. There was no need to. It would have been obvious to all that he had transgressed the unwritten codes of architectural language.

Experiencing Architectural Aesthetics

If we consider that the visitor to the great house understood the meaning of the lodging range, we can appreciate that both visitor and building were manipulated to display the lord's identities. The two case studies in this chapter demonstrate how the position of the lodging ranges was a deliberate choice in order to utilise uniformity and homogeneity to create architectural illusions. This manipulation of the view bolstered, even exaggerated, the identities of the lord. To fully grasp the effect of the theatre of display, we must think of the view and experience of a male guest to the great house.

Both examples discussed in this chapter were multi-courtyard great houses whose configuration allowed the lodging ranges to be viewed by visitors on their way to the hall. The hall, which connected to the parlour in later examples of great houses, can be considered the epicentre of power, as this was where a lord would meet guests and entertain. Its position was therefore deliberate, as was its spatial relationship to the lodging range. The position and size of the hall appears to have changed over the course of the medieval period, reflecting a developing function. As fireplaces replaced central hearths, the hall's ceiling became lower, and as the number of rooms within the house increased with the addition of spaces such as a parlour, the hall became smaller.[56] In later examples it appears that the hall was more often in the inner courtyard, rather than in the cross-range as in earlier examples. For example, Dartington, built c.1390, had a hall in the cross-range, directly opposite the gatehouse. The gatehouse itself was unassuming, while the substantial courtyard and entrance porch into the hall range created an elaborate display. In contrast, the hall at Wingfield, built in the mid-fifteenth century, was almost hidden in the manor, dwarfed by the high towers in the inner courtyard. Similarly, at Thornbury, the hall was located in the early sixteenth-century inner courtyard on the range furthest from the outer court: again, it was hidden from view from the house's main entrance. By locating the hall at the furthest possible point

56 Wood, *House*, p. 49.

from the entrance, the walk to the hall was extended, allowing maximum display during this route. This development was not without variations. Haddon Hall, despite being mainly a fifteenth-century house, had a hall in its cross-range. This is probably due to the earlier date of the hall and the later addition of the double-courtyard plan. The hall's development hints at a change in function. As with all rooms during this period, it became more specialised in use, particularly as the parlour was introduced for meeting guests, entertaining and conducting business. Furthermore, the hall was no longer the only elevation for elaborate display. In the fourteenth century the H-plan house was common; that is, a house with the hall in the centre with the high and low ends as standard in the cross-wings. There was limited scope for architectural display when compared to the later multi-courtyard great house. This allows a tentative suggestion that the hall became less important as a feature of architectural display in favour of the courtyards, gateways and lodging ranges. While it is important to note this development, the hall was at no point an unimportant space. Even with the addition and increased use of the parlour, and if 'it became one of several living-rooms,'[57] the hall remained the focus of the house. Whether it was the main room for receiving guests or the formal entrance into the parlour,[58] the route of visitors to the hall allows an insight to how lodging ranges displayed the lord's identities.

Considering a walk through the great house requires a degree of informed imagination. While the effect of the lodging ranges' architecture still has a considerable impact on the modern viewer, we must strip back post-medieval additions and add roofs, window glass, people and activity. By doing so we can see the illusory quality that was created. When walking past the ranges, the uniformity – the repeated features, the consistent spacing and so on – create, even today, a visual deception: the impression that the range is longer than it actually is. The features create a seemingly endless appearance rather than having one key feature stand out and attract attention. From outside Thornbury's outer courtyard, the exterior of the north range was dotted with garderobe towers. The uniformity drew the eye along the range, rather than focusing attention on the fairly sparse north gate through which one entered the outer courtyard. Once within the courtyard, the inner elevation was similarly decorated with a confusion of stair turrets (Figure 36). If we consider that the viewer understood the use of the lodging range, and knew that it housed retainers, he was made aware of Stafford's authority over people, his wealth, which allowed the hiring of so many staff, and his social prestige which drew them to his service. Each of these facets of a lord's identity was heightened by the

57 Wood, *House*, p. 49.
58 As suggested by Nicholas Cooper, *House of the Gentry* (London, 1999), p. 297.

FIG. 36 PHOTOGRAPH OF THE LODGING RANGE AT THORNBURY CASTLE, VIEWED FROM WITHIN THE OUTER COURTYARD. THE THREE STAIR TURRETS ON THE EASTERN END OF THE NORTH RANGE CAN BE SEEN, AS WELL AS A FURTHER TWO ON THE WESTERN END. ALTHOUGH INCOMPLETE AND CONCEALED BY FOLIAGE, THE UNIFORMITY OF THIS COMPILATION IS PERCEPTIBLE.

uniformity which made the ranges seems boundless. As such, the lord's authority, wealth and social prestige seemed equally endless.

Dartington Hall was built by John Holland, Duke of Exeter, to exploit uniformity to its full potential. One entered the great house through a gateway. Unlike Wingfield Manor, where the intimidation commenced at this point, with the entrance set deep between protruding walls, Dartington's gateway was barely distinguished from the remainder of the range. Once under the semi-circular archway, however, the visitor was faced with the largest undivided courtyard in fourteenth-century England (see Figure 6). The 80-metre walk to the cross-passage porch, which led to the hall, was flanked by a lodging range to the right and probably further household accommodation to the left. The west range on the right-hand side displayed a uniform façade composed of five sections. In four of the sections were four doors, two on the ground floor and two directly above; the fifth section, at the southern end, had two doors across two floors. On either side of each group of doors was a four-light window, mimicking the formation of the doors and creating symmetry within each section. The spacing between the doors and windows was uniform along the entirety of the range. A visitor to the house would walk past eighteen doors and twenty windows on the way to the porch, a display suggesting the size of

FIG. 37 PHOTOGRAPH FROM THE HALL PORCH, LOOKING ALONG THE FULL EXTENT OF DARTINGTON HALL'S LODGING RANGE. EVEN WITH LATER ADDITIONS AND REMOVALS, THE OVERT UNIFORMITY CONFUSES THE VIEWER AND EXAGGERATES THE LENGTH OF THE RANGE. THE CLOSER ONE STANDS TO THE LODGING RANGE THE MORE THE ILLUSORY EXPERIENCE IS HEIGHTENED.

Holland's retinue. It is likely, however, the viewer did not actively count the features. The architecture was created to confuse; the uniformity made it difficult to focus attention on one element, meaning it was (and is, even today) difficult to quantify the number of features while moving (Figure 37). Adding to the illusion, the position of the gateway into the courtyard did not bisect the southern range evenly, but was closer to the west range. To walk directly from gateway to porch meant staying closer to the west range and this made it harder to see the full extent of the range (even with a wide-lens camera, it was difficult to capture the full lodging range). This aided the visual trickery, as, by reducing the spatial context, it became impossible to judge how many doors and windows there were. The repetition of features exaggerated the length of the range, making it seem never-ending. The visitor would see countless doors and countless windows, suggesting countless retainers. By the end of the walk across the courtyard, just before entering the hall, there was no doubt of Holland's wealth, status and social prowess. Therefore this range exploited repetition, symmetry, pairing and equal spacing to exaggerate the length of the range, and thus the lord's identities (Figure 37).

Uniformity may appear to be a subtle architectural feature when considered in isolation, but when we consider the viewer as well, its impact is revealed. It demonstrates the level of planning adopted to display the lord's identities whichever way someone looked, and the effect was further heightened by other methods of architectural manipulation. At Wingfield the entrance to the outer courtyard was via the gatehouse in the south-east corner. As one turned towards the cross-range connecting to the inner courtyard, household accommodation appeared on the right-hand, eastern side, which, like Dartington, was in close spatial context. The west range is considerably less well preserved, and thus its medieval use can only be surmised. However, if it too accommodated household members, and utilised a uniform pattern of architecture, this may have enhanced the architectural display confronting the visitor as they entered. The visitor was then faced with the cross-range adorned with Cromwell's heraldic panel. This is a more explicit form of display, but it would have been of equal importance with the architecture – and had an equal impact on the medieval audience. Indeed, the twin entrance dominated by flanking turrets and substantial chimneys was an extremely powerful statement of identity. Likewise, at Thornbury the gatehouse pierced the north range, forcing the guest to turn left towards the inner courtyard, and as they did this, the lodging range appeared. The repetition of the stair turrets upon its façade created an illusion of endlessness. Therefore the guest was immediately faced with the retainer accommodation and the identities it communicated (Figure 36). As at Dartington, spatial immediacy was used at Thornbury to manipulate the guest's view. Thornbury's gateway was not in the centre of the range, but much closer to the cross-range. As the visitor entered through the gateway and turned to the left, they were faced with the cross-range immediately in front of them, with the vastness of the courtyard now at their back. This compact view of the cross-range meant it could not be seen fully in its spatial context, but instead was directly and closely in front of the viewer, thus exaggerating the height and width (Figure 33). The necessity to turn at both Thornbury and Wingfield implies that twists and turns were not accidental but strategic features in the great house. Johnson argues that this was an echo of liturgical processions in the secular great house;[59] it may also have served to slow down the visitor, ensuring that no feature of the lodging range was missed. The lord wanted the visitor to see every window, entrance and stair turret because they showed the owner's control of vast numbers of retainers. This management of views, even architectural coercion, was present throughout the house; it appears that no opportunity was missed to construct the ideal representation of the lord's power and control.

To heighten the experience of walking past the ranges, the courtyards were tapered. At Wingfield the outer courtyard tapered towards the inner, creating a sense of power closing in. As one moves from the gateway past at least one range of household accommodation towards the cross-range, the courtyard's width reduces by more than 10 metres. Once within the inner courtyard, with the lodging range to the left and possibly Cromwell's apartments to the right, the width reduces once again as one moves towards the hall porch. It may have felt as though the walls were closing in – as they were. This instilled a degree of power as the space contracted. A sense of compression can be perceived; as the lord's identity intensified, the guests' identity was diminished. At Thornbury, the tapering was used in a different way: the width of the outer court increased as it approached the inner court. The result was a cross-range which appeared exceedingly wide, exaggerated by the shorter range opposite. The full effect of this is reduced by later additions in the outer court; however, the full extent of the cross-range was approximately 40 metres longer than its low-end counterpart. This architectural tool presents another facet of the lord's identity: one of instilling fear.

Johnson's description, discussed earlier, of a visitor entering the great house and being engulfed in darkness before being admitted into the outer courtyard expresses a distinctly defenceless experience.[60] It was shown how the guest may have been deliberately made to feel vulnerable through their position, waiting for entry, beneath battlements and arrow slits. At Thornbury and Wingfield this vulnerability was further accentuated once

---

59   Johnson, *Castle*, p. 83.
60   Johnson, *Castle*.

through the gateway and into the house proper. Given the social norm of meeting the lord in the hall, the visitor might have looked for the hall's location, but it was not visible from the outer courtyard. Their destination was nowhere to be seen. Therefore it was not only the view of the lodging ranges and other displays which may have instilled fear: the lack of seeing may have heighted the intimidation.

In the present, we cannot feel the full impact of viewing the illusory architecture during the medieval period, nor experience entirely the walk through a great house, and this risks underplaying the impact it had on the intended audience. As discussed earlier, medieval viewing was affective, almost akin to touching that which was seen. The contemporary visitor, therefore, may have *felt* the identities presented, rather than merely noting the display. The impact this had should not be underestimated, as is demonstrated by Thornbury's lodging ranges and Stafford's demise.

When Stafford began to rebuild Thornbury with extensive lodging ranges he was creating a physical manifestation of his view of himself; indeed, he had a 'love of ceremony and personal display'.[61] He planned to construct 'service lodgings' which 'surpassed' in size all of those in his other houses, alongside a moat, gunports, and portcullis.[62] Until now we have focused on the viewpoint of a visitor whose social status was equal to or lower than that of Stafford; but how were audiences of higher rank impacted by the display? Henry VIII was already mistrustful of Stafford because the latter's father, Henry Stafford, second Duke of Buckingham, had led a failed rebellion against Richard III in October 1483.[63] By 1518 the Thornbury rebuild was, as described by Rawcliffe, 'near enough completion to confirm all of Henry VIII's worst suspicions' of insurgency. Rawcliffe credits this, in part, to the lodging ranges, surmising that it is 'easy to see how these fears were generated'.[64] There can be no doubt of the substantial impact of a building's architecture in the medieval period: the very fabric of Thornbury, including, or especially, the lodging ranges, was enough to tip the scale against Stafford. He had built above his station and was executed in 1521, leaving Thornbury incomplete.

It is sometimes supposed that Henry VIII took issue with the lodging ranges' potential for the owner to quickly muster an army, due to the individual doors, location in the courtyard and the separation from servants' dormitories, but, as we have seen, a lodging range had a myriad of functions and uses, of which gathering an army was not one, and this

---

61 Rawcliffe, *Staffords*, p. 36.
62 Rawcliffe, *Staffords*, p. 86.
63 Rawcliffe, *Staffords*, p. 31.
64 Rawcliffe, *Staffords*, p. 86.

is the case for Thornbury, despite how Stafford's life ended.[65] Indeed, there was little evidence in his surviving wardrober's accounts to suggest he was planning treason. Rather, his father's failed rebellion, his own ill-considered actions such as his lavish hospitality at Penshurst in 1519, his references to his de Bohun (and therefore royal) descent, and finally a request for an armed bodyguard to assist his control of Wales, pushed the king's trust too far and gave Cardinal Wolsey the ammunition to remove a political rival.[66] There is no evidence to suggest that the king's disquiet with the lodging range was a fear that it would be used for an armed rebellion, particularly as lodging ranges were commonplace in great houses by the sixteenth century. What was unacceptable was that Stafford had created a physical impression of how he saw his own identity: he saw himself as equal to the crown and he was building palatially in accordance with his vision. This explicit and impactful architectural display was the tipping point in an uneasy relationship with Henry VIII and Cardinal Wolsey. What Stafford may have planned as ostentatious self-promotion and architectural coercion for a lower-status guest became, for the crown, architectural antagonism.

CONCLUSION

This chapter has re-centred the lord in the discussion of lodging ranges whilst retaining the focus on meaning over use. It has been made clear that lodging ranges had central roles in the display of the lord's status at least equal to, and arguably greater than, the gatehouse, hall and other parts of the great house. Status was not the only facet of the lord's identity for which lodging ranges were an important illustration. We have seen how authority, wealth and social prestige were presented to the medieval audience through lodging ranges.

The architecture of lodging ranges reveals their function in representing these facets of identity. The uniformity of their elevations was created through consistency, repetition, symmetry and pairing, an unusual combination of architectural features in the medieval period and otherwise seen only in the comparable vicarial and collegiate ranges. The illusion it created belied the true length of the lodging range, tricking the eyes to see more doors and windows than were there, convincing the viewer of more retainers therein. This architectural intimidation was heightened by tapering courtyards, utilised differently at Wingfield and

---

65 *Contra.* Rawcliffe, *Staffords*, p. 86; *Contra.* William Douglas Simpson, 'Bastard Feudalism and the Later Castles', *The Antiquaries Journal*, 26:3–4 (1946), pp. 145–71 at pp. 163–70.
66 Rawcliffe, *Staffords*, pp. 31, 41, 100.

Thornbury but both creating a sense of the lord's authority in stone and space. At the former, the courtyard draws in as one moves through the house, diminishing the visitor in contrast to the lord's identity, while at the latter, the courtyard expands outwards, towards what would have been a tower-laden cross-range, emphasising its size. Employing architectural illusions in spaces where the hall could not be yet seen was a deliberate construct to conceal the final destination of the guest's journey. Although a little speculative, we can imagine how a sense of relief may have struck the visitor to Wingfield and Thornbury once they were through the outer courtyard and cross-range and the hall was finally before them.

This combination of the lodging ranges' architecture, their spatial relationship with the rest of the house, and the movement around them created a theatre of display. Adopted from Wotton's theatre of hospitality,[67] it has been argued that each element of the house was a deliberate choice to construct a certain representation of the lord's identities. As with the retainers' identities, the lord's had to be performed. In this chapter it has been shown how the lord's identities were performed through the movement of others. The movement of a visitor was manipulated and curated to perform the lord's identities which were iterated and repeated and consolidated through what the visitor could and could not see.

This may have seemed a tortuous trip of vulnerability through the great house and, as Johnson states, a visitor simply had to trust their host.[68] The social acceptance of a safe visit may have allowed lords to play with architectural intimidation more freely. They could instil fear and a sense of lack of control in the visitor due to this unspoken trust. These unwritten rules were clearly universally understood, so much so that breaching acceptable parameters could become cause for execution. When Stafford rebuilt Thornbury, he pushed these boundaries, as he presented a view of himself which was beyond what was reasonable for a Duke. This shows that architecture had meaning that was read and understood by its audience. The next chapter will build on this understanding and include space as an actor in communicating meaning.

---

67 Wotton, *Elements*.
68 Johnson, *Castle*.

4

THE SPACES BETWEEN

EXPLORING SPACE

The north-east corner of Middleham Castle, North Yorkshire, comprised an impressive gatehouse connected to a bridge crossing the moat. The doorway was surrounded by subtle articulation and led to the inner courtyard via a vaulted passageway. Within the passageway there were horizontal stone slabs running lengthways: benches. The gatehouse's stone narrative reveals its function and use. Its use was to allow entry into the courtyard. But what of the *functions* of the gatehouse, beyond the utilitarian? The benches suggest a pause in a journey; guests may have been delayed here before they were granted further access to the house, and some juridical activities may have taken place in the spacious vault. It was both a thoroughfare and a place which prevented access. There were cavities which held the portcullis and the wooden gates which would have secured the gatehouse. A distinction between outside and inside was created. The use of the gatehouse was to give access, but one could not walk through easily or unhindered. Its function was one of separation: access was granted for some, not all. The lived experience of the gatehouse takes shape.

It has been argued over the course of the previous chapters that the placement of lodging ranges within the great house was highly planned and deliberate. And, like the gatehouse, their functions were multi-faceted, practical and explicit in one sense but subtly persuasive in another. The layers of understanding derive not only from the fabric of the buildings, but also from the space in and around the stones. The space exists only because of the fabric and the fabric only makes sense because of the space. Fabric disrupts space as much as it encloses it. Therefore we should not separate one from the other in building analysis.

This chapter considers space more fully in the discussion of lodging ranges through the examples of Middleham Castle and Bishop's Waltham Palace. On visiting the sites today, they seem starkly different. While both are in ruins, Middleham appears better preserved due to its compactness. It seems that Middleham has more to tell the viewer due to the extent of the remains, whereas at Bishop's Waltham there are swathes of dandelion-dotted grass between the surviving sections. In the late medieval period, too, they would have looked rather different. Bishop's Waltham was a multi-courtyard house at least 130 metres from north to south, and Middleham was possibly half the size. However, they only seem different when we focus on the fabric. As Graham Fairclough argues, 'it may sometimes be instructive to disregard physical form' in order to fully understand a building.[1] When we delve into the space in and around the fabric, we find parallels in the construction, the reasons behind the what and the where, and in the lived experience of the household. This chapter adds yet another layer to the function of lodging ranges: the representation of social distance, which was the non-locational separation of different social groups.

Distance: Social and Spatial

Spatial analysis essentially means examining not only the 'things' but also the spatial relationships between things. The term encompasses many different approaches, some of which are better suited to one context than another. Some methods map the location of artefacts rediscovered through excavation or field walking. Some researchers use nearest neighbour analysis to seek a quantification of spatial distribution, which can then be compared across periods or areas, while others utilise a more heuristic approach. In the past three decades spatial analysis has increasingly been used to investigate architectural space, coinciding with the increase of its use in medieval contexts. Pierre Bourdieu's concept of *habitus*, the taken-for-granted understanding of the world, has been hugely influential in this area.[2] He established that actors in a lived space have an innate sense of understanding of their role and place therein. Within each environment, there is a practical logic and sense of order that is culturally transmitted. Henri Lefebvre had similar ideas and stated that each culture 'produces a space, its own space'.[3] As such, he is more concerned with the social production of space rather than its physical configuration, with his idea of

---

[1] Graham Fairclough, 'Meaningful Constructions – Spatial and Functional Analysis of Medieval Buildings', *Antiquity*, 66:251 (1992), 348–66, at. p. 351.
[2] Pierre Bourdieu, *Outline of a Theory of Practice* (Cambridge, 1977).
[3] Henri Lefebvre, *The Production of Space* (Malden, 1991, orig. 1974), p. 31.

space being 'at once a precondition and a result of social superstructures'.[4] As discussed in the introductory chapter, Bill Hillier and Julienne Hanson's work on the syntax of space has had a great impact on the study of medieval space, as has the work of Thomas Markus and Amos Rapoport.[5] To summarise Hillier and Hanson's ideas, differentiation of space relates to the organisation of society. Therefore, due to this connection, or 'strong relationship' as they describe it, when we explore the organisation of space we can better understand the order of society.[6] We can see their impact appearing in archaeological discourse from around the start of the 1990s in Roberta Gilchrist's work on medieval nunneries, Matthew Johnson's on post medieval vernacular houses, Sally Foster's on brochs, and Jane Grenville's on medieval rural and urban houses.[7]

Hillier and Hanson use access analysis, whereby penetration diagrams are created to show the varying 'depths' of different spaces within a house. This focus on movement, direction and access is used effectively in the medieval context by Amanda Richardson and Katherine Weikert, but it is not without its flaws.[8] A considerable limitation is the consideration of space as something that was *used* rather than something with multiple, overlapping and ebbing functions; a distinction which has been crucial in this study. This is somewhat addressed by Patrick Faulkner's planning analysis, which developed quite separately from Hillier and Hanson's work.[9] His work as part of the Ministry of Public Buildings and Works sets out that a building's plan reveals the 'mode of living of those for

---

4   Lefebvre, *Space*, p. 85.
5   Bill Hillier and Julienne Hanson, *The Social Logic of Space* (Cambridge, 1984); Thomas Markus, *Buildings and Power: Freedom and Control in the Origin of Modern Building Types* (Abingdon, 1993); Amos Rapoport, *The Meaning of the Built Environment* (Tucson, 1990).
6   Hillier and Hanson, *Logic*, pp. 142–143, 18.
7   Roberta Gilchrist, *Gender and Material Archaeology: The Archaeology of Religious Women* (Abingdon, 1994); Matthew Johnson, *Housing Culture: Traditional Architecture in an English Landscape* (London, 1993); Sally Foster, 'Analysis of Spatial Patterns in Buildings (Access Analysis) as an Insight into Social Structure', *Antiquity*, 63:238 (1989), 40–50; Jane Grenville, 'Urban and Rural Houses and Households in the Late Middle Ages', in Maryanne Kowaleski and P. J. P. Goldberg (eds), *Medieval Domesticity: Home, Housing and Household in Medieval England* (Cambridge, 2008), pp. 92–123.
8   Amanda Richardson, 'Corridors of Power: A Case Study in Access Analysis from Medieval England', *Antiquity*, 77:296 (2003), pp. 373–84; Kate Weikert, *Authority, Gender and Space in the Anglo-Norman World, 900–1200* (Woodbridge, 2020).
9   Patrick Faulkner, 'Domestic Planning from the Twelfth to the Fourteenth Centuries', *Archaeological Journal*, 115 (1958), pp. 150–184; Patrick Faulkner, 'Castle Planning in the Fourteenth Century', *Archaeological Journal*, 120:1 (1963), pp. 215–35.

whom the building was designed'.[10] As such, he considers the interaction between the building and its occupants, as well as its visitors. He argues that this demonstrated the approach of the designers which reveals more of the building's function, not simply its use.[11] Fairclough's 'Meaningful Constructions' has possibly had the greatest influence on this chapter on lodging ranges. He argues that close consideration of the plan of a building is important but there must be an equal emphasis on the 'hidden and unspoken' meanings.[12]

Spatial analysis requires us to tread carefully, because our modern understanding of space is arguably different from that in the past. Aristotle's container view of space suggested an envelope in which life took place. From the late fourteenth century the idea of space as something that exists between things emerged, a step towards a more abstract and infinite understanding. No singular consideration of space is correct, and today we consider space in different and contradictory ways. We accept its abstract and endless nature and then we try to box it up in measurements, directions and shapes. So is spatial exploration doomed to fail? To avoid imposing modern ideas on the past, I accept that medieval people had different conceptions of space, while seeking connections between space and society that aid our understanding. These connections are the principles of spatial analysis.

The starting point of spatial analysis is the understanding that culture shaped the way in which society negotiated space, and was the main influence on how space was used.[13] This is evidenced by buildings. Buildings were constructed deliberately to segment, connect or create space. Second, the influence of society was continuous. That is, the social affects did not end with a building's construction. Society's influence continued to shape how we understand space, its use, ownership and functions. Combined, these principles allow us to view space as a reflection of social norms, and consider buildings as deliberate decisions which create a particular sense of place, forms of identity, social relations and political power.[14]

Third, as well as continuously shaping our understanding of space, society's rules were in turn reinforced by space. Therefore space should be considered an active participant in the medieval – and indeed modern – lived experience. These three principles mean that this chapter, while looking at space, uses few measurements, plans or maps.

10   Faulkner, 'Domestic', p. 150.
11   Faulkner, 'Castle'.
12   Fairclough, 'Meaningful', p. 351.
13   Fairclough, 'Meaningful'; Rapoport, *Meaning*; Amos Rapoport, *Culture, Architecture, and Design* (Chicago, 2005).
14   Kate Giles, 'Seeing and Believing: Visuality and Space in Pre-modern England', *World Archaeology*, 39:1 (2007), 105–21, at p. 106.

Social distance is the non-physical distinction between social groups, based on their attributes. These attributes may be wealth, social status or culture, and the ways in which these vary create separation between groups. It is relational: that is, it can change in different social, cultural and spatial contexts. Consider an intern and a CEO (Chief Executive Officer) within the same company. Each has a different social position due to their role, and social distance is the distinction between these intangible social positions. When in the workplace they are intangibly separated by considerable social distance. However, if they both attend a sector-wide conference as delegates their social distance is reduced, and their social positions in this context may be the same. Social distance is not measured in metres nor is it tangible. However, it is *represented* in a myriad of ways which can be either tangible or intangible: for example, precedence, or who can approach whom and when. The CEO and the intern may interact rarely in their workplace, and when they do the CEO may initiate the interaction: this is an indication of their social distance. It can also be physically represented. If the intern and the CEO have a meeting, there may be a board table between them. Yet when the intern takes a break with peers, they may stand side-by-side or commune around a coffee table. Furthermore, social distance may be spatially represented. Consider the offices of the CEO and the intern; they may be separated by a wall or located on different floors, or in different buildings or countries altogether. These tables, walls and spaces are representations of social distance.

In the late medieval great house there were equally numerous manifestations of social distance, both explicit and subtle. John Blair suggests that, by 1100, substantial houses were already divided into spaces, imperfectly termed 'public' and 'private'.[15] He usefully highlights the physical representations of social difference between those who would access the *aula* (hall) and *camera* (chamber).[16] Within the hall, people sat 'in respect of their dignity', which reflected their status and position within the social hierarchy.[17] This was so engrained in society that most medieval halls followed the same plan; the layout was accepted and appropriated from house to house.[18] This was a spatial representation of social distance: those who were far from the lord socially were far physically within the

---

15 John Blair, 'Hall and Chamber: English Domestic Planning 1000–1250', in Gwyn Meirion-Jones and Michael Jones (eds), *Manorial Domestic Buildings in England and Northern France*, Society of Antiquaries Occasional Papers 15, (London, 1993), pp. 1–21.
16 Blair, 'Hall', p. 2.
17 Edith Rickert (ed.), *The Babees' Book: Medieval Manners for the Young: Done into English from Dr. Furnivall's Texts* (London, 1923), p. 71.
18 Blair, 'Hall', pp. 11, 15.

hall. As Mark Gardiner states: the hall was not merely a room, but a 'hierarchical space'.[19] Space in the medieval hall equated to social distance; but it could be demonstrated through a variety of means, regardless of how physically close people were. After all, social distance is a *non-locational* difference, so it may be represented even when people are grouped together in a compact space, and the medieval hall, again, shows us this. The lord and family would sit at the high end of the hall, often on a dais. This raised them physically and metaphorically above the others in the hall, including their retainers, and they would be closest to the heat. Fireplaces in high medieval halls were often centrally-placed with smoke escaping through a louvre in the roof, but in the late medieval period they were more commonly in the long walls, located towards the high end, ensuring the lord was kept warm to the disadvantage of the retainers and others in the hall. The high end was better lit, with a grand window such as the recycled bay window at Gainsborough Hall. The screen passage separated the low end of the hall from the draught and the noise emanating from the services, but remained comparatively colder and darker than the high end of the hall.[20] The relational aspect of social distance can also be detected through the hall. The low end might be colder and darker than the high end but what of those household members who did not dine in the room at all? Their physical position, outside the hall, represented their social distance from the lord, family and retainers within.

The representation of social distance was arguably more crucial in this time period than in preceding centuries.[21] The increased social mobility of the late medieval period created a convoluted social hierarchy. This was accelerated by the Wars of the Roses and the development of bastard feudalism which allowed a snakes-and-ladders type of social dynamism, particularly for those in the middle and upper ranks. Therefore, during what Christine Carpenter calls the 'age of ambition', people wanted to ensure their rank was displayed physically, and nowhere is this more evident than with retainers.[22] It would not do for someone of an upper rank to be mistaken for or surpassed by someone of a lower rank. K. B. McFarlane described the upper classes as living in fear of 'being swamped

---

19   Mark Gardiner, 'Buttery and Pantry and the Antecedents: Idea and Architecture in the English Medieval House', in Maryanne Kowaleski and P. J. P. Goldberg (eds), *Medieval Domesticity: Home, Housing and Household in Medieval England* (Cambridge, 2008), pp. 37–65, at p. 38.
20   Gardiner, 'Buttery', p. 38.
21   Michael Hicks, 'Bastard Feudalism, Overmighty Subjects and Idols of the Multitude during the Wars of the Roses', *The Journal of the Historical Association*, 85:279 (2000), 386–403, p. 392.
22   Christine Carpenter, *Locality and Polity: A Study of Warwickshire Landed Society, 1401-1499* (Cambridge, 1992), p. 152.

by the mass of invaders', creating a picture of almost a tsunami of retainers vying for the place of their lord.[23] Whether or not this was a genuine fear, distinct social distance was certainly desired.[24]

The need to display social distance is apparent in the sumptuary laws which restricted the type of livery certain groups could wear.[25] Henry II restricted the use of scarlet, sable, vair and gris by those not in his own retinue.[26] As a result, those donning the fur of a sable or red squirrel could rest assured that it was clear they were of the King's retinue and not that of a lesser lord. Likewise, retainer badges reinforced the social distance created by livery. The Dunstable Swan, excavated at the Dunstable Dominican Friary, Bedfordshire, is one such badge. It was produced in either England or France c.1400 by the *émail en ronde bosse* method, whereby molten glass was applied to gold to produce a three dimensional sculpture. It was an exceptional badge for a high-ranking retainer of either Henry IV or V, as the former adopted the swan emblem after his marriage to Mary de Bohun in c.1380. A copper alloy retainer badge depicting the white boar emblem of Richard III was found at Middleham Castle, on the exterior of the north range. It was created in a mould and then gilded, suggesting that a considerable number were produced, unlike the Dunstable Swan. Thousands of badges would have been produced of fustian cloth for the lower ranking supporters of Richard III, Henry IV and Henry V. This created a hierarchy of badges which reflected the hierarchy of the livery. Combined, these were a visual display of social distance between those retained and those not, and between higher- and lower-ranked retainers. When we return to look at lodging ranges, we see that they were also graduated in accordance with rank. At Gainsborough this was represented in the type of room and the access to it, while at Caister Castle there were two distinct ranges separating those of different status, and at Thornbury Castle and Wingfield Manor the ground-floor rooms lacked provisions granted to the upper floors. This shows that each aspect of the retainers' lives was graduated by rank, in a reflection of their social distance from those above and below them.

Once we deconstruct social distance it is clear that it determined all aspects of the medieval lived experience,[27] and indeed of our lived experience today. This was not restricted to the upper echelons of society. As P. J. P. Golberg and Maryanne Kowaleski state, houses of varying status

---

23 K. B. McFarlane, *The Nobility of Later Medieval England* (Oxford, 1973), p. 122.
24 Hicks, 'Overmighty', p. 403.
25 Gordon McKelvie, *Bastard Feudalism, English Society and the Law. The Statutes of Livery 1390–1520* (Woodbridge, 2020), p. 57.
26 Frédérique Lachaud, 'Liveries of Robes in England, c.1200–c.1330', *The English Historical Review*, 111 (1996), pp. 279–98, at p. 281.
27 Hicks, 'Overmighty'.

were organised to reflect both conscious and unconscious social values.[28] One single representation of social distance did not determine one's place in society; instead, there was a compilation of tangible and intangible manifestations reinforcing one another. Therefore, while the hall's organisation shows how spatial distance could equate to social distance, this cannot be stretched to give a physical measurement of its representation. Social distance was considerably more nuanced than that: it was not fixed. Retainers or guests sitting midway down the hall would be aware of the presence of those above and below them. But when they returned home? Sitting on the dais at the high end of one's own hall presented a different social dynamic. Therefore discussing social distance is akin to viewing a snapshot of society which changed as soon as another person entered or left the space. This chapter will look at space around lodging ranges and discuss what elements of social distance can be detected.

MIDDLEHAM CASTLE, NORTH YORKSHIRE

There has been a castle at Middleham, in Wensleydale, North Yorkshire, since before the Norman Conquest. There are remains of a motte and bailey located *c.*450m south of the current Middleham Castle, on a high mound. This was probably built by Alan the Red *c.*1086 and subsequently passed to his brother, Ribald. The latter's grandson or great grandson constructed the central tower or keep, *c.*1170–80, in the great house we see today. It measured 32 by 24 metres with ashlar-faced walls up to 3.7 metres thick in places. While it is not as tall as other Northern towers of a similar date, it covers a much larger area.[29] It was divided longitudinally and contained the great hall on the east side, the great chamber, privy chamber and chapel on the west side, and two small chambers within the turrets. All of this was above the kitchen and storage rooms on the ground floor, which appears as a basement due to the first-floor, eastern entrance.

Ralph Fitzranulph, born *c.*1218, died without a male heir in 1270, and his daughter Mary married Robert Neville of Raby.[30] Their son, Ralph, first Lord Neville of Raby (d. 1331), inherited the great estates of Raby and Brancepath in County Durham and Sheriff Hutton in East Yorkshire; commencing centuries of Neville ownership and expansion. As the Neville

---

28 Maryanne Kowaleski and P. J. P. Goldberg, *Medieval Domesticity: Home, Housing and Household in Medieval England* (Cambridge, 2008), p. 4; see also Richard Suggett, 'Peasant Houses', in Christopher Gerrard and Alejandra Gutiérrez (eds), *The Oxford Handbook of Later Medieval Archaeology in Britain* (Oxford, 2018), pp. 226–41, at p. 239.
29 L. Poultney, *Middleham Castle* (London, 1998), p. 22.
30 C. Peers, *Middleham Castle* (London, 1965), p. 1.

family gained power and importance throughout the medieval period, most of them had some role in the control of the Marches – a role which required what could be described as 'a private army'.[31] In c.1300, Ralph, Lord Neville, added a chapel on the east side of the keep and rebuilt the outer defences of the castle, replacing timber palisades with a stone curtain wall and corner towers. The wall had shallow pilaster buttresses which remain *in situ*, dwarfed by later additions from the fifteenth century.

Ralph was succeeded by his son, also Ralph, who was appointed Warden of the Marches under King Edward III.[32] His successor, John, the third Lord Neville, became steward of the royal household during Edward III's reign. He fought in the Battle of Neville's Cross, was retained by John of Gaunt in 1370, whom he joined in France, and later became a chief lieutenant.[33] Under Richard II he became Seneschal of Gascony, then later Warden of the East March. The wealth from these appointments, profits from the war, plus inheritances from two marriages, was not spent on Middleham. He rebuilt Raby and Sherriff Hutton, and made considerable benefactions to Durham Cathedral.[34]

John's son, Ralph, fourth Lord Neville (b. 1364), became the wealthiest and most powerful lord of the northern counties, serving Richard II, Henry IV and Henry V over the course of his career. Under Richard II he was Joint Keeper of the Town and Castle of Carlisle, Joint Warden of the West March, Earl of Westmorland and Honour of Penrith. He received a huge inheritance and went on to marry Joan Beaufort, daughter of John of Gaunt, in 1396. He changed his allegiance to the Lancastrian effort soon after and was rewarded with more titles, including that of Marshal of England, and was granted the Honour of Richmond.[35] It is his social-ladder-climbing ability that we see at Middleham. He converted Middleham from what was visually a high medieval castle into a great house typical of the period, including ranges on the south and west sections of the curtain wall. This required an increase in the height of the curtain wall and corner towers. The fourth Lord Neville was thus able to accommodate a large household and provide the hospitality expected by his guests, including in 1410 King Henry IV.

Neville may have prioritised the south range, as it appears to have included his accommodation on the first floor. It is likely there were barrel-vaulted, ground-floor rooms in existence already, incorporating the fourteenth-century curtain wall. In the south west of the courtyard lies the

---

31 Poultney, *Middleham*, p. 27.
32 Poultney, *Middleham*, p. 24.
33 Poultney, *Middleham*, p. 24.
34 Poultney, *Middleham*, p. 24.
35 Poultney, *Middleham*, p. 25.

FIG. 38 PHOTOGRAPH SHOWING THE NORTHERN EXTENT OF THE LODGING RANGE AT MIDDLEHAM CASTLE. THE FORMER PRESENCE OF A GROUND-FLOOR VAULT CAN BE IDENTIFIED THROUGH THE AREAS OF STONE-ROBBING. THE ROOMS THAT DID NOT ABUT THE GARDEROBE TOWER, THOSE ON THE RIGHT-HAND SIDE, WERE GRANTED THE PROVISION ON THE EXTERIOR WALL, SEEN IN THE CENTRE OF THE IMAGE. THE DISPARITY BETWEEN THE FIRST- AND GROUND-FLOOR WINDOWS IS EVIDENT. THE LOBBY CAN JUST BE SEEN IN THE LOWER RIGHT CORNER.

only circular tower at Middleham. Referred to today as the Prince's tower, as Richard III's only legitimate son was supposedly born there in c.1474, it was called 'the Round Tower' in a sixteenth-century survey.[36] There is evidence for at least six rooms on the ground floor of the south range, including that on the ground floor of the south-east tower. At the west end of the range there was an unusual arrangement possibly indicating one or two suites. Two stone walls terminate in doors against the curtain wall: one voussoir survives, indicating a four-centred or ogee arch. With two doors from the courtyard, this space may have been two two-room suites, divided by a timber partition, although the presence of only one garderobe could indicate that it was one three-room suite.

The first floor was added, along with an external straight staircase. This indicates a slightly earlier date than the other first floors added, as the west range had both internal and external stairs while the north range

---

36 Poultney, *Middleham*, p. 30; Peers, *Middleham*, p. 5.

had only internal staircases. The stairs provided access to the eastern end of the first floor and it is likely that the floor was subdivided, probably with a timber partition at the point where two garderobes met on the south wall. The western end of the first floor was a space separate from the east, and the provisions created a grand space. It was equipped with a substantial fireplace, two or three windows, and the garderobe on the south wall. Roughly opposite the fireplace appears to be the only access into the western end of the south range: a bridge from the keep over the courtyard. If this access via the keep was the only way in, this space was the most hidden area in the house.

The lodging range was located in the courtyard's west range and appears to have been divided into eight large rooms: four on each of the ground and first floors. The ground floor comprised four barrel-vaulted rooms, two on either side of the garderobe tower (Figure 38). All bar one were entered directly from the courtyard; the room located at the north end of the range was prefixed with a small lobby. Small loop windows punctured the curtain wall with evidence for some windows on the inner elevation.

The ground and first floors were roughly identical in plan, showing the uniformity seen in other lodging ranges, with provisions similarly located in comparable rooms. As expected, the first-floor windows were considerably larger versions of those below, although no decoration remains intact. In a deviation from uniformity, however, the ground floor fireplaces were on the inner, courtyard-facing elevation, while those on the first floor were on the exterior wall; the latter was a much more common arrangement. This may have been due to the earlier curtain wall: rather than demolish parts of it when the lodging range was added, the ground floor fireplaces were sited on the newly built inner elevation. Access to the room at the north end of the first floor was via an external staircase, extending above the small lobby, and there may have been something similar for the room at the southernmost extent. Access to the central two first-floor rooms was via the central garderobe tower.

Each of the eight rooms had access to a single garderobe: the two rooms on the ground floor and two on the first floor room that abutted the garderobe tower were provided with the utility within the tower. The other four rooms (two on each floor) at either end of the range were provided with a garderobe built within the thickness of the exterior, western wall (Figure 38). The central garderobe tower had two entrances directly from the courtyard (Figure 39). The first door led to a newel staircase providing access to the adjoining rooms on the first floor, and to a second floor which had a low pitched roof. The second door provided access to a third garderobe on the ground floor. This was something like a 'public' garderobe, as seen at Wingfield Manor.

The garderobe tower was a key feature of this range. It contained a space where the first-floor rooms met and opened to a bridge leading to

FIG. 39 PHOTOGRAPH OF THE GARDEROBE TOWER CENTRALLY LOCATED IN MIDDLEHAM CASTLE'S LODGING RANGE. OF THE TWO GROUND-FLOOR DOORS VISIBLE, ONE LED TO A 'PUBLIC' GARDEROBE. THE SECOND DOOR LED TO A NEWEL STAIRCASE AND INTO THE FIRST-FLOOR ROOMS ON EITHER SIDE OF THE TOWER. THE FIRST-FLOOR DOOR CONNECTED THE TOWER AND KEEP (ON LEFT OF IMAGE) WITH A BRIDGE NOW LOST. THE CORBELS THAT SUPPORTED THE BRIDGE CAN JUST BE DETECTED.

the keep. This was the second bridge from the courtyard ranges to the south-west corner of the keep. When the keep was constructed in the late twelfth century the western side of the longitudinal spine was the great chamber, with the hall on the east side. By the late fourteenth or early fifteenth century it appears that Neville's chamber had moved to the western end of the south range, with the original chamber becoming a chamber of presence, accessible from the hall, the lord's chambers, and the first floor of the lodging range (Figure 43).

Ralph Neville's son Richard, Earl of Salisbury, continued the redevelopment of the courtyard after the death of Joan Beaufort, his mother, by building the north range. There may have been three rooms on the ground floor, west of the gatehouse, with small one-light windows. The westernmost room was entered via a lobby, while the remaining two chambers were accessed directly from the courtyard. An internal newel staircase led from the courtyard to the first floor. An off-centre garderobe tower extended upwards to the second floor and the wall-walk above. The north-west tower's height was increased, and the upper part of the gatehouse was remodelled to include diagonal buttresses, turrets and machicolations. After the Battle of Bosworth, Middleham was confiscated by Henry VII, remaining as Crown property until 1604. It is now managed by English Heritage.

THE PERFECT HOUSE

As we turn to focus on lodging ranges we begin to see how they too played a role in the construction of social distance. But first we must explore and understand the spatial configuration of lodging ranges, and this requires an explanation of courtyards. At both Middleham and Bishop's Waltham Palace, the lodging ranges comprised a wing of a courtyard. That is, they enclosed a space which was part of the great house. Access to the lodging range was via this enclosed space, creating a sense of inward-looking buildings. There are few examples of lodging ranges which were distinct from a courtyard, and they tend to be slightly misleading. At Brook Hall, the lodging range appears to stand alone, but this is due to the demolition of the remainder of the great house. At Brympton d'Evercy, Somerset, built by John Sydenham between 1434 and 1464, what appears to be a lodging range is separated from all surrounding medieval buildings. However, the spatial configuration actually reflects that of a courtyard, even though the buildings were not physically connected. All known examples of lodging ranges were part of a courtyard system, and this requires some unpacking. The integral features of the great house, that is, the hall, principal chamber and services, had been separate entities until the thirteenth century, at which point they became more commonly integrated in secular houses.[37] This tight integration happened sooner in bishop's palaces, such as Wolvesey, Winchester, as they drew on ecclesiastical planning, including cloisters.[38] Over the course of the late thirteenth century, the elements of the house were built 'under one roof' and the courtyard became a standard feature in the great house plan by the mid-fifteenth century.[39] Larger and wealthier houses might have double or multi-courtyard systems, while lesser lords had smaller houses which may have had only one courtyard; however, the reasons behind the plan, whether single, double or multi, were the same. A courtyard reflected practicality, social order, identity and social distance. In these ways, as features of the great house, courtyards and lodging ranges go hand in hand, with their functions, uses and meanings overlapping considerably.

The first reason behind the courtyard plan was practicality. From the thirteenth century, household numbers grew as they became less

---

37 Blair, 'Hall', p. 15.
38 Blair, 'Hall', pp. 10–11.
39 Blair, 'Hall', p. 15.

peripatetic. Courtyards provided the space to accommodate these swollen numbers, which included retainers. They were also practical in that they provided just enough protection to deter intruders. The exterior elevation of the lodging range at Middleham appeared foreboding with its garderobe tower and buttresses flanked by corner towers, but it was not defensible against a genuine attack. A courtyard was a visual deterrent and an obstacle to those daring enough to intrude. Courtyards were a barrier between those in the household and those without, as well as between those who *could* enter and who could not. Therefore courtyards represented social distance between these groups.

The space and rooms within the courtyards further exemplified the social distances within the household. Blair intimates that all places where one could sleep were reflections of social difference. He uses King Alfred's paraphrase of St Augustine's soliloquies to outline the hierarchy within royal houses: 'some men are in the chamber, some in the hall, some on the threshing floor, some in prison'.[40] It is as though social stratification within the medieval hall seeped out to the courtyards and through the remainder of the estate. This is perhaps perceptible most clearly in a double-courtyard plan: the ideal house in the late medieval period as described by contemporary writer Andrew Boorde.[41] The upper or inner courtyard was a higher-status space, socially distant from the lower or outer courtyard. The inner space usually contained the lord's and family's chambers and the hall, although the latter was sometimes located in the cross-range between the courtyards, as at Haddon Hall. Compared to the outer courtyard, it was quieter, with fewer people allowed access to it or to the rooms leading from it. Much like the inner and outer chambers within lodging ranges, the outer courtyard was more open and accessible. It contained the gatehouse, sometimes stables, and lower-status accommodation such as the porters' or guards' rooms.[42] This standard domestic plan, created time and time again by elites, reflected society's wider hierarchical order. Therefore the plan was not only for reasons pertaining to health, as was Boorde's focus, but a confirmation that social and moral order was instilled in the house. Social distance between those who occupied each courtyard was represented spatially: the further someone lived and worked from the inner courtyard, the further socially they were from the lord. However, much like the lower end of the hall, the outer courtyard and the remainder of the estate were not

---

40 Blair, 'Hall', p. 2.
41 Andrew Boorde, *A compendyous regyment or a dyetary of healthe made in Mountpyllyer, by Andrewe Boorde* (1542); after Christopher Woolgar, *The Great Household in Late Medieval England* (New Haven, 1999), p. 69.
42 Jane Grenville, *Medieval Housing* (London, 1997), p. 103; Woolgar, *Household*, pp. 68–9.

unimportant. Each was a representation of the social distance between those who could enter a space and those who could not. Therefore the courtyard system further represents the relational characteristics of social distance.

As each great-house plan varied, so did the location of the lodging ranges: they were constructed in both the inner and outer courtyards and in houses with single, double or multi-courtyards. At Dartington Hall, two lodging ranges probably faced one another to create an expansive outer courtyard. At the south end the perpendicular cross-range comprised the hall and services, and beyond this lay an inner courtyard with the living quarters for the Holland family. The social distance was represented through the double courtyard plan, creating almost a hierarchical pyramid tipped flat: the vast outer courtyard occupied by a huge number of household members, set socially and spatially apart from the occupants of the smaller, quieter, calmer inner courtyard. At Haddon Hall the inner and outer courtyards were more comparable in size: the outer, only slightly larger, contained the lodging range opposite the cross-range. The social distance between lord and retainer was demonstrated spatially through this separation.

This may present an impression of diversity in configuration across great houses, but there are connective threads of similarity in the construction and representation of social distance. While this was, and indeed is, the non-locational separation of different social groups, it was spatially represented throughout the great house: in the hall, courtyards and the position of the lodging ranges. At Dartington and Haddon, the spatial representation of medieval social distance is explicit in the buildings' plans. This discussion will now look at what appears to be more subtle representations in spatially restricted, multi-phase houses.

BISHOP'S WALTHAM PALACE, HAMPSHIRE

Bishop's Waltham was one of the largest late-medieval episcopal great houses in England, consisting of several small and large courtyards, a great park, gardens and fishponds.[43] The bishops of Winchester obtained the land, nine miles from their seat to the north-west, in AD 904, and it was added to and extended over five centuries. The chapel crypt, parts of the west tower and bishop's chambers are the oldest extant buildings, dating to the mid/late twelfth century. These were probably constructed

---

43 Anthony Emery, *Greater Medieval Houses of England and Wales 1300–1500* (3 vols, Cambridge, 2006), Vol. 3, p. 312.

FIG. 40 PHOTOGRAPH SHOWING THE REMAINS OF THE LODGING RANGE AT BISHOP'S WALTHAM PALACE. THE FOOTINGS RETAIN THE FIREPLACES, INDICTING THE NUMBER OF ROOMS, WHILE THE FARMHOUSE REVEALS THE FORM OF THE TIMBER-FRAMED STRUCTURE, INCLUDING FIRST-FLOOR PENTICE. TO THE RIGHT IS THE SUBSTANTIAL BAKE–BREWHOUSE. THE SPACE BETWEEN THE FARMHOUSE AND THE BAKE–BREWHOUSE WAS TRAVERSED WITH A FIRST-FLOOR BRIDGE. IT EXTENDED ALONG THE COURTYARD-FACING ELEVATION OF THE BAKE–BREWHOUSE, PROVIDING ACCESS TO ITS FIRST FLOOR.

by Henry of Blois (d. 1171), King Stephen's brother, after he returned from exile in 1158, and Richard Ilchester, between 1174 and 1188.[44]

The majority of the remains, above ground level, were the product of two of the most powerful bishops of Winchester: Wykeham and Beaufort. William of Wykeham (d. 1404) gained a reputation in royal service under the rule of Edward III before acquiring Bishop's Waltham in 1367.[45] He managed the building works at Windsor, and, as a result, became an important member of the king's service, holding the post of Keeper of the Privy Seal from 1364 to 1367.[46] Wykeham's success before and during his tenure of the See of Winchester meant that he had the ability to transform Bishop's Waltham, expanding it in all directions. He began by building a substantial range for baking and brewing, to the east, the size of which demonstrates the scale of the household (Figures 40 and 41). Roughly opposite this range, he remodelled the hall and services, adding five large windows which overlooked the moat.[47] Beyond the high end of the hall, to the south, Wykeham widened and added a first floor to the Norman-period block which connected the hall to the west tower. This allowed access from the high end of the hall directly to the first-floor gallery of the block and then into the tower. The ground floor of the block was accessible from a small courtyard at the southern extent of the house. To the east of the west tower were rooms over two floors set around the south courtyard. The bishop's suite of chambers was likely to have been on the first floor, as indicated by the large windows, which were described in the manorial account rolls as panelled and glazed in 1395.[48] The services and kitchen were also reconstructed at this time, on the same scale as the bake-brewhouse. Bishop's Waltham under Wykeham was a period of considerable growth in scale and comfort.

Henry Beaufort (d. 1447) succeeded Wykeham in 1404. As the half-brother of Henry IV he was a significant figure in government, particularly during the reign of Henry V.[49] He left royal service in 1417 and moved to the Continent, returning with a cardinalship which had not been approved by the king.[50] He managed to retain the bishopric, probably by loaning almost £18,000 to the Crown.[51] He occupied Bishop's Waltham between 1405 and

---

44 Emery, *Greater Medieval Houses*, Vol. 3, p. 312.
45 John Hare, 'Bishop's Waltham Palace, Hampshire: William of Wykeham, Henry Beaufort and the Transformation of a Medieval Episcopal Palace', *Archaeological Journal*, 145 (1988), 222–54, at p. 226.
46 Hare, 'Waltham', p. 226.
47 Hare, 'Waltham', p. 227.
48 Hare, 'Waltham', p. 229.
49 Hare, 'Waltham', p. 233.
50 Hare, 'Waltham', p. 233.
51 Hare, 'Waltham', p. 234.

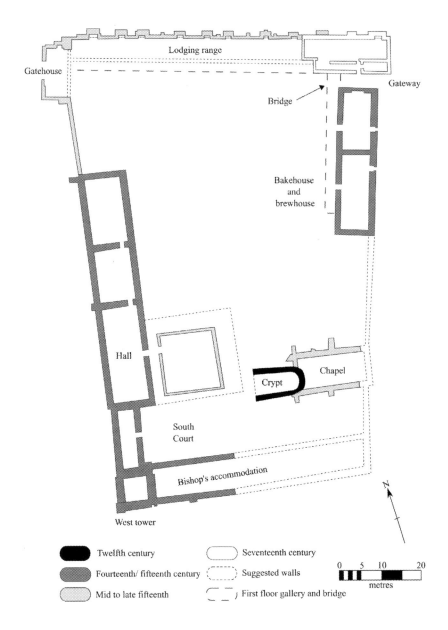

FIG. 41 PLAN OF BISHOP'S WALTHAM PALACE. THE APPROXIMATE POSITIONS OF THE GALLERY AND BRIDGE HAVE BEEN INDICATED. THE BRIDGE CONNECTED THE FIRST FLOOR OF THE LODGING RANGE TO THE FIRST FLOOR OF THE BAKE-BREWHOUSE. THE DISTANCE BETWEEN THE LODGING RANGE AND THE BISHOP'S ACCOMMODATION IN THE SOUTH COURTYARD CAN BE SEEN, SUGGESTING THAT SOCIAL DISTANCE BETWEEN LORD AND RETAINER WAS REPRESENTED THROUGH SPACE AND THE SENSES.

1447, during which period he added a third floor to the west tower. The corner of a decorated fireplace lintel can be seen in the remaining part of this floor, hinting at the opulence of the small south courtyard. At the other end of the house, he added a gatehouse, the cloisters at the east of the hall, and a new chapel above the twelfth-century crypt. Although less of his work has survived, Beaufort's additions created a multi-courtyard, palatial house typical of the mid-fifteenth century, and included an extensive lodging range.

The lodging range was located on the north range of the site, running from Beaufort's western gatehouse to a smaller gateway at the east. The lodging range remains as intermittent flint foundations with the east end incorporated into a seventeenth-century farmhouse (Figure 40). This has preserved elements of a chimney stack, revealing that these were built of brick on the flint foundations on the northern, external elevation. The remainder of the range surrounding the chimney stack was timber-framed, filled in with wattle and daub.[52] The entrance to each room was on the southern elevation, not centrally positioned but to the east side, on both the ground and first floors. This would have displayed a uniform façade, as seen on other examples of lodging ranges.

The number of extant fireplaces indicate there were eleven rooms with one further fireplace at the west end probably providing heat to the room within the western gatehouse. The backs of the fireboxes were decorated with thin, diaper-pattern brickwork, but no jambs or lintels survive. There is no evidence for garderobes here; these often appear on the rear wall in other lodging ranges. This is unlikely to be due to the lack of fabric remaining, as an outshot for a garderobe tower would usually be perceptible in the foundations. Therefore chamber pots may have been used. This is particularly unusual as the range is located beside the moat, therefore it would have been relatively easy to create garderobes which expelled into the water. First-floor fireplaces would have been directly above the ground-floor counterparts, suggesting the same number of rooms, with the same provisions. As with other examples of lodging ranges, these first-floor rooms were of slightly higher status. The remains of a low-pitch rafter in the timber framing of the farmhouse indicates a higher ceiling height.

The rooms on the ground floor were accessed directly from the courtyard while those on the first floor opened on to a gallery. The gallery ran along the southern elevation of the lodging range then continued to the bake-brewhouse, which was located perpendicular to the lodging range; thus a bridge extended over the narrow space indicated in Figure 41. The bake-

---

52   R. Warmington, 'Beaufort's Range of Lodgings', in John Hare, 'Bishop's Waltham Palace', *Archaeological Journal*, 145 (1988), pp. 246–51, at p. 246.

brewhouse range was on the eastern side of the courtyard, stretching north–south. It predated the lodging range; however, it was altered when the latter was built next to it. Contemporary with the construction of the bake-brewhouse were two doors on the east-facing elevation and two on the west-facing, the latter two accessible from the courtyard (and just seen in Figure 40). When the lodging range was built, the doors on the west-facing elevation were lowered, and a first floor was inserted, while the east-facing doors remained at their original level. This adaptation allowed the gallery from the lodging range to connect to the first-floor room in the service range. The first floor of the bake-brewhouse may have been a large dormitory, as suggested by the fireplace within.

LODGING RANGES AND SOCIAL DISTANCE

The spatial configuration of lodging ranges shows that representing social distance was a consideration in their construction. At Bishop's Waltham the lodging range was located at the opposite end of the multi-courtyard complex from Beaufort's chambers (Figure 41). His accommodation opened from a small courtyard located at the southern extent of the house, which could be considered the most 'inner' courtyard. The retainers' lodging range was located in the north courtyard. The space between them represented their social difference. Space equated social distance here, as it did at Dartington and Haddon, but was exaggerated through the presence of multiple courtyards. While the majority of the walls within the complex are lost, there was at least a cloister and another courtyard, which contained the chapel, between the lodging range and Beaufort's accommodation. Therefore the social distance was reinforced by a lack of communication between the spaces.

As we know from the features of the lodging ranges, retainers were mid-ranking in the household hierarchy. Therefore there was social distance between these individuals and lower-status household members. How was this represented? Livery and retainer badges would set them apart from kitchen staff or those working the land, and the position of lodging ranges shows that their social distance was also spatially represented. At Bishop's Waltham, the lodging range was in the same courtyard as the bake-brewhouse. Those who worked in the services may have lived there, close to their place of work, and there seems to have been further accommodation in the form of a dormitory on the first floor. Therefore, within the one courtyard, there were at least three different types of accommodation, each with different provisions and status. Despite being grouped in one courtyard, the social distance between the occupants was clear. The space *within* each courtyard, not only *between* them, contributed to the representation of social distance.

At Bishop's Waltham the construction of a bridge allowed social distance to be represented between retainers and lower-status household members (Figure 41). Those in the lodging range and those living above the bake-brewhouse were, to a degree, grouped together through the inclusion of the bridge, stretching over the eastern gateway. This separated them, as a collective, from those working and probably sleeping in the service rooms below. While it is likely that the space above the bake-brewhouse was a dormitory, it may have been a mess hall for the retainers. Beaufort's household was substantial, so the retainers may have dined outside the main hall. There is tentative evidence for parallels in other great houses with lodging ranges, such as Gainsborough, and the purpose of the mess hall was to provide retainers with their own space for dining, instilling their social distance from the lord, and from lower-status household members, while reinforcing a collective identity. A mess hall illustrated the dynamic tug-of-war in the display of social distance. It would have set the retainers apart as being clearly not of such high status as the lord, but above the more numerous low-status household members.

The position of lodging ranges within the courtyard system created two clear spatial representations of social distance: between the lord and the retainer, and between the retainer and lower-status household members. This might create a visualisation in our minds of the great house as a tripartite system with a strong sense of vertical association, as discussed in Chapter 2.[53] This is a sterile understanding of a space where humans lived, and when we delve further into to the spatial configuration of lodging ranges we see that social distance is more convoluted and messier than that. Space around lodging ranges was manipulated not only to create social distance between retainers and others but between the retainers themselves.

One way in which social distance was created between retainers was through the spatial relationship between the lodging range and hall. At Middleham, the retainers living in the west range were grouped together, separated from other household members, but sub-divided into those who lived on the ground floor and those on the first. Those who lived on the ground floor walked around the keep and up the staircase to the hall on the east side of the keep (Figure 42). Those living on the first floor used the bridge from the garderobe tower to the keep (Figure 43). Reducing the distance to the hall indicates the higher status of the occupants of the first floor, and this is supported by larger windows in these rooms. While the difference between 5 metres and 70 metres is not great, this space had a social meaning. The bridge provided access to a space which may have

---

[53] Christine Carpenter, *Locality and Polity: A Study of Warwickshire Landed Society, 1401-1499* (Cambridge, 1992); McKelvie, *Bastard*.

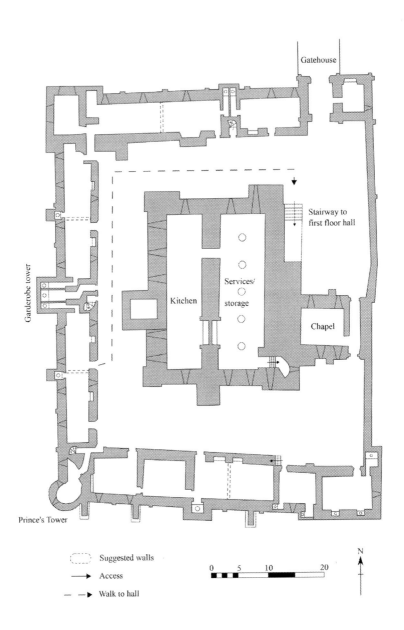

FIG. 42 GROUND-FLOOR PLAN OF MIDDLEHAM CASTLE. ACCESS TO THE HALL FROM THE LODGING RANGE IS INDICATED: THIS INVOLVED WALKING AROUND THE KEEP AND THROUGH THE COURTYARD BEFORE ASCENDING A FLIGHT OF STAIRS. THIS IS A CRUCIAL DISTINCTION WHEN COMPARED TO THE FIRST-FLOOR ACCESS SHOWN IN FIGURE 43.

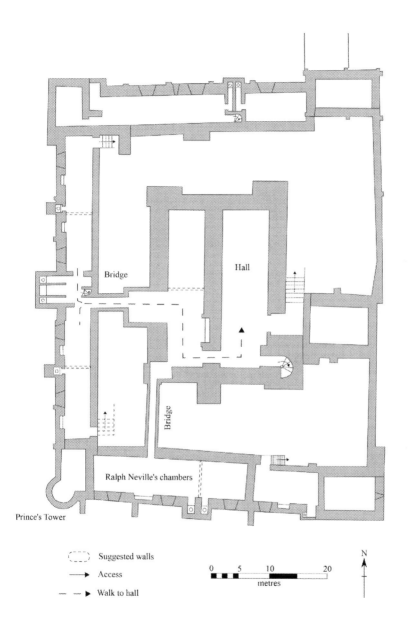

FIG. 43 FIRST-FLOOR PLAN OF MIDDLEHAM CASTLE. THE CENTRAL ROOMS OF THE LODGING RANGE WERE CONNECTED TO THE KEEP VIA A BRIDGE THAT ALLOWED RETAINERS TO ACCESS THE HALL. THIS DIFFERENCE WAS EXPERIENCED NOT ONLY IN DISTANCE BUT THROUGH SENSORY PERCEPTIONS.

been a chamber of presence, suggesting the retainers with access engaged in discussions with the lord outside the hall. Each group of retainers entered the hall from a different door: those living on the ground floor entered via the east and those from the bridge from the west. Entering the hall by the same door as the lord would not have gone unnoticed by those who did not have this privilege. Once again, we return to the relational aspect of social distance: the first-floor retainers were socially distant from the ground-floor retainers, while both groups were perceived as socially distant from those altogether forbidden to dine in the hall.

The second aspect of the bridge's role in representing social distance is more sensory in nature. The bridge divided the space into two segments, each with different sensory experiences. The first-floor retainers were somewhat removed from the noise, smells and activities of the courtyard. This reinforced the social distance between them and those retainers who walked through and lived beside the sounds and smells of the courtyard. Sounds in the medieval period were intertwined with identity and, in a world quieter than ours today, any noise made a strong impression on the listener.[54] Uncontrolled noise was associated with the devil and madness; therefore silence was preferred for its connection to order and sanctity.[55] As with seeing in the medieval period, which was akin to a tangible experience, smelling, as argued by Emma Wells, was more active than we consider it today.[56] Scent was a point of contact and, in the ecclesiastic context, proof of a material presence and existence.[57]

Furthermore, there were different visual experiences. The first-floor retainers were less visible to others when using the bridge and were therefore seen less frequently by lower-status people. This spatial and visual separation created fewer opportunities for personal interaction between the first-floor and ground-floor retainers and, indeed, other household members in the courtyard. The bridge also provided a degree of comfort. The putlog holes in Middleham's keep indicate that the bridge to the lodging range was covered, partially or fully. Similarly, at Bishop's Waltham, the timber remains indicate the use of a pentice running along the southern

---

54 Stephen Mileson, 'Sound and Landscape', in Christopher Gerrard and Alejandra Gutiérrez (eds), *The Oxford Handbook of Later Medieval Archaeology in Britain* (Oxford, 2018), pp. 713–728, at p. 714.
55 Christopher Woolgar, *The Senses in Late Medieval England* (New Haven, 2006), pp. 68, 75; Mileson, 'Sound' p. 714.
56 Emma Wells, 'Overview: The Medieval Senses', in Christopher Gerrard and Alejandra Gutiérrez (eds), *The Oxford Handbook of Later Medieval Archaeology in Britain* (Oxford, 2018), pp. 681–98, at p. 681.
57 Wells, 'Senses'; see also, C. Classen, D. Howes and A. Synnott, *Aroma: The Cultural History of Smell* (Abingdon, 1994); S. A. Harvey, *Scenting Salvation* (Berkeley, 2006).

elevation of the first floor. These were further ways of representing social distance: they provided a degree of comfort by protecting users from the elements. A difference was created between those working in or walking through the elements to the hall, and those not. A pentice is usually open-framed, with intermittent supports and spaces between. At Middleham, the bridge may also have been open framed; either way, the open frames allowed those permitted to use the high-status features to be seen.

Being seen in the medieval period created a connection between the viewer and the viewed.[58] The lord and lady were seen only at certain times and in certain circumstances. The lady's apartments have been considered the most 'hidden' in the great house: that is, they could not be accessed without permission, or stumbled upon easily, reflecting her control over when she could be seen.[59] By being viewed rarely, social distance was created between her and all others.[60] Her handmaids would have spent time with her regularly and travelled with her: these roles were high-status in comparison to the servants in the kitchen, for example, who would have rarely seen her.[61]

Further consideration of the bridges at Middleham and Bishop's Waltham shows that being seen may have heightened the retainers' social distance from others rather than diminished it. Those with access to the bridge and gallery were seen from below as they made use of a feature which indicated their status as being higher than that of those viewing them. They were viewed less frequently on the same level, literally and metaphorically, by those who occupied the ground floor in both ranges. When they were seen, it was through the prism of social distance. It was not by chance that the lower-status staff would have to look *up* to catch a glimpse of the retainers using the bridge. Medieval writers, including Roger Bacon and St Bernard in the twelfth century, argued that only through presentation in front of one's eyes – that is, seeing something for oneself – could truth and accuracy be revealed.[62] Therefore, when the ground-floor retainers saw the first-floor retainers using the bridge, it established the latter's place as truly above them in the social hierarchy.

---

58 Weikert, *Authority*, p. 90; Simon Roffey, 'The Medieval Afterlife', in Christopher Gerrard and Alejandra Gutiérrez (eds), *The Oxford Handbook of Later Medieval Archaeology in Britain* (Oxford, 2018), pp. 868–86, at p. 877.
59 Gilchrist, *Religious*; Amanda Richardson, 'Gender and Space in the Later Middle Ages: past, present, and future routes', in Christopher Gerrard and Alejandra Gutiérrez (eds), *The Oxford Handbook of Later Medieval Archaeology in Britain* (Oxford, 2018), pp. 805–18, at p. 813.
60 Richardson, 'Corridors'.
61 Roberta Gilchrist, *Gender and Archaeology: Contesting the Past* (Abingdon, 1999).
62 Wells, 'Senses', p. 691; Michael Camille, *Gothic Art* (London, 1996).

What is particularly interesting about the use of bridges is the creation of social distance in a small space. This is a different approach to representing social distance than those discussed previously, such as the double courtyard or the hall, where spatial distance equated to social distance. Instead, at Middleham and Bishop's Waltham, chasms of social distance were created between those in close proximity, even just metres apart.

The use of bridges was no doubt due to the multi-phase nature of both Middleham Castle and Bishop's Waltham Palace. New elements were added, adapted and adjusted over centuries, with each house expanding upwards and outwards to accommodate the requirements of the late medieval lords.[63] When Neville and Beaufort added lodging ranges, they were physically constrained by the space which was available to them: Middleham had an earlier curtain wall surrounded by a moat, and Bishop's Waltham was within a curated, moated landscape. It is tempting, therefore, to minimise the bridges as representations of social distance and consider them implicit or less impactful. They could be viewed as less emphatic representations of social distance than the double-courtyard plan, almost ubiquitous in late medieval great houses built on virgin sites. Were Neville and Beaufort simply making the most of an imperfect situation? This was not the case: in fact, it would be folly to assume that social distance was not as clearly represented in a small space or multi-phase house. This is clear when the multi-phase sites are compared with one built anew.

Wingfield Manor comprised two architecturally, spatially and socially different ranges for household accommodation. The east range of the outer courtyard contained at least two dormitories, each with one garderobe and rebates for beds. The west range of the inner courtyard demonstrated provisions for higher-status occupants, such as individual garderobes and doors per room. These ranges were separated by the cross-range, representing spatially the social distance between the groups living within each. As Cromwell built his house anew, having demolished Swyllington's house when he gained ownership, he had the freedom of great, even unlimited space. With this, he could distance spatially those who were different socially from one another. This dispersed approach to demonstrating social distance incorporated many of the elements perceived at Middleham and Bishop's Waltham. The occupants of Cromwell's inner courtyard were not visible to those living in the lower-status range. They were hidden until such times that they would meet, which may have been in the hall where their status was demarcated by their seating.

---

63 Woolgar, *Household*, p. 46; Phillip Dixon and Beryl Lott, 'The Courtyard and the Tower', *Journal of the British Archaeological Association*, 146 (1993), 93–101.

This meant they were seen at a time when their status was clear – much like the retainers being seen while crossing the bridge at either Middleham or Bishops' Waltham. Cromwell's high-status retainers were separated from the noises, smells and activities of the lower courtyard, as the first-floor retainers at Middleham were distinct from the same in the space below their bridge. The representation of social distance is multi-threaded and relational: no one element sets a social group in place. It was a combination of livery, spatial demonstration, retainer badges, and non-physical representations such as who should approach whom, who could see whom, what sights and smells were experienced, all created and reinforced through lived experience.

SOCIAL DISTANCE THROUGHOUT THE HOUSE

The examples demonstrate that the position of a lodging range was in part determined by the desire to represent social distance. The spatial configuration within the great house shows that there was a wish to exhibit the social difference between retainers, their lord, lower-status household members and between groups of retainers themselves. In some great houses, spatial connections between lodging ranges and other buildings indicate further layers of social distance between groups.

Gatehouses are another feature of late medieval great houses, as seen at Middleham and Bishop's Waltham. At first glance a gatehouse appears to be a symbol of defence, suggesting that hidden behind was an impenetrable fortress. However, a number of clues indicate that defence was not a priority: at Bishop's Waltham, for example, to the left of the east gateway there were two doors leading into the bake-brewhouse. Instead, a gatehouse demonstrated the identity of the lord and acted as a social barrier to those who were not part of the household. The lack of visibility beyond the gatehouse entrenched the separation between those who could easily enter and those who could not. Essentially, a gateway can be considered a physical manifestation of social distance.

At Bishop's Waltham the western gatehouse was not enormous as at Middleham, but it was constructed of red brick, which was a fashionable material in the mid-fifteenth century. The gatehouse led directly into the outer courtyard with the long lodging range displayed on the left-hand side. This close spatial relationship is shown in a number of great houses with lodging ranges. At Amberley Castle, Sussex, the fourteenth-century lodging range was directly opposite the gatehouse on the other side of a relatively small courtyard. The courtyard at Amberley is so small that it was probably free of ancillary buildings, allowing the lodging range to be perceived immediately by visitors. This manipulation of space reveals another representation of social distance: that between a visitor and the lord. It appears that all visitors to the great house were to be made aware of the lodging ranges, and their visibility as a guest entered the house was a crucial consideration in the configuration. As they viewed the lodging range, and understood its purpose of housing retainers, a visitor would have their social distance from the lord impressed upon them.

The lodging range at Amberley was located in an unusual position, not replicated in other great houses: between services at the low end of the hall. It was located beside a protruding kitchen at the north-east and an oven at the south-west. The principle of Occam's razor suggests that the simplest explanation is correct; which in this case means we would assume a functional relationship between service rooms and the accommodation in close proximity. For example, a room above stables was often occupied by the stable hands, and a room in the gatehouse was generally for the porter. However, much of the narrative here has stressed the relatively high status of lodging ranges and people who lived therein. As with all lodging ranges, those at Amberley demonstrated grandeur (see Figure 17). The garderobe tower, comprising four garderobes, each with an individual entrance, indicates the position of the partitions creating separate rooms. The two ground-floor rooms had cruciform windows with huge splays, set beside fireplaces with flat monolithic lintels. On the first floor the pattern was repeated, but each feature hinted at a higher-status space. The fireplaces had segmental arches while the windows were large and ornate, with two trefoil-headed lights and an open quatrefoil in the spandrel.

The distinct status of the rooms jars with their physical position between the service rooms. The explanation lies in the physical restrictions of a multi-phase house situated upon a natural mound. The early to mid-fourteenth century hall was built perpendicular to an earlier thirteenth-century hall located to the south-east of the mound. The second hall was built to utilise the first hall as a receiving chamber or parlour, as it connected to the bishop's apartments, which continued to be in the same location throughout the house's use. The surrounding ranges were constructed in the late fourteenth century, post-dating both halls. Therefore the position of all later elements was determined by the location of the earlier hall. For example, the high end of the second hall was at the south, to connect to the first hall. To adhere to the configuration of a medieval hall, the low end with kitchen, buttery and pantry was at the opposing, northern end; therefore the services had to be located here. Yet why was the lodging range positioned in between the services? Only by being situated there could it be viewed instantly upon entering the house. If it were in the west or south range of the courtyard, it would be somewhat hidden from the visitor's view. It appears that the visibility of the range was crucial, and took precedence over removing retainers from lower-status service spaces. There are several houses discussed here in which the hall was opposite the gatehouse, and the impact of placing either lodging range or hall in this position was the same: an indication of social distance between lord and guest. At Amberley, there was ingenuity and compromise in the planning to achieve the desired visual impact.

The spatial connection between lodging ranges and services at Amberley allows some comparison with Bishop's Waltham. Bridges were used at Bishop's Waltham to create social distance between the occupants of the lodging range and those working in the ground floor of the bake-brewhouse, whereas at Amberley, occupants of the lodging range and those working in the services worked side-by-side and probably lived side-by-side. This reinforces the understanding of social distance as multi-stranded: there were numerous representations alongside each other.

There was rarely a direct relationship between a lodging range and a chapel, but Cotehele House, Cornwall, is an exception. In this multi-courtyard house, the Retainers' Court was added to the earlier Hall Court, extending south-west from the chapel range. Access to the chapel for the Edgecumbe family was from the parlour in the Hall Court, while there was a secondary door leading from the Retainers' Court. This spatial representation of social distance was similar to that seen in the hall, with a high and low end of the chapel. A small window on the Retainers' Court side of the chapel indicates that social distance extended beyond its walls. Too small and low to allow in any light, yet decorated with a hood moulding and label stops, its function was to allow those not permitted into the chapel to listen to the service. This indicates another sensory demonstration of social distance: what one was permitted to hear and see represented one's place in the social hierarchy.

CONCLUSION

As with all buildings, lodging ranges were built with purpose. They were created for use as accommodation but their functions were somewhat more complex than that. They were representations of social distance between retainers and the lord, retainers and lower-status household members, and between the retainers themselves. They were built to manipulate space and maintain social distance between a lord and a visitor to the great house. Each example of a lodging range did this in a different way, as each great house was unique. However, I want to steer away from separating late medieval great houses from one another. Instead we can accept their architectural uniqueness but see the similarities which connect them. Anthony Emery described the development of Middleham as a transformation from a 'castle into a palace-fortress',[64] but this term has been avoided here as it separates Middleham from other great houses, such as Bishop's Waltham. Indeed, Middleham was a palatial house with token features of defence. However, its architecture and spatial configuration created social distance between the lord and visitors, between different ranks of retainers, and between the household and those from the rest of the estate. This shaped how people experienced living in and visiting the great house, meaning that to medieval society these houses were much more similar than they seem to us today. Despite different appearances, Middleham is comparable to the great houses that had a protracted plan. You would be forgiven, however, for considering those built at virgin sites, such as Dartington or Wingfield, as more ordered or less messy in plan than the multi-phase Middleham and Bishop's Waltham, but this viewpoint only appears when we focus on the buildings' fabric. When we include space in our reading of a great house, we see the parallels of order and control being administered through the representation of social distance, with lodging ranges contributing to this. Elites were able to create the ideal house even when earlier constructions prohibited the creation of the commonplace double-courtyard plan.

Regardless of whether a great house was built anew or added to over centuries, social distance was represented spatially or through sensory experiences. The addition of bridges at Middleham created a shorter access route, while removing the sensory experience of the courtyard for some retainers. Instead, members of the select group were viewed from below, their status spatially and literally above others. At Bishop's Waltham the bake-brewhouse doors were lowered and the bridge added to connect the first floor to the neighbouring lodging range. This horizontally bisected the service range, denoting a social distinction between those on the ground floor and the first floor. In the physically constrained houses there were ingenious ways to demonstrate social difference. These methods could be considered as compromises in comparison to the great houses built with vast spaces demonstrating social distance, but if they are considered compromises, this should not be extended to considering these representations of social distance as less impactful than others. Rather, the desire for displaying social distance overcame any restrictions imposed by an earlier construction, such as the thirteenth-century curtain wall at Middleham. Regardless of how social distance was represented, the impacts were the same. They controlled what could be heard, smelt, seen and, crucially, who could be seen; they altered movement, access, scope for interaction, and comfort. Therefore representing social distance was a key feature in the lived experience of the late medieval great house.

64 Emery, *Greater Medieval Houses*, Vol. 2, p. 368.

The plethora of ways in which social distance was represented in the great house suggests a social rigidity at odds with the permeability of the middle and upper echelons of late medieval society. Such spatial configurations may have provided structure and control within society, but we must wonder if this encouraged competition and discontent between the social ranks and rival retinues.

We see a tension between what we decipher in the great house: rigidity and flexibility, the lords' identity and the retainers', the group and the individual. It must be remembered, however, that these were not binaries or mutually exclusive but co-existed alongside one another, ebbing and flowing in different circumstances.

ENVOI: NARRATIVES IN STONE AND SPACE

Medieval architecture was imbued with individual rationale and wider social norms. Each stone was a deliberate choice, whether it created a window of a precise size, demarcated a certain door or articulated a particular fireplace. This accumulation of form, and the space it divided, has been described as a building's architectural language. As with a textual source, architecture can be considered a snapshot of the society from which it derived as well as the composite individual decisions involved. When a building is examined – when the architectural language is read – it is an opportunity to decipher both society's ideals and each decision in its creation. This was one of the fundamental premises of this book: that the medieval fabric is the primary source material. A few other threads pertinent to my approach will be summarised here: in particular, the prioritisation of function over use; striving for greater granularity through deconstructing common terms such as status and identity; and embracing dynamism throughout evaluations, whether detecting dominant identities or assigning the functions of architectural forms.

This book has aimed to introduce fully the lodging ranges of the late medieval great house and consider the 'why': functions, uses and meanings. Within buildings archaeology the dominant focus has, until recently, been on their use. This focus influenced the methods and analyses used, resulting in a prioritisation of use over function, thus rendering the functions less explicit. This book centres the exploration of function over use: the reasons (beyond the utilitarian) why they were built in the places they were, in those particular forms. None the less, understanding the use of lodging ranges is a principal step in comprehending their functions. As such, it was established at the beginning of this book that lodging ranges were used as high-status accommodation, as evident in their architecture. This was not the conclusion of the analysis, but rather a foundation for exploring meanings and functions through spatial examination, architectural analysis and visuality. Through this lens it was revealed that lodging ranges had varying, multi-faceted, and even conflicting functions. These included displaying the retainers as a uniform collective of subordinates; acquiescing in the identities of retainers as individuals, each with a particular rank, agency, ownership and role; and promoting the lord's authority, social and financial capital, and permanence.

Identifying lodging ranges as accommodation provided an indication of the lived experience in the great house, but this designation contradicts, or even overwrites, our knowledge of the flexible use of space which occurred throughout the medieval period. Therefore a complete examination of the rooms, including the spatial ordering, was required. A number of key features of the architectural language pointed to the lodging ranges' use. Timber or stone partitions, and the duplication of features, revealed that the ranges were divided into rooms. Within each room the inclusion of garderobes, fireplaces, windows and access through individual doors indicated their use as accommodation, and indicated warm, well-lit and comfortable spaces. Comparing this degree of comfort to other types of accommodation supported the assertion that these rooms were considered to be of relatively high status in the late medieval period.

Evidence from Haddon Hall revealed that some rooms were further sub-divided. The exceptional survival of a timber screen indicated that each first-floor room there comprised two unequal-sized spaces. The accepted spatial ordering seen elsewhere in medieval buildings, such as inner and outer courtyards, and the hall's upper and low ends, was superimposed upon these spaces and evaluated alongside descriptions from earlier surveys. It was posited that the inner space may have been a bedchamber, primarily for sleeping, while the outer was an office, primarily for working.

It would be misleading to extrapolate this plan across all lodging ranges without careful consideration of each lodging range's social and architectural uniqueness. However, there were some instances in which the spatial ordering, layout of provisions and size of room allowed the tentative projection of a similar use of space. The overall homogeneity across examples of lodging ranges, even without other intact timber screens, allowed a confident deduction that the rooms were primarily used for sleeping and working, with other secondary uses as needed.

The identification of such uses revealed that lodging ranges were part of a wider late medieval movement in which space was becoming compartmentalised and specialised. Sleeping was emerging as an activity for which separation from others was desired, although the spaces were not what we would now consider private sleeping quarters. The separation of the bedchambers in the lodging ranges is indicative of this shift in social expectations towards the privacy which emerged later. Similarly, the office was a specialised space, behind the individual door and separated from, but adjoining, the bedchamber, drawing comparisons with a hall or parlour. Adding this granularity to the use of the rooms reinforced our understanding of the retainers. They were not unruly soldiers who would leave their lord for a better pay day; they were mid- to high-ranking household members with roles essential to the running of the house. The discussion of the social bonds, in addition to the political and financial relationships, between lord and retainer suggested that other activities, such as playing at dice and joining the lord in hunts, were also part of the retainer's role. This aided the appraisal of their permanence in the great house: they were probably in attendance when the lord was present, which might have been for several months at a time. As such, their role was important in understanding this facet of their identity, but they should not be considered solely in terms of their relationship with their lord. The rooms were probably spaces for socialising, meeting with other staff, or hosting the retainer's family at times. This reinforced the high-status description initially bestowed on the lodging range based on the provisions; that is, the variety of uses for the rooms, and the types of usage, further demonstrated that lodging ranges were high-status spaces.

Just as the lodging ranges' use was written in their stones, so, too, their function could be read. Once the high-status character of lodging ranges had been determined, it was possible to extend this to the occupants; that is, the use as high-status spaces translated to the function of representing the retainer's status. This could have been somewhat naïve and transactional, and therefore unsatisfactory, without contextualisation, so it was explored through an explanation of the lived experience and without reductive use of status. In the same way in which I aimed to dissect lodging ranges into use, functions and meanings, I have similarly argued for a faceted evaluation of identity. We see that status was a facet of the medieval retainer's identity, alongside privacy, ownership, independence and authority; these were detected within the architecture, and particularly evidenced by the individual doors. Medieval privacy was the ability to isolate oneself from others, and the individual doors were employed to create separation from the majority, if not all, of the household: they were used to enact privacy. Doors were both the physical barriers creating separation between people yet they were also full of meaning. The ability to separate oneself required not only the physical capacity to do so, but the social capacity too; that is, privacy was determined by social status. So the door was a physical representation of the status of the occupant – a status which permitted privacy. It also represented social distance, the intangible difference between people, particularly between those who could enter and who could not. We can consider, therefore, the individual door as an embodiment of these facets of identity: hints of privacy in its medieval conception, authority over the space beyond the door, and independence from others. Identifying specific facets of individual identity further supported the reading of lodging ranges as high-status accommodation. This was crucial for the later discussion on the juxtaposition of these identities with the overall control held by the head of the household.

The significance of determining the relative social status of the retainers was reflected in the definition of lodging ranges and coining the typology of collective-living buildings. I stated earlier that typologies are not without limitations. When they *are* useful is when their parameters are clearly set, and can be adhered to or changed by the next scholar, to suit the purpose of a particular discussion. I sought to set the parameters of lodging ranges here in order to highlight their specificity and their collective rather than communal character: a lodging range housed a group, made up of individuals with different social ranks, jobs and identities, in a series of low-occupancy rooms. The lodging ranges were imbued with both of these identities; that is, the architecture reflected both togetherness and individualism. Acknowledging this required a term other than 'communal', since describing them as communal accommodation would restrict our understanding and awareness of these contrasting identities. Collectivity accommodates both identities and allows this duality to exist.

The individual doors were central to identifying collective living, as these were not present in communal spaces such as dormitories, and it was important to accentuate this distinction, due to the use of both types of space throughout the late medieval period. The presence in the great houses of both lodging ranges, with a door per room, and dormitories, with a single door, such as at Bishop's Waltham Palace, allowed a clear deduction of the higher status of the former. Distinguishing collective from communal was also important due to the temporal shift from one to another, since dormitories were a particularly prevalent form of accommodation prior to the construction of lodging ranges. As discussed, lodging ranges emerged in the plan of the great house with little evidence of a development towards them, unlike other types of collective-living buildings which show a development in their architectural and archaeological remains. The lack of proto-lodging ranges and the comparison with vicarial and collegiate ranges suggests that dormitories were used by staff as the household grew. It was reasoned that collective-living buildings are evidential of the wider changes within late medieval society's relationship to space: the emergence of something akin to privacy, robust displays of social distance, and specialisation of space.

The parallels between lodging ranges and other types of collective-living buildings, particularly collegiate and vicarial ranges, were identified, including their high-status provisions, comparatively small rooms and inclusion as part of a wider household, be it secular, academic or ecclesiastical. All these ranges were roughly contemporaneous, indicating the emergence of a distinct mid-ranking group with strong horizontal identities: the middling sort. By including the other ranges in the discussion, it became clear that the middling sort's status demanded acquiescence in these emerging ideals regarding social distance and privacy. Rather than living in dormitories, as they had in earlier decades, they now lived in much smaller groups. In colleges there were a handful of fellows per room, while in vicarial ranges the *cubiculi* or houses were occupied by individuals. It is not clear how many people occupied each room within a lodging range, and I have not tried to assign a definitive number. The evidence from Caister Castle revealed that some rooms may have been occupied by single retainers at least some of the time. This cannot be assumed for other houses, as it was dependent on the plan of the house, wealth of the lord, number of retainers, number of guests at that time, and so on. While rooms in the great house were becoming increasingly specialised, each was still flexible in its use, potentially housing more people at certain times of the year, especially during festivities. Therefore an understanding of lodging ranges' low occupancy levels, regardless of actual numbers per room, revealed a great deal about the retainers, households and society. It was apparent that the identities of retainers, and indeed occupants across the collective-living ranges, were no longer appropriately reflected in dormitories: individualism was emerging from the collective and growing in importance. Despite this, each of these groups were under the jurisdiction of a college master, canon or lord, so their collective, subservient identity was equally ever-present, as the terminology indicates.

Extending the examination of the lodging ranges' architecture to include comparison with other collective-living buildings supported the identification of high-status spaces for sleeping and working and their function as a display of identities, including status, authority and individualism. This assessment allowed for further granularity to be introduced. A consideration of Caister Castle's inventories allowed possible names and jobs to be assigned to retainers in the lodging ranges there. We saw that the retainers had mid- to high-ranking jobs within the household, prompting further movement away from the militaristic view of retainers and a war-contingent relationship with their lord. The documentary evidence suggested that lodging ranges were occupied by educated men of gentry level or higher in the social hierarchy, but an awareness of the entrenched limitations of contemporary documents, particularly the gender partiality, is essential. Furthermore, it was accepted that a name and job are not sole representations of an identity. Rather, the inclusion of Caister's inventories helped to assign further layers to the retainers, such as their social relationship with the lord, and assisted complexification of the household's structure in a step away from a simplistic tripartite hierarchy.

Returning to the duality embedded in collectivity, the term was chosen to show that the indications of individualism were evident almost in spite of each person's inclusion in the wider retinue and household. There was a strong collective identity embedded in the retainers' lived experience, and examination of the lodging ranges' architecture revealed the ways in which this was displayed. Uniform façades were identified as a consistent feature of lodging ranges and consequently included in their definition. The components of consistency, repetition, symmetry and pairing created an overall display of sameness and a distinct uniformity, associated more usually with Renaissance houses rather than medieval buildings. This allowed those ideals which were fundamental to the post-medieval house to be drawn into the medieval period, such as the desire to conceal the configuration of a household from outside. This concealment was evident at Gainsborough Hall, in which three different room-types were juxtaposed against the overtly uniform external elevation; the latter belied any indication of the variation within. As with the retainers, there was a contrast between the individual identities which were present, but hidden from view, and the visible sameness on the outside. The individual and collective identities were both represented but the latter disguised, even veiled, the former. Individualism was permitted, but enforced collectivity was of utmost importance. The awareness of yet another meaning written into the fabric of the lodging ranges allowed acknowledgement of the fact that the identities on display might be, and indeed in lodging ranges were, contrasting and even contradictory.

This discussion reintroduced bastard feudalism and the horizontal identities it created through indentures, displays of livery, and retainer badges. Just as these were representations of the feudal relationship, so too were lodging ranges. Livery, retainer badges and indentures were broadly the same across the retinue, with varying quality, materials or descriptions based on individual role and status. The façades of lodging ranges displayed sameness in an equally overt way, yet they too had variations to reflect the inner hierarchy. This discussion placed lodging ranges firmly among the elements of bastard feudalism.

At the apex of the bastard feudal relationship was the lord. They placed a horizontal and collective identity upon the group of individuals in their retinue in order to unify them and make them uniform. It was supposed that this intimated an erasure of those identities discussed previously: an elimination of each retainer's individualism. The lord's position of dominance and control suggested a removal of the retainer's authority over space or independence from others: after all, each retainer was in the lord's house. I have argued that they were in fact in equilibrium. One did not expunge the other; instead, they were dominant at different times of the lived experience. This complicates the duality of collective living by the incorporation of yet another identity: that of the lord. As the retainer moved through the great house, each of these identities fluctuated in their perceptibility: their subordination was perhaps more obvious in the hall than in their own office. There were clear parallels between the lodging range and retinue: just as the collective-living range comprised individual small rooms beneath one roof, so too the retinue encompassed people from different houses, brought together under the lord's banner.

It was posited that lords may have constructed uniform architecture to enforce a collective identity and even subdue any desire of over-mighty subjects. Even without an exaggerated modern perception of a late medieval society in which social mobility aided the toppling of the uppermost nobility, lords may still have wanted a solidified household hierarchy and its physical representation in order to strengthen their control. Demonstrating the collective identity certainly aimed to enhance the presentation of the lord's identity; it was one of many elements of the great house deliberately constructed to do so. Much like the retainers' identities, the lord's was multifaceted. The lodging ranges displayed the lord's wealth and social power, since both were needed to attract retainers and build the range, and to ensure the upkeep of both. The uniformity reinforced these facets by ensuring that perceptions of retainers' individuality did not dominate, and instead the lord's control over the group was explicitly displayed. The sameness instilled through the architecture was passed on to the retainers to identify them as household members, emphasising their service over their individuality.

Considering the display of the lord's identity through lodging ranges allowed a detection of the wider theatre of display; that is, how each and every element of the great house was precisely constructed to display identities. Turning the discussion from those who had their identity imposed upon them to those who constructed their own does not mean that some identities were less contrived and distorted than others. The great house was not created as an accurate portrayal of identity; rather, it was a communication of a *desired* identity. By examining the experience of a visitor to the great house, and their passage from gatehouse to hall, it can be seen that the display of the lord's manipulated identity was omnipresent, with lodging ranges having an especially significant role.

Exploring the spatial organisation of lodging ranges revealed that their position in the great house was carefully curated so that they were on display to visitors. In some instances, such as at Thornbury Castle, the journey towards the hall required visitors to turn towards the lodging range, creating a visual awareness of the lord's retinue. At Amberley Castle the lodging range was front and centre when one entered through the gatehouse, demanding to be noticed upon arrival. The lodging range as the focus of attention was emphasised by the position of the hall, which, in some instances, was hidden from view. This augmented attention towards that which could be seen and, although there were different layouts in each great house, the lodging range was always on display. This added another layer to our understanding of a lord's identity; they had complete control over those visiting the house. This control was in addition to the status, wealth and authority communicated to the medieval audience through the lodging range.

It was evident that the uniformity of lodging ranges enhanced these facets of the lord's identity. The case studies showed that architectural deceptions were employed to do so: in particular, the façades' uniformity created visual illusions. Repetition denied the viewer an accurate observation of the features, cheating the eyes to see more doors and windows. This exaggerated the length of the range to the viewer, and the illusion was then bolstered by further architectural tools, such as tapering or expanding courtyards, which embellished further the extent of ranges. The effect was that the lodging ranges seemed endless as one walked towards the hall.

Returning to the analogy of architectural language, I must emphasise that these meanings were not written into the fabric for the buildings archaeologist: the encoded communication was for the contemporary audience. It was made clear that the medieval viewer comprehended the use of lodging ranges, as they were essentially homogeneous across great houses; that is, it was known that they accommodated retainers. The architectural illusions revealed that there was a deliberate attempt to exaggerate how many retainers the lord appeared to have within their command. Rather than viewing this as a display of military prowess, or a threat to ensure no violence occurred, it was a clear intention to exaggerate those facets of the lord's identity suggested earlier: control, status, authority and wealth. This in turn revealed that the lodging ranges' fabric and the space in and around it created a specific stage with the actors, and the roles they were to play, already in mind. Viewing the great house as a theatre assisted recognition of each element as a prop contributing to the overall narrative of the lord's desired identity, with the lodging range a principal character in the play.

The discussion of multiple, overlapping, contested and contrasting identities showed that each was performed. An identity was not bestowed or created to then remain static; instead, different facets took centre stage at different times and had to be enacted to exist. The bastard feudal relationship, the identity of being retained or being able to retain, was highly performative. Maintenance, for example, was in essence a playing-out of these identities in court, while the act of donning livery presented one as a retainer. Lodging ranges, as further products of feudal identities, can also be considered as performative. They were not solely a stage for further performances, but were elements of the lived experience that reinforced, enacted and contributed to identities. In particular, the individual door performed the retainer's identity. The physical and social ability to close the door was a performance of privacy. Allowing a guest in – or not – performed authority over space. If the steward of the household, or the lord, wanted access, then the retainer was performing a different facet of their identity: one of submission to social superiors. Individualism gave way to performances of collectivity when the retainer joined the retinue to travel with their lord or sat amongst peers in the hall. The household hierarchy would be performed in these instances through precedence and who could approach whom, or physically through the hall's seating plan. It was made clear that each person performed their own identity which shifted, for example, as they entered the hall, returned to the outer courtyard, or left the house clothed in livery. Similarly, a lord's identity was performed through their personal movements and actions. Considering the theatre of display, however, demonstrated that their identity was also performed through the actions of others, such as a guest moving within the house, or the retainer's activities.

The discussion on social distance pulled together much of what had been discussed, from identities and their representations to physical and sensory manifestations. It centred space rather than fabric, emphasising the spatial configuration of lodging ranges within the house. It was evident that were a number of social distinctions to be seen within the great house; it was not simply binary, high and low status, but rather a network of different identities that required perceptible displays. Social distance, therefore, was represented between the lord and retainers, retainers and lower-status staff; between the household and those beyond; between a lord and a guest; and between retainers themselves. Social distance and its representations were ubiquitous across the great house in all manner of displays beyond architecture and space. There was a considerable determination in ensuring social distance was displayed, with lodging ranges contributing to this in multiple tangible and intangible ways.

The sprawling plan regularly adopted in late medieval great houses meant that social distance was frequently represented through physical separation. It might be shown through the position of the lodging ranges in a separate courtyard from the lord's accommodation, allowing the physical distance between these spaces to equate to the social distance between their occupants. This could be exaggerated when there were many courtyards, as at Bishop's Waltham Palace. As well as physical distance there was a sensory dimension to this: the lack of visibility reinforced the social distance between those social strata. In other instances, the space within the courtyard represented social distance. This was also often represented physically, through smaller or larger rooms, restricted access to spaces, or different provisions in the rooms, though the variations might be barely perceptible from outside the range. For example, the provision or absence of garderobes at Haddon Hall created a social distance between retainers on the ground floor and those on the first, but this was not evident from outside the rooms. The representations of social distance across lodging ranges and across the rooms within them correlated to displays of identity elsewhere in the retinue. Livery was graded according to status, with expensive coloured furs reserved for higher-status retainers; similarly, retainer badges could be made of precious metal, alloy or fustian cloth. This showed how, from their accommodation in the lodging range to their seat in the hall, to the clothes they wore, to their passage through different spaces, all aspects of the retainer's life were curated in line with social distance and the correct displays of identity.

Access from different parts of the courtyard could be used to represent social distance within the lodging range, with Middleham Castle's lodging range clearly demonstrating this. The addition of a bridge from the lodging range's first floor to the keep created and maintained social distance between the ground- and first-floor retainers. This had an obvious physical dimension, but that was only one element of how the social distance was experienced; sensory experiences further contributed to maintaining the distinction. The separation from the courtyard's noise, smells and activities, by being literally placed above them, permitted the first-floor retainers social distance and reinforced their distinction from those who were of a lower social status. The use of the first-floor bridges at both Bishop's Waltham and Middleham placed those retainers metaphorically and literally above the others. In addition, they introduced a crucial element of visuality. The use of pentices rather than fully-covered roofs meant others could see this performance of social distance when the bridges were crossed. It was clear that representing social distance was elemental to the lived experience – so much so that any spatial restrictions were overcome.

Although this book has focused on lodging ranges, it does not consider the remainder of the great house, or other houses, any less important; rather, this was an attempt to highlight that individual elements impacted on the medieval lived experience. And within each element there were more, seemingly minor, features which were of great importance. Stressing the significance of granularity at this point is important, since it impacted those who lived in the houses but also provides a lens through which we in the present can discern the meanings of lodging ranges and attain a greater understanding of medieval society.

The degree of subtlety employed in the construction of lodging ranges seems almost dissenting against the bigger-is-better mentality seen in other elements of the great house. These were not at odds as such but in tandem. Shifting our focus from the grand features to individual details allows the significance of each element to be highlighted. The lodging ranges' uniformity was overwhelming, and in contrast to the remainder of the architecture, yet it contained irregularities which reveal complex and overlapping messages in the stones. A single external stairway at Dartington Hall which ascended in the opposite direction to the other external stairways was an indication to the medieval audience that the retainers within that space were different from the others. Also at Dartington, the imitation of the four grouped doors in its four-light windows was not merely a pleasant architectural touch but created an architectural illusion. Focusing on such granularity demonstrated that each and every element was carefully selected: lodging ranges were deliberate constructions.

These physically minor details were impactful socially, and the extent of this impact was exposed when their spatial organisation was considered. The addition of a bridge at Middleham Castle imbued apparently identical rooms with utterly different meanings. Including consideration of smells, sight and noise indicated that the impact of each architectural feature was reinforced: they affected the lived experiences across the household. Understanding these individual, smaller-scale features was an essential insight to the present understanding of lodging ranges. In turn, however, it utterly shifted the understanding of the wider great house. Furthermore, the extension from the lodging ranges to shifts in wider society was evident, particularly that lodging ranges were indicative of changes in relation to the development of privacy, compartmentalisation of the house and the specialisation of spaces.

The meanings of lodging ranges have been at the forefront of this discussion, revealed through the reading of architecture and space. I have used the verb *read* when describing architecture of the great house, whether it is I who am reading or the medieval audience. It might be useful to extend this further, at the point of conclusion, to reading an entire book. If we consider the house a book to be read, then we should accept that there are overlapping meanings and interpretations that may not be the same for each reader. This is true of the lodging ranges as well. A lower-ranking guest might be intimidated by the explicit display of a retinue through an exaggerated range while a high-ranking guest could see the same range as an indication of excessive self-promotion. But just as the medieval viewers would read different interpretations from the fabric, so too will the modern archaeologist. I have included my interpretations in the hope these will be supported and contested in future examinations of lodging ranges, as well as considered and disputed in other buildings.

I described viewing medieval architecture as seeing a snapshot of time in the past. I alter that slightly here and suggest that it is a glimpse of an active production. Lodging ranges were dynamic and ever-changing. We perceived collective and individual identities taking it in turns to have centre stage, each with multiple facets beyond status, as well as various representations of social distance ebbing and flowing in and out of focus. Scrutinising the functions with the same rigour as the uses exposed the level of planning in the medieval patron's design. They created lodging ranges full of messages to inform, confuse, delight, terrify; this multiplicity of meanings is transcribed to the viewer through the careful consideration of each and every stone.

GLOSSARY

Aperture Opening in a wall, such as a door, window, arrow slit, or vent. It is composed of jambs at either side, a lintel or arch at the top and a cill at its base.

Arch brace In timber-framed structures, such as a roof, a curved brace (a brace is a diagonal timber beam stiffening the frame). A pair creates an arched shape.

Arch: elliptical, flat, four-centred, ogee, relieving, semi-circular, shouldered

An arch is a series of wedge-shaped stones or bricks, called voussoirs, which form a curved structure usually spanning an opening. Arches support a superimposed weight, similar to a lintel which is one horizontal piece performing the same function. The stones are held together by mutual pressure and supported only at the sides, called the springs. The space between the springs is called the springing line.

An elliptical arch is a half-ellipse drawn from the springing line.

A flat arch, sometimes called *a straight arch*, has a level soffit or underarch. The voussoirs appear almost like a lintel.

A four-centred arch, sometimes called *a Tudor arch*, is a depressed pointed arch. This is composed of two pairs of arcs, the lower pair is drawn from two centres on the springing line while the upper pair is drawn from centres below the springing line.

An ogee arch is a pointed arch formed of two convex arcs above two concave arcs, creating two S-shaped curves.

A relieving arch is built within and flush with the wall's fabric above a lintel to dissipate the weight of the masonry above.

A semi-circular arch has its centre on the springing line.

A shouldered arch has protruding stone resting on the horizontal course.

Arrow slit Narrow vertical aperture with deeply splayed inner jambs through which an arrow could be fired. Sometimes referred to as a loop window.

Barrel vault Uninterrupted vault (an arched roof or ceiling), semi-circular in section. Appears like a continuous arch.

Bastion Projection from the outer wall of a building, usually a castle.

Bay The regular structural subdivision of a building marked by the units of vaulting, roof compartments or main supporting timbers. Note the subdivision is not based on the position of internal walls.

Belvedere Raised turret to provide a viewing point for pleasure rather than strategy.

Boss Richly decorated projection at the intersection of a vault's ribs. That in the centre of a vault is called a central boss.

Bouche of court Food, drink, accommodation and other necessities, such as firewood, provided to those staying in the lord's residence.

Bretèche Single small protrusion from a wall, with or without a roof, with machicolation. Appears similar to a box machicolation.

Buttery Store room, usually for drink. Invariably beyond the screen at the low end of the hall beside the pantry.

Buttress Mass of stone or brick built against a wall to provide stability or to counteract the outward thrust of an arch or vault.

Chamfered edge Edge formed when a square angle is cut away obliquely.

Cloister Walkway around an open space.

Cofferer Household member who controlled the money chests or coffers.

Collar Lateral beam connecting the principal rafters (the main inclined beams indicating a building's bays) below the apex of the roof.

Crenellations Indented parapet. The raised parts are referred to as merlons and the openings are crenelles or embrasures.

Cross frame Part of the skeletal structure of a timber-framed building.

Cross-passage Passageway separating the hall and the services, while providing access to both. Access to passageway through doors at either end.

Cross-wing Wing attached perpendicular to the hall range.

Crow stepped Steps or indentations created in brick along the edge of a gable.

GLOSSARY

Cruciform loops Narrow vertical aperture in the shape of a cross, usually with deeply splayed inner jambs.

Cusp Point formed by the intersection of two arcs, called foils, in tracery (decoration within a window frame created by branching mullions). Usually referred to by the number of foils present, such as trefoil, quatrefoil, cinquefoil cusp, and so on. A quatrefoil has four sections separated by cusps, resembling a flower.

Dais Raised platform at the high end of the hall.

Diaper pattern Pattern of small lozenge shapes.

Dormant table Table in a fixed position, that is, it does not collapse.

Fustian Heavy fabric composed of cotton and linen.

Gablet Small termination point in the shape of a gable, often atop a buttress or chimney stack.

Gallery Balcony or upper-floor projecting platform providing access or seating for viewing the area below. Also a room acting as both a corridor and space for recreation and display of paintings or tapestries.

Gargoyle Drain spout to take water away from the wall to eject onto the ground. Often decorated and sometimes entirely ornamental.

Hood moulding Projection over the top of an aperture, such as a window, usually terminating in label stops.

Jamb Composes the vertical side of an aperture.

Label stop Termination of hood moulding, often decorated.

Light (in windows) Section of a window; that is, each segment separated from one another by mullions, transoms and tracery.

Lintel Horizontal piece of stone or wood spanning the top of an opening to carry the weight of the fabric above.

Lobby Relatively small space leading into a larger room.

Loop window See *Arrow slit*.

Louvre Outlet in a roof to allow smoke to escape.

Machicolation Opening between the corbels (supportive projections) supporting a parapet (low protective wall).

Marshalsea Household department concerned with the maintenance and care of horses.

Mortice Space hollowed out in timber to receive a tenon (projection at the end of another timber).

Moulding Any continuous projecting or recessed decoration, with a contoured profile, upon a surface.

Mullion Vertical member dividing a window into individual lights.

Newel Type of stair in a spiral form. It winds around a central pillar, which is known as a newel or newel post.

Offset Sloping ledge.

Palisade Enclosure wall composed of stakes fixed to the ground.

Pantry Store room, usually for bread. Invariably beyond the screen at the low end of the hall beside the buttery.

Pentice Extension of the roof to create a covered walkway.

Perpendicular style English Gothic architectural style characterised by strong lines of vertical tracery.

Pilaster buttress Rectangular column attached to the wall and protruding only slightly, not as much as a buttress.

Postern Small ancillary entrance.

Putlog hole Small hole within the wall's fabric to hold beams, used, for example, to support wooden stairs or scaffolding.

Quoin Stone at the external angle of a building, often articulated in some way – for example, by the use of a different stone type to the remainder.

Rafter Inclined timber used in the construction of pitched roofs.

Rebate Recess within a wall to receive or support another feature.

Rib vault Vault comprising rib framework concealing the groins (crease-like edge where two vaults intersect). The ribs support the infilling of the vault.

Spandrel Quasi-triangular-shaped area beyond the exterior curve of an arch, often within a window's tracery.

Spine wall Load-bearing wall.

Splay Diagonal surface between the opening of an aperture and the face of the wall. Found at the inner face of windows and arrow loops.

Squinch Small arch built across an angle or corner to act as a support.

Stone course Stone of uniform height laid in regular layers.

Stud Vertical post in a timber-framed partition or wall. Spaces between the studs are often filled with another material.

Tie-beam Beam connecting two wall plates (horizontal beams at the top of the wall). The lowest member of the roof truss (the roof's structural framework).

Tracery Decorative segmentation of a window frame created by branching mullions. May also appear on panels, screens or vaults due to moulded bars or ribs.

Transom Horizontal member dividing a window into individual lights.

Turret Small tower, part of a larger structure.

Undercroft Vaulted underground room.

Undressed stone work Walls comprising rough uncut stone.

Vault Arched roof or ceiling where the depth of the arch is greater than the span. May also refer to a room, the ceiling of which is vaulted. Its elements are mutually supportive, thus keeping each other in place, as in an arch.

Voussoir One of a series of stone or brick wedges which together create an arch or a vault.

Wind brace Diagonal brace (a brace is a diagonal timber beam stiffening the frame) crossing the rafter to stiffen the roof longitudinally.

GAZETTEER A

This lists the lodging ranges discussed in the main body of the book. Since each example is discussed there, only a brief description is included here. These were deemed the examples most useful to the discussion, due to the survival of medieval fabric which was usually, but not always, at least one wall of the lodging range at full or nearly full height.

Amberley Castle, Sussex

Two-storey lodging range constructed by Bishop Rede *c.*1377. Located in the outer courtyard between the kitchen and other service rooms, directly opposite the gatehouse. It comprised four rooms.

Bishop's Waltham Palace, Hampshire

Lodging range built by Bishop Beaufort between 1438 and 1442. Located in the north range of the multi-courtyard, multi-phase great house. Comprised a total of twenty-two rooms across two floors. The upper floor had a gallery which extended to a bridge connecting it to the first floor of the bake-brewhouse.

Brook Hall, Wiltshire

Two-storey lodging range built by Robert Willoughby, the first Baron of Brook between 1491 and 1502. Located in the north range of the three-sided courtyard, it comprised six rooms.

Brympton d'Evercy, Somerset

Two-storey building, possibly a lodging range, built by John Sydenham I between 1434 and 1464. It was free-standing, although its spatial context was similar to an outer, three-sided courtyard. It may have comprised five rooms.

Caister Castle, Norfolk

Two-storey brick-built range, possibly with accommodation on the first floor only, located in either the north-west or south-east range of the inner courtyard. Built by John Fastolf c.1431–45 and extant only in parts.

Cotehele, Cornwall

The Retainers' Court was built by Piers Edgecumbe between 1530 and 1545 and may have been completed by his son Richard Edgecumbe. The courtyard was to the west of the inner court, connected by a range which included the chapel. The Retainers' Court comprised two ranges, including a variety of different room types and sizes.

Dartington Hall, Devon

Two-storey lodging range, comprising eighteen rooms, built by John Holland between 1390 and 1400 in the west range of the expansive outer courtyard. Possibly a second lodging range in the east range.

Gainsborough Hall, Lincolnshire

Three-storey, timber-framed lodging range built by Thomas Burgh c.1479 in the west range of a three-sided courtyard. A variety of accommodation types were included, such as suites, one-bay rooms and a two-bay dormitory.

Haddon Hall, Derbyshire

Two-storey lodging range located in the west range of the outer courtyard. Built by Henry Vernon between 1470 and 1490 opposite the hall range. Contained six rooms of varying sizes plus two further rooms accessible from either end of the range.

Ince Manor, Cheshire

Two-storey lodging range, free-standing, perpendicular to the high end of the hall. The founder is unknown and the architecture suggests a mid-to-late fourteenth century date of construction.

Middleham Castle, Yorkshire

Three-storey lodging range constructed against an earlier curtain wall by Ralph, fourth Lord Neville c.1400–25. Located in the west range of the courtyard, with eight rooms across the ground and first floors and an unknown number on the second floor. A bridge connected the garderobe tower to the central keep.

Old Newnham, Devon

Two-storey lodging range built by the Strode family in the early sixteenth century. Located in the west range of what is now an L-shaped house, bisected by the gateway. Extensively restored and occupied.

Thornbury Castle, Gloucestershire

Three-storey lodging range built by Edward Stafford, third Duke Buckingham, between 1510 and 1521; never finished. Located in the north range of the outer courtyard, bisected by a gateway. On the eastern side there were five rooms on the first floor with more on the ground floor and an unknown number planned for the never-completed second floor. Probable further lodging range in the west range of the outer courtyard.

Wells Palace, Somerset

A very early example of a two-storey lodging range, built between 1230 and 1240, although possibly only the first floor provided accommodation. Extant with Victorian alterations to the front façade and internally changed for new purpose. This has concealed much of its medieval character and little of the original form can be determined.

Wingfield Manor, Derbyshire

Built by Ralph Lord Cromwell between 1440 and 1456. Three-storey lodging range located in the west range of the inner courtyard with a possible second range in the east range of the outer courtyard.

GAZETTEER B

This list comprises great houses which appear to have encompassed at least one lodging range. A brief description is included, which relates to the lodging range as opposed to the great house itself. Where the construction date of the lodging range is known, this has been added. These examples were not included in the main discussion due to a lack of extant medieval fabric as a result of either demolition, ruinous current condition or extensive restorative work. Combined with those in Gazetteer A, there are sixty-five known examples which once stood: I hope this provides a useful foundation for greater exploration of this building type.

Ampthill Castle, Bedfordshire

Constructed in the early fifteenth century. Two ranges within the double-courtyard house, both with projecting stair turrets. Entire site was demolished in the early seventeenth century.

Apethorpe Hall, Northamptonshire

Late fifteenth-century with considerable remodelling from the eighteenth century. Two-storeyed, comprising the west range of the outer court beside the gatehouse. Extant and remodelled.

Ashby de la Zouch, Leicestershire

Built c.1462–70. A two-storeyed range in the inner courtyard, to the east of the site. Two external walls remain.

Askerton Castle, Cumbria

Late fifteenth-century two-storey range located in the north range of the courtyard. Currently inhabited with extensive restoration.

Bodiam Castle, Sussex

Late fourteenth-century two-storey range with accommodation possibly only on first floor. Ruinous condition except the outer walls.

Bolton Castle, North Yorkshire

Constructed in the late fourteenth century. Possibly two storeys of a three-storey range located to the east alongside the gatehouse. Now in ruins.

Broughton Castle, Oxfordshire

Possible lodging range built in the mid-fifteenth century to the east of the gatehouse in the outer courtyard. Extant with many recent alterations.

Burwell, Cambridgeshire

Mid-fourteenth century, two-storey range, located on the high street and extensively restored.

Cawood Castle, Yorkshire

Two-storey range constructed between c.1425–52 in brick. Extant but ruinous.

Charing Palace, Kent

Two two-storey ranges built between 1333 and 1348 on the south and west of the outer courtyard. Part now converted into two cottages.

Codnor Castle, Derbyshire

Possibly late fifteenth century. Two-storey range located on the west side of the outer courtyard. A low wall remains.

Cothay Manor, Somerset

Two-storey ranges built c.1480 on either side of the gatehouse. Only that to the north remains.

Compton Wynyates, Warwickshire

Possibly built between 1481 and 1493 in the north and west of the courtyard. Standing but heavily remodelled.

Croydon Palace, Surrey

Two two-storey ranges built in brick between 1454 and 1486. Both demolished.

Dunster Castle, Somerset
Two three-storey ranges built *c.*1419–21. Extant fabric incorporated into the seventeenth-century mansion.

Edlington Castle, Northumberland
Courtyards added in a piecemeal fashion; lodging range date and form unknown. Currently foundation-level ruins.

Eltham Castle, Kent
Lodging range located within a courtyard possibly added between 1475 and 1483. No remains are standing.

Ewelme Manor, Oxfordshire
Early or mid-fifteenth century. Construction of a two-storey range possibly began in 1430 or 1444. Remains have been converted into a Georgian house.

Farleigh Hungerford Castle, Somerset
Lodging ranges built *c.*1370 were connected to a five-storey tower which contained garderobes. Much of the double-courtyard house remains as low footings.

Fotheringhay Castle, Northamptonshire
Built in the late fourteenth century and added to in the fifteenth and sixteenth centuries; no fabric extant.

Giffords Hall, Suffolk
Two-storey range built *c.*1520 in the west range of the courtyard. Remains survive in a heavily altered condition.

Hampton Court, Surrey
Possibly built in the early-to-mid fifteenth century to the north-west of the gatehouse, but no extant remains.

Harewood Castle, Yorkshire
Constructed *c.*1366; the current ruin prevents access above basement level.

Hedingham Castle, Essex
Lodging range constructed on the north side of the courtyard in the late fifteenth or early sixteenth centuries. Nothing remains extant.

Herstmonceux Castle, Sussex

Two separate ranges with first-floor accommodation only: one in the range between the Pump Court and the Green Court and a second on the south side of the Green Court. Possibly built c.1438–49 and later demolished before renovations of the remainder of the castle.

Holme Pierrepont Hall, Nottingham

Two-storey ranges of unknown date flanked the entrance into the manor in the south range. Remains survive in a heavily altered state.

Howden Manor, East Yorkshire

Possible two-storey lodging range constructed c.1388–1405, located in the east range. Now demolished.

Kirby Muxloe Castle, Leicestershire

Two storey lodging range built c.1480–85, possibly located in the north range, extant as low footings.

King's Langley Palace, Hertfordshire

Foundations of a lodging range revealed during excavation, suggesting a timber-framed construction of early fourteenth century date.

Knole, Kent

Two-storey lodging range built in the north range of the Stone Court between 1456 and 1486. Extant but extensively remodelled.

Leconfield Manor, East Yorkshire

Two two-storey ranges of unknown date were located in the east and west ranges with a galleried first floor. Demolished 1608–09.

Lichfield Palace, Staffordshire

Possible lodging range built in the early fourteenth century beside the gateway. Nothing remains extant.

Llawhaden Castle, Pembrokeshire

Two-storey range connected to the tower at the south side of the great house. Constructed between 1361 and 1389. One wall remains in ruins.

Maxstoke Castle, Warwickshire

Partially timber-framed two-storey ranges located in the north and south ranges. Constructed c.1342–46. Only an external wall survives.

Minster Lovell Hall, Oxfordshire

Two-storey lodging range located in the west range of the courtyard. Constructed between 1431 and 1440 and remains only at foundation level.

Ockwells Manor, Berkshire

Lodging range of *c*.1450–59 probably in the west range of the outer courtyard. Partial extant remains.

Okehampton Castle, Devon

Two-storey lodging range of late fourteenth century date was located opposite the hall range. Partial remains of one wall.

Pooley Hall, Warwickshire

Two-storey lodging range of early sixteenth century date. No standing remains.

Powderham Castle, Devon

Two-storey lodging range built *c*.1415, located in the south range of the courtyard. Now a church and hall.

Raby Castle, Durham

Identified tentatively as a lodging range comprising three floors within a tower, built *c*.1367–77, each with outer and inner chambers. Extant and extensively altered.

Raglan Castle, Monmouthshire

Two two-storey ranges, one in the Pitched Stone Court and a second in the Fountain Court which included a grand staircase. Constructed between 1455 and 1469. Very little remains in the Pitched Stone Court; most of one wall remains in the Fountain Court.

Sheriff Hutton Castle, North Yorkshire

Possible lodging range built in the lower courtyard between 1382 and 1402. It was of unknown form and nothing remains.

Shute Barton, Devon

Lodging range located in the north range opposite the hall and services. Possibly constructed *c*.1503–23, although parts may have been built earlier between 1427 and 1449. Now demolished.

Sudeley Castle, Gloucestershire

Two-storey lodging range, with rooms on both floors, constructed *c.*1572 in the outer courtyard. Standing but restored in the nineteenth and twentieth centuries. Possibly the last known lodging range to be built.

South Wraxall Manor, Wiltshire

Two-storey lodging range built in the late fifteenth century in the inner courtyard and extended in the early sixteenth century. Extant with later modifications.

Tattershall Castle, Lincolnshire

Possible lodging range of unknown form built *c.*1434–52 in the outer courtyard beside surviving guard house. No extant remains.

Wardour Castle, Wiltshire

Possible four-storey lodging range built within the south-eastern segment of the great house *c.*1390. Now in ruins with small section extant.

Warwick Castle, Northumberland

Possible lodging range built in the late fourteenth century abutting the curtain wall. Form unknown and no remains are extant.

Windsor Castle, Berkshire

Two-storey ranges, with rooms on both floors, constructed by 1370 and replacing earlier household accommodation. Located along two sides of the substantial upper ward. Currently intact but extensively altered.

Wressle Castle, East Yorkshire

Two-storey lodging range constructed *c.*1364–1403 between two corner towers in the courtyard. No extant remains.

BIBLIOGRAPHY

MANUSCRIPTS

Additional MS 39848, *British Library, London.*
Additional MS 39849, *British Library, London.*
MCO Fastolf paper 43, *Magdalen College, Oxford.*

SECONDARY SOURCES

Alcock, N. W. and Michael Laithwaite, 'Medieval Houses in Devon and their Modernization', *Medieval Archaeology*, 17 (1973), 100–25.
Amyot, Thomas, 'Transcript of two rolls, containing an inventory of the effects formerly belonging to Sir John Fastolfe', *Archaeologia* 21 (1827), pp. 232–80.
Baker, Hannah, *That Most Precious Merchandise: The Mediterranean Trade in Black Sea Slaves, 1260-1500* (Philadelphia, 2019).
Barlow, Frank, *The Feudal Kingdom of England: 1042-1216* (Abingdon, 2014).
Barnes, H. D. and W. D. Simpson, 'Caister Castle', *Antiquaries Journal*, 32:1–2 (1952), 35–51.
Barrett, C. R. B., 'Caister Castle and Sir John Fastolfe', *Journal of the British Archaeological Association*, 2 (1896), 37–47.
Barry, Jonathon, 'Introduction', in Jonathon Barry and Christopher Brooks (eds), *The Middling Sort of People* (Basingstoke, 1994), pp. 1–27.
Barry, Jonathon and Christopher Brooks (eds), *The Middling Sort of People* (Basingstoke, 1994).
Barthélemy, Dominique, 'Civilizing the Fortress', in Georges Duby (ed.), *A History of Private Life II* (London, 1988), pp. 397–424.
Bean, J. M. W., *From Lord to Patron: Lordship in Late Medieval England* (Manchester, 1989).
Beaumont James, Tom, 'Medieval Palaces and Royal Houses', in Christopher Gerrard and Alejandra Gutiérrez (eds), *The Oxford Handbook of Later Medieval Archaeology in Britain* (Oxford, 2018), pp. 371–85.

Biernoff, Suzannah, *Sight and Embodiment in the Middle Ages* (Basingstoke, 2002).

Blair, John, 'Hall and Chamber: English Domestic Planning 1000-1250', in Gwyn Meirion-Jones and Michael Jones (eds), *Manorial Domestic Buildings in England and Northern France*, Society of Antiquaries Occasional Papers 15 (London, 1993), pp. 1-21.

Boorde, Andrew, *A compendyous regyment or a dyetary of healthe made in Mountpyllyer, by Andrewe Boorde* (1542).

Bourdieu, Pierre, *Outline of a Theory of Practice* (Cambridge, 1977).

Brown, Elizabeth A. R., 'The Tyranny of a Construct: Feudalism and Historians of Medieval Europe', *The American Historical Review*, 79 (1974), 1063-88.

Brown, F., 'Comment on Chapman: Some Cautionary Notes on the Application of Spatial Measures to Prehistoric Settlements', in Ross Samson (ed.), *The Social Archaeology of Houses* (Edinburgh, 1990), pp. 93-109.

Butler, Judith, 'Performative Acts and Gender Constitution: An Essay in Phenomenology and Feminist Theory', *Theatre Journal*, 40:4 (1988), 519-31.

Camille, Michael, *Gothic Art* (London, 1996).

Campbell, Jill, 'Architectural design and exterior display in gentry houses in 14th- and 15th-century England' (unpublished Ph.D. dissertation, Queen's University Belfast, 2012).

Carpenter, Christine, *Locality and Polity: A Study of Warwickshire Landed Society, 1401-1499* (Cambridge, 1992).

Clark, Catherine, 'Place, Identity and Performance: Spatial Practices and Social Proxies in Medieval Swansea', *Journal of Medieval History*, 41:3 (2015), 256-72.

Clark, David, 'Archaeology: The Loss of Innocence', *Antiquity*, 47:185 (1973), 6-18.

Clark, Gregory, 'Regression to Mediocrity? Surnames and Social Mobility in England, 1200-2009', *Social Science Research Network* (2010) <https://papers.ssrn.com/sol3/papers.cfm?abstract_id=1651904> [accessed 4 August 2022].

Clark, M. V., 'The West Range', in Philip Lindley (ed.), *Gainsborough Old Hall* (Lincoln, 1991), pp. 43-56.

Classen, C., D. Howes and A. Synnott, *Aroma: The Cultural History of Smell* (Abingdon, 1994).

Conkey, Margaret W. and Janet D. Spector, 'Archaeology and the Study of Gender', *Archaeological Method and Theory*, 7 (1984), 1-38.

Cooper, Nicholas, *House of the Gentry* (London, 1999).

Coss, Peter, 'Knights, Esquires and the Origins of Social Gradation in England', *Transactions of the Royal Historical Society*, 5 (1995), 155-78.

——, *The Origins of the English Gentry* (Cambridge, 2003).

Coulson, Charles, 'Fourteenth-century Castles in Context: Apotheosis or Decline?', in Robert Liddiard (ed.), *Late Medieval Castles* (Woodbridge, 2016), pp. 19–40.

Creighton, Oliver, *Castles and Landscapes: Power, Community and Fortification in Medieval England* (Sheffield, 2005).

——, *Designs upon the Land: Elite Landscapes of the Middle Ages* (Woodbridge, 2009).

——, 'Overview: Castles and Elite Landscapes', in Christopher Gerrard and Alejandra Gutiérrez (eds), *The Oxford Handbook of Later Medieval Archaeology in Britain* (Oxford, 2018), pp. 355–70.

Creighton, Oliver and Robert Liddiard, 'Fighting Yesterday's Battle: Beyond War or Status in Castle Studies', *Medieval Archaeology*, 52 (2008), 161–9.

Crittall, Elizabeth, *A History of the County of Wiltshire: Volume 8, Warminster, Westbury and Whorwellsdown Hundreds* (London, 1965).

Cunliffe, B., C. Gosden and R. Joyce (eds), *The Oxford Handbook of Archaeology* (Oxford, 2009).

Davis, Norman, *Paston Letters and Papers of the Fifteenth Century*, 2nd edn (Oxford, 2004).

Dempsey, Karen,
'Understanding Hall-Houses', *Medieval Archaeology*, 61 (2017), 372–99.

——, 'Gender and Medieval Archaeology: Storming the Castle', *Antiquity*, 93:369 (2019), 772–88.

——, 'Planting new ideas: A feminist gaze on medieval castles', *Château Gaillard: Études de Castellologie Médiévale*, 29 (2021), 85–98.

Dixon, Philip, 'The Manor-Houses of the Anglo-Scottish Border', in Gwyn Meirion-Jones and Michael Jones (eds), *Manorial Domestic Buildings in England and Northern France*, Society of Antiquaries Occasional Papers 15 (London, 1993), pp. 22–48.

——, 'Design in Castle-Buildings: The Controlling of Access to the Lord', *Chateau Gaillard*, 18 (1996), 47–57.

——, 'The Donjon of Knaresborough: The Castle as Theatre', in Robert Liddiard (ed.), *Late Medieval Castles* (Woodbridge, 2016), pp. 333–48.

Dixon, Philip and Beryl Lott, 'The Courtyard and the Tower', *Journal of the British Archaeological Association*, 146 (1993), 93–101.

Dobson, Barrie, 'The English Vicars Choral: an Introduction', in Richard Hall and David Stocker (eds), *Vicars Choral in English Cathedrals* (Oxford, 2005), pp. 1–10.

Dovey, Kim, *Framing Places: Mediating Power in Built Form* (London, 1999).

Duby, Georges (ed.), *A History of Private Life II* (London, 1988).

Dunham, William Huse, *Lord Hastings' Indentured Retainers, 1461–1483: The Lawfulness of Livery and Retaining under the Yorkists and Tudors* (New Haven, 1970).

Earle, Peter, 'The Middling Sort in London', in Jonathon Barry and Christopher Brooks (eds), *The Middling Sort of People* (Basingstoke, 1994), pp. 141-58.

Emery, Anthony, *Dartington Hall* (Oxford, 1970).

——, 'The Development of Raglan Castle and Keeps in Late Medieval England', *Archaeological Journal*, 132 (1975), 151-86.

——, *Greater Medieval Houses of England and Wales 1300-1500* (3 vols, Cambridge, 2000-6).

——, 'Late-Medieval Houses as an Expression of Social Status', *Historical Research*, 78 (2005), 140-61.

Everitt, Alan, 'The English Urban Inn 1560-1760', in A. Everitt (ed.), *Perspectives in English Urban History* (London, 1973), pp. 91-137.

Fairclough, Graham, 'Meaningful Constructions – Spatial and Functional Analysis of Medieval Buildings', *Antiquity*, 66:251 (1992), 348-66.

Faulkner, Patrick,

'Domestic Planning from the Twelfth to the Fourteenth Centuries', *Archaeological Journal*, 115 (1958), 150-84.

——, 'Haddon Hall and Bolsover Castle', *Archaeological Journal*, 118 (1961), 180-7.

——, 'Castle Planning in the Fourteenth Century', *Archaeological Journal*, 120:1 (1963), 215-35.

Fernie, Eric, 'Technical Terms and the Understanding of English Medieval Architecture', *Architectural History*, 44 (2001), 13-21.

Field, N., 'Excavations and the West Range', in Philip Lindley (ed.), *Gainsborough Old Hall* (Lincoln, 1991), pp. 34-42.

Fisher, Kevin D., 'Placing Social Interaction: An Integrative Approach to Analyzing Past Built Environments', *Journal of Anthropological Archaeology*, 28:4 (2009), 439-57.

Fisher, Peter, Chris Farrelly, Adrian Maddocks and Clive Ruggles, 'Spatial Analysis of Visible Areas from the Bronze Age Cairns of Mull', *Journal of Archaeological Science*, 24:7 (1997), 581-92.

Foster, Hal, *Vision and Visuality* (Seattle, 1988).

Foster, Sally, 'Analysis of Spatial Patterns in Buildings (Access Analysis) as an Insight into Social Structure', *Antiquity*, 63:238 (1989), 40-50.

Fox, Cyril and FitzRoy Richard Somerset Raglan, *Monmouthshire Houses: A Study of Building Techniques and Smaller House-plans in the Fifteenth to Seventeenth Centuries* (Cardiff, 1953).

Frantzen, Allen J. and Douglas Moffat (eds), *The Work of Work Servitude, Slavery and Labor in Medieval England* (Glasgow, 1994).

Frazer, William, 'Identities in Early Medieval Britain', in William Frazer and Andrew Tyrell (eds), *Social Identity in Early Medieval Britain* (Leicester, 2000), pp. 1-22.

French, H. R., *The Middle Sort of People in Provincial England, 1600-1750* (Oxford, 2007).

——, 'The Search for the "Middle Sort of People" in England, 1600-1800', *The Historical Journal*, 43:1 (2000), 277-93.
Gairdner, James (ed.), *The Paston Letters 1422-1509* (4 vols, Westminster, 1901).
Gardiner, Mark, 'Vernacular Buildings and the Development of the Later Medieval Domestic Plan in England', *Medieval Archaeology*, 44 (2000), 159-79.
——, 'Buttery and Pantry and the Antecedents: Idea and Architecture in the English Medieval House', in Maryanne Kowaleski and P. J. P. Goldberg (eds), *Medieval Domesticity: Home, Housing and Household in Medieval England* (Cambridge, 2008), pp. 37-65.
——, 'Conceptions of Domestic Space in the Long Term – the Example of the English Medieval Hall', in Mette Svart Kristiansen, Else Roesdahl and James Graham-Campbell (eds), *Medieval Archaeology in Scandinavia and Beyond: History, Trends and Tomorrow* (Aarhus, 2015), pp. 313-33.
——, 'What is Building History? Emergence and Practice in Britain and Ireland', in Liz Thomas and Jill Campbell (eds), *Buildings in Society: International Studies in the Historic Era* (Summertown, 2018), pp. 1-8.
Gardiner, Mark and Susan Kilby, 'Perceptions of Medieval Settlement', in Christopher Gerrard and Alejandra Gutiérrez (eds), *The Oxford Handbook of Later Medieval Archaeology in Britain* (Oxford, 2018), pp. 210-25.
Gilchrist, Roberta, 'Women's archaeology? Political feminism, gender theory and historical revision', *Antiquity*, 65:248 (1991), 495-501.
——, *Gender and Material Archaeology: The Archaeology of Religious Women* (Abingdon, 1994).
——, *Gender and Archaeology: Contesting the Past* (Abingdon, 1999).
——, 'The archaeology of sex and gender', in B. Cunliffe, C. Gosden and R. Joyce (eds), *The Oxford Handbook of Archaeology* (Oxford, 2009), pp. 1029-47.
Giles, Kate, 'Seeing and Believing: Visuality and Space in Pre-modern England', *World Archaeology*, 39 (2007), 105-21.
Girouard, Mark, *Life in the English Country House: A Social and Architectural History* (New Haven, 1978).
Gomme, Andor and Alison Maguire, *Design and Plan in the Country House. From Castle Donjons to Palladian Boxes* (New Haven, 2008).
Goodall, John, *The English Castle: 1066-1650* (New Haven, 2011).
Gotch, John Alfred, *Early Renaissance Architecture in England* (London, 1901).
Graves, C. Pamela, 'Social Space in the English Medieval Parish Church', *Economy and Society*, 18 (1989), 297-322.
——, *The Form and Fabric of Belief* (York, 2000).
Grenville, Jane, *Medieval Housing* (London, 1997).

———, 'Urban and Rural Houses and Households in the Late Middle Ages', in Maryanne Kowaleski and P. J. P. Goldberg (eds), *Medieval Domesticity: Home, Housing and Household in Medieval England* (Cambridge, 2008), pp. 92–123.

Gunn, S. J., 'The Rise of the Burgh Family, c. 1431–1550', in Philip Lindley (ed.), *Gainsborough Old Hall* (Lincoln, 1991), pp. 8–13.

Hadley, Dawn, *Masculinity in Medieval Europe* (London, 1999).

Halliwell, J. O. (ed.), *A Chronicle of the First Thirteen Years of the Reign of King Edward the Fourth by John Warkworth*, The Camden Series, 10:1 (London, 1839).

Handley, Sasha, *Sleep in Early Modern England* (New Haven, 2016).

Hanscam, Emily and Robert Witcher, 'Women in Antiquity: An Analysis of Gender and Publishing in a Global Archaeology Journal', *Journal of Field Archaeology*, 48:2 (2023), 87–101.

Hare, John, 'Bishop's Waltham Palace, Hampshire: William of Wykeham, Henry Beaufort and the Transformation of a Medieval Episcopal Palace', *Archaeological Journal*, 145 (1988), 222–54.

———, 'Inns, Innkeepers and the Society of Later Medieval England', *Journal of Medieval History*, 39:4 (2013), 477–97.

Harvey, S. A., *Scenting Salvation* (Berkeley, 2006).

Hawkyard, Alasdair, 'Sir John Fastolf's "Gret mansion By Me Late Edified": Caister Castle, Norfolk', in Linda Clark (ed.), *The Fifteenth Century V: 'Of Mice and Men': Image, Belief and Regulation in Late Medieval England* (Woodbridge, 2005), pp. 39–68.

Heal, Felicity, *Hospitality in Early Modern England* (Oxford, 1990).

Hexter, Jack H., *Reappraisals in History* (London, 1961).

Hicks, Leonie, 'Magnificent Entrances and Undignified Exits', *Journal of Medieval History*, 35 (2009), 52–69.

Hicks, Michael, *Bastard Feudalism* (London, 1995).

———, 'Bastard Feudalism, Overmighty Subjects and Idols of the Multitude during the Wars of the Roses', *The Journal of the Historical Association*, 85:279 (2000), 386–403.

Hill, Nick and Mark Gardiner, 'The English Medieval First-floor Hall: Part 1 – Scolland's Hall, Richmond, North Yorkshire', *Archaeological Journal*, 175 (2018), 157–83.

———, 'The English Medieval First-floor Hall: Part 2 – The Evidence from the Eleventh to Early Thirteenth Century', *Archaeological Journal*, 175 (2018), 315–61.

Hillier, Bill and Julienne Hanson, *The Social Logic of Space* (Cambridge, 1984).

Hinton, David A., '"Closing" and the Later Middle Ages', *Medieval Archaeology*, 43:1 (1999), 172–82.

——, 'Symbols of Power', in Christopher Gerrard and Alejandra Gutiérrez (eds), *The Oxford Handbook of Later Medieval Archaeology in Britain* (Oxford, 2018), pp. 418–34.

Holmes, George, *The Estates of the Higher Nobility in Fourteenth-century England* (Cambridge, 1957).

Horning, Audrey and Dan Hicks, 'Historical Archaeology and Buildings', in Mary Beaudry and Dan Hicks (eds), *Cambridge Companion to Historical Archaeology* (Cambridge, 2006), pp. 273–93.

Hughes, Jonathan, 'Scrope, Stephen' (2015), *Oxford DNB* <https://doi.org/10.1093/ref:odnb/66283> [accessed 23 August 2021].

Ingold, Tim, *The Perception of the Environment* (London, 2000).

Johnson, Matthew, *Housing Culture: Traditional Architecture in an English Landscape* (London, 1993).

——, *Behind the Castle Gate: From Medieval to Renaissance* (London, 2002).

——, *Lived Experience in the Later Middle Ages* (Oxford, 2017).

Keene, Derek, 'Wardrobes in the City: Houses of Consumption, Finance and Power', *Thirteenth Century England*, VII (1999), 61–80.

Kekewich, Margaret, *Sir John Fortescue and the Governance of England* (Woodbridge, 2018).

Kerr, Sarah, 'A study of lodging ranges in late medieval England' (unpublished Ph.D. dissertation, Queen's University Belfast, 2016).

——, 'Collective Living and Individual Identities in Late Medieval England', *Archaeological Journal*, 177 (2020), 83–98.

——, 'The Future of Archaeology, Interdisciplinarity and Global Challenges', *Antiquity*, 94:377 (2020), 1337–48.

King, Christopher, 'The Organization of Social Space in Late Medieval Manor Houses', *Archaeological Journal*, 160:1 (2003), 104–24.

——, 'The Interpretation of Urban Buildings: Power, Memory and Appropriation in Norwich Merchants' Houses, c. 1400–1660', *World Archaeology*, 41:3 (2009), 471–88.

Kowaleski, Maryanne and P. J. P. Goldberg, *Medieval Domesticity: Home, Housing and Household in Medieval England* (Cambridge, 2008).

Krausman Ben-Amos, Ilana, *The Culture of Giving* (Cambridge, 2008).

Lachaud, Frédérique, 'Liveries of Robes in England, c.1200–c.1330', *The English Historical Review*, 111 (1996), 279–98.

Lake, M. W., P. E. Woodman and S. J. Mithen, 'Tailoring GIS Software for Archaeological Applications', *Journal of Archaeological Science*, 25 (1998), 27–38.

Lefebvre, Henri, *The Production of Space* (Malden, 1991, orig. 1974).

Liddiard, Robert (ed.), *Late Medieval Castles* (Woodbridge, 2016).

Lindley, Philip (ed.), *Gainsborough Old Hall* (Lincoln, 1991).

McClain, Aleksandra, 'Theory, Disciplinary Perspectives and the Archaeology of Later Medieval England', *Medieval Archaeology*, 56:1 (2012), 131–70.

McDonald, Nicola, 'Fragments of (Have Your) Desire', in Maryanne Kowaleski and P. J. P. Goldberg (eds), *Medieval Domesticity: Home, Housing and Household in Medieval England* (Cambridge, 2008), pp. 232–58.

McFarlane, K. B., *The Nobility of Later Medieval England* (Oxford, 1973).

——, *England in the Fifteenth Century: Collected Essays* (London, 1981).

McKelvie, Gordon, *Bastard Feudalism: English Society and the Law. The Statutes of Livery 1390–1520* (Woodbridge, 2020).

McNeill, Tom, *Castles* (London, 1992).

Markus, Thomas, *Buildings and Power: Freedom and Control in the Origin of Modern Building Types* (Abingdon, 1993).

Martin, G. H., 'Road Travel in the Middle Ages', *The Journal of Transport History*, 3:3 (1976), 159–78.

Meech, S. B. and H. E. Allen (eds), *The Book of Margery Kempe* (London, 1940).

Meirion-Jones, Gwyn, Edward Impey and Michael Jones (eds), *The Seigneurial Residence in Western Europe AD c.800–1600*, British Archaeological Reports International Series, 1088 (Oxford, 2002).

Meirion-Jones, Gwyn and Michael Jones (eds), *Manorial Domestic Buildings in England and Northern France*, Society of Antiquaries Occasional Papers 15 (London, 1993).

Mercer, Eric, *English Vernacular Houses* (London, 1975).

Mertes, Kate, *The English Noble Household 1250–1600* (Oxford, 1988).

Mileson, Stephen, 'Sound and Landscape', in Christopher Gerrard and Alejandra Gutiérrez (eds), *The Oxford Handbook of Later Medieval Archaeology in Britain* (Oxford, 2018), pp. 713–28.

Mitchell, Linda E., 'The Lady Is a Lord: Noble Widows and Land in Thirteenth-Century Britain', *Historical Reflections/Réflexions Historiques*, 18:1 (1992), 71–97.

Moen, Marianne, 'Gender and Archaeology: Where Are We Now?', *Archaeologies*, 15 (2019), 206–26.

Morgan, Hollie, *Beds and Chambers in Late Medieval England: Readings, Representations and Realities* (York, 2017).

Nelson, Robert, *Visuality Before and Beyond the Renaissance* (Cambridge, 2000).

Nevell, M. D., R. Nevell and B. H. Grimsditch, 'Power, Status and War', in B. H. Grimsditch, M. D. Nevell and R. Nevell, *Buckton Castle and the Castles of North West England* (Salford, 2012), pp. 1–35.

Nightingale, Pamela, 'Knights and Merchants: Trade, Politics and the Gentry in Late Medieval England', *Past & Present*, 169 (2000), 36–62.

Oosthuizen, Susan, 'Culture and Identity in the Early Medieval Fenland Landscape', *Landscape History*, 37:1 (2016), 5–24.

O'Sullivan, Aidan, 'Early Medieval Houses In Ireland: Social Identity and Dwelling Spaces', *Peritia*, 20 (2008), 225–56.

Pantin, William,
'The Recently Demolished Houses in Broad Street, Oxford', *Oxoniensia*, 4 (1939), 171–200.

——, 'Tackley's Inn, Oxford', *Oxoniensia*, 7 (1942), 80–93.

——, 'Chantry Priests' Houses and Other Medieval Lodgings', *Medieval Archaeology*, 3 (1959), 216–58.

——, 'Medieval English Town-House Plans', *Medieval Archaeology*, 6:1 (1962), 202–39.

Payling, S. J., 'Social Mobility, Demographic Change, and Landed Society in Late Medieval England', *The Economic History Review*, 45:1 (1992), 51–73.

Peers, C., *Middleham Castle* (London, 1965).

Platt, Colin, 'Excavations at Dartington Hall', *Archaeological Journal*, 119 (1962), 208–24.

——, *The Architecture of Medieval Britain: A Social History* (New Haven, 1990).

Plummer, Charles (ed.), *The Governance of England* (Oxford, 1885).

Pollard, J. and A. Reynolds, *Avebury: The Biography of a Landscape* (Cheltenham, 2002).

Poultney, L., *Middleham Castle* (London, 1998).

Pounds, Norman, *The Medieval Castle in England and Wales: A Social and Political History* (Cambridge, 1990).

Powicke, Michael, *Military Obligation in Medieval England* (Oxford, 1962).

Quiney, Anthony, *Town Houses of Medieval Britain* (London, 2004).

Rapoport, Amos, *The Meaning of the Built Environment* (Tucson, 1990).

——, *Culture, Architecture, and Design* (Chicago, 2005).

Rawcliffe, Carole, *The Staffords, Earls of Stafford and Dukes of Buckingham: 1394–1521* (Cambridge, 1978).

Reynolds, Susan, *The Middle Ages without Feudalism: Essays in Criticism and Comparison on the Medieval West* (London, 2012).

Richards, Julian, 'The Bedern Foundry', *Archaeology of York*, 10:3 (London, 1993), 149–210.

Richardson, Amanda, 'Corridors of Power: A Case Study in Access Analysis from Medieval England', *Antiquity*, 77:296 (2003), 373–84.

——, 'Gender and Space in English Royal Palaces c.1160–c.1547: A Study in Access Analysis and Imagery', *Medieval Archaeology*, 47 (2003), 131–65.

——, 'Gender and Space in the Later Middle Ages', in Christopher Gerrard and Alejandra Gutiérrez (eds), *The Oxford Handbook of Later Medieval Archaeology in Britain* (Oxford, 2018), pp. 805–18.

Rickert, Edith (ed.), *The Babees' Book: Medieval Manners for the Young: Done into English from Dr. Furnivall's Texts* (London, 1923).

Riddy, Felicity, '"Burgeis" Domesticity in Late-medieval England', in Maryanne Kowaleski and P. J. P. Goldberg (eds), *Medieval Domesticity: Home, Housing and Household in Medieval England* (Cambridge, 2008), pp. 14–36.

Rippon, Stephen, Piers Dixon and Bob Silvester, 'Overview: The Form and Pattern of Medieval Settlement', in Christopher Gerrard and Alejandra Gutiérrez (eds), *The Oxford Handbook of Later Medieval Archaeology in Britain* (Oxford, 2018), pp. 171–92.

Roberts, Brian and Stuart Wrathmell, *Region and Place: A Study of English Rural Settlement* (London, 2002).

Roberts, Edward, 'A Fifteenth Century Inn at Andover', *Proceedings of the Hampshire Field Club and Archaeological Society*, 47 (1991), 153–70.

——, 'Inns, Taverns and Alehouses in Hampshire 1300–1600', *Hampshire Studies*, 75:1 (2020), 75–87.

Roffey, Simon, 'Constructing a Vision of Salvation', *Archaeological Journal*, 163 (2006), 122–46.

——, *The Medieval Chantry Chapel: An Archaeology* (Woodbridge, 2007).

——, 'The Medieval Afterlife', in Christopher Gerrard and Alejandra Gutiérrez (eds), *The Oxford Handbook of Later Medieval Archaeology in Britain* (Oxford, 2018), pp. 868–86.

Sand, Alexa, 'Visuality', *Studies in Iconography*, 33 (2012), 89–95.

Sanders, Ivor, *Feudal Military Service in England: A Study of the Constitutional and Military Powers of the Barones in Medieval England* (Oxford, 1956).

Saul, Nigel, *Knights and Esquires* (Oxford, 1981).

——, 'The Commons and the Abolition of Badges', *Parliamentary History*, 9 (1990), 302–15.

Schofield, John, 'The Topography and Buildings of London, ca. 1600', in Lena Cowen Orlin (ed.), *Material London, ca. 1600* (Philadelphia, 2012), pp. 296–321.

Senecal, Christine, 'Keeping Up with the Godwinsons: In Pursuit of Aristocratic Status in Late Anglo-Saxon England', *Anglo-Norman Studies*, 23 (2000), 251–66.

Siddons, Michael Powell, *Heraldic Badges in England and Wales* (3 vols, Woodbridge, 2009).

Simpson, William Douglas, '"Bastard Feudalism" and the Later Castles', *Antiquaries Journal*, 26:3–4 (1946), 145–71.

Smith, J. T., 'Timber-framed Building in England', *Archaeological Journal*, 122 (1965), 133–58.

——, *English Houses 1200–1800: The Hertfordshire Evidence* (London, 1992).

Smith, Sally, 'Materializing Resistant Identities Among the Medieval Peasantry', *Journal of Material Culture*, 14:3 (2009), 309–32.

Speight, Sarah, 'British Castle Studies in the Late 20th and 21st Centuries', *History Compass*, 2:1 (2005) <https://compass.onlinelibrary.wiley.com/doi/full/10.1111/j.1478-0542.2004.00086.x> [accessed 4 August 2022].

Spencer, Andrew, *Nobility and Kingship in Medieval England: The Earls and Edward I, 1272–1307* (Cambridge, 2014).

Stocker, David, 'The Quest for One's Own Front Door: Housing the Vicars' Choral at the English Cathedrals', *Vernacular Architecture*, 36 (2005), 15–31.

Stone, Lawrence and Jeanne C. Fawtier Stone, *An Open Elite? England 1550–1880* (Oxford, 1984).

Stubbs, William, *The Constitutional History of England in Its Origin and Development*, Vol. 1 (Oxford, 1903).

Suggett, Richard, 'Peasant Houses', in Christopher Gerrard and Alejandra Gutiérrez (eds), *The Oxford Handbook of Later Medieval Archaeology in Britain* (Oxford, 2018), pp. 226–41.

Thomas, Hugh M., *The Norman Conquest: England after William the Conqueror* (Plymouth, 2008).

Thomas, Liz and Jill Campbell, 'Introduction', in Liz Thomas and Jill Campbell (eds), *Buildings in Society: International Studies in the Historic Era* (Summertown, 2018), pp. iii–1.

Thompson, Michael, *The Decline of the Castle* (Cambridge, 1978).

——, *The Medieval Hall: The Basis of Secular Domestic Life, 600–1600 AD* (Aldershot, 1995).

Thompson, Michael W., 'The Architectural Context of Gainsborough Old Hall', in P. Lindley (ed.), *Gainsborough Old Hall* (Lincoln, 1991), pp. 13–20.

Thorstad, Audrey, 'Living in an Early Tudor Castle: Households, Display, and Space, 1485-1547' (unpublished Ph.D. dissertation, University of Leeds, 2015).

——, *The Culture of Castles in Tudor England and Wales* (Woodbridge, 2019).

Timbs, John and Alexander Gunn, *Abbeys, Castles and Ancient Halls of England and Wales* (3 vols, London, 1872).

Turner, J., M. Hogg, P. Oaks, S. Reicher and M. Wetherell, *Rediscovering the Social Group: A Self-categorization Theory* (Cambridge, 1987).

Vernon, J., 'A Fine Wreck of the Feudal Age', in Philip Lindley (ed.), *Gainsborough Old Hall* (Lincoln, 1991), pp. 27–33.

Walker, Simon, *The Lancastrian Affinity, 1361–99* (Oxford, 1990).

——, *Political Culture in Later Medieval England: Essays*, ed. Michael Braddick (Manchester, 2006).

Ward, Jennifer, *English Noblewomen in the Later Middle Ages* (London, 1992).

Ward, Matthew, *The Livery Collar in Late Medieval England and Wales: Politics, Identity and Affinity* (Woodbridge, 2016).

Warmington, R., 'Beaufort's Range of Lodgings', in John Hare, 'Bishop's Waltham Palace, Hampshire: William of Wykeham, Henry Beaufort and the Transformation of a Medieval Episcopal Palace', *Archaeological Journal*, 145 (1988), 246–51.

Webb, Diana, *Privacy and Solitude in the Middle Ages* (London, 2007).

Weikert, Katherine, *Authority, Gender and Space in the Anglo-Norman World, 900–1200* (Woodbridge, 2020).

Wells, Emma, 'Overview: The Medieval Senses', in Christopher Gerrard and Alejandra Gutiérrez (eds), *The Oxford Handbook of Later Medieval Archaeology in Britain* (Oxford, 2018), pp. 681–98.

West Wiltshire District Council, *Brook Hall Brokerswood: Statement of Significance and Development Brief* (2004).

Wickham, Chris, 'The Other Transition: From the Ancient World to Feudalism', *Past & Present*, 103 (1984), 3–36.

Wood, Margaret, 'Lincoln – 3 Vicars' Court', *Lincolnshire Historian*, 1:7 (1951), 281–6.

——, *The English Medieval House* (New York, 1965).

Woolgar, Christopher, *The Great Household in Late Medieval England* (New Haven, 1999).

——, *The Senses in Late Medieval England* (New Haven, 2006).

Wotton, Henry, *The Elements of Architecture* (London, 1624).

Wrightson, Keith, '"Sorts of People" in Tudor and Stuart England', in Jonathon Barry and Christopher Brooks (eds), *The Middling Sort of People* (Basingstoke, 1994), pp. 28–51.

Wylie, Alison, 'Gender Archaeology/Feminist Archaeology', in Elisabeth A. Bacus (ed.), *A Gendered Past: A Critical Bibliography of Gender in Archaeology* (Ann Arbor, 1993).

WEB SOURCES

Harriss, G. L., 'Fastolf, Sir John' (2004), *Oxford DNB* <https://doi.org/10.1093/ref:odnb/9199> [accessed 23 August 2021].

Historic England, *Caister Castle*, List Entry Number: 1287573 (2014) <https://historicengland.org.uk/listing/the-list/list-entry/1287573> [accessed 23 August 2021].

Historic England, *The Outer Court of Thornbury Castle and Walls of Kitchen Court*, List Entry Number: 1321132 (2021) <https://historicengland.org.uk/listing/the-list/list-entry/1321132> [accessed 8 August 2021].

Historic England, *Thornbury Castle*, List Entry Number: 1000569 (2021) <https://historicengland.org.uk/listing/the-list/list-entry/1000569> [accessed 8 August 2021].

Nigota, Joseph, 'Vernon family' (2004), *Oxford DNB* <https://doi.org/10.1093/ref:odnb/52800> [accessed 10 August 2021].

OED, 'chamber' (2021) <https://www.oed.com/> [accessed 10 August 2021].

OED, 'lodge' (2021) <https://www.oed.com/> [accessed 17 June 2021].

INDEX

Academic
    colleges 3, 19, 20, 84
    fellows *see* Fellows
    halls 20
    household 215
    ranges *see* Collegiate ranges
Access analysis 43–4, 49, 88, 100, 143–4, 181 *see also* Spatial analysis
Aesthetics 40, 102, 158, 169–76
    experiencing 169–76
Agency, of an individual 96, 98, 99, 116, 136, 212
Alehouses *see* Inns
Alfred, King 192
All Souls, Oxford 84, 94
Amberley Castle 52, 53, 57, 59, 61, 62, 69, 76, 92, 94, 105, 205–7, 217, 229
Animals 102
Aragon, Catherine of 156
Archaeology 12, 27, 41, 42, 54
    Gender archaeology 12
    Prehistoric archaeology 44
Archaeology of buildings 12, 40–5, 53, 74, 211
    development of 40–4
Architectural language or grammar 47, 48, 50–1, 61, 89, 95, 103, 104, 105, 156, 168, 169, 211, 212, 218
    of lodging ranges 50–63
Architectural principles 83, 106, 125, 126, 127, 206 *see also* Inner/outer, *see also* Spatial order, *see also* Social order

Arundel, Archbishop 136
Ashby de la Zouch 33, 233
Auditor 86, 88, 123, 128
Audley, Hugh de 155
Audley, Margaret 155
Aula see under Hall
Avenell, Alice 76
Avenell, William de 76
Aydon Castle 17

Bacon, Roger 203
Badges, for retainers 29, 35, 37–8, 40, 131, 136, 185, 198, 205, 216, 220
    see also Collars
    material of 38, 185, 220
    of Richard II 37, 64
    of Richard III 38, 185
Baking and brewing, spaces for 72, 78, 194, 195, 196, 197–9, 205, 207, 208, 229
Barns *see* Stables
Bastard feudalism 25, 30–40, 46, 134, 135, 167, 216, 218, 219 *see also* Feudalism
Battle 34, 37, 48, 155
    battlefield 114
    of Barnet 108
    of Bosworth 26, 191
    of Hastings 30
    of Mortimer's Cross 29
    of Neville's Cross 187
    of Patay 117
Battlements 174 *see also* Machicolations
Beauchamp, Joan 33

Beaufort, Bishop Henry   195, 197–9, 204, 229
Beaufort, Joan   187, 190
Beaufort, Margaret   155
Beckington, Bishop   83
Bedchamber *see under* Chamber
Beds   15 n.56, 21, 84, 87, 89, 90, 91, 93, 119, 126, 127, 148 *see also* Furniture
  rebates for   204
Bishop's Waltham Palace   52, 62, 72, 92, 94, 180, 191, 193–9, 202–5, 207–8, 214, 219, 220, 229
Black Death   9
Blackmore Farm   93
Bletchingly   88
Blois, Henry of   195
Boar emblem   38, 185 *see also* Badges
Bodiam Castle   55, 234
Bohun family   176
Bohun, Mary de   185
Bokking   119, 125, 129
Boorde, Andrew   192
Bossherde, John   126
Bouche of court   1, 35, 39, 128, 167, 224
Bradley Manor   64
Braziers   61, 89
Bretèche style   54, 224
Brickwork   107, 111, 112, 113, 114, 117, 119, 121, 129, 197, 205, 223, 224, 227, 230, 234
Bridges   118, 119, 125, 127, 152, 179, 189–90, 194, 196, 197, 199, 201, 202–5, 207, 208, 220, 221, 229, 230
Brome, Adam de   20
Brook Hall   26, 52, 60–1, 92, 94, 191, 229
Brympton d'Evercy   52, 94, 191, 229
Buckingham, Katherine Dowager Duchess of   155
Burgh, Edward   114
Burgh, Elizabeth de   33
Burgh, Thomas   106, 108, 113, 114, 135, 230
Burgh, Thomas fifth Lord   108, 111, 114
Buttery   13, 14, 17, 78, 108, 206, 224, 226 *see also* Services
Buttress   119, 121, 148, 149, 187, 191, 192, 224, 225, 226

Caister Castle   29, 86, 89, 90, 93, 103, 104, 116–26, 131, 136, 143, 185, 215, 230
Camera see under Chamber
Canon (occupation)   19, 131, 133, 215
Canterbury (city)   158
Caps and hats   38
Carpenter (occupation)   23
Carpenter, Robert   126
Cash and Money   1, 26, 31, 32, 33, 36, 101, 167
  Money chests   13, 224
  New money/*nouveau riche*   25, 26, 27, 99, 156
Castle terminology   4, 14, 23, 48, 208
Cellars   20
Central Province   6–7
Chamber   17, 18 n.66–7, 20–2, 24, 49, 66, 73, 83–4, 86–91, 109, 123, 126, 152, 183, 186, 192, 206
  bedchamber   1, 4, 16, 83, 84, 88–91, 96, 116, 212–13
  camera   91, 183
  chamber block   88, 95, 152
  lord's   47, 49, 50, 72, 83, 86–91, 95, 105, 106, 108, 127, 144, 186, 190, 191, 193, 195, 195, 198
  of presence   202, 206
  unheated   89
  women's   15, 16, 86, 93
Chamber pots   50, 55, 56, 197
Chamberlain   13, 123
Chantry houses   3, 23
  chantry chapels   144
Chapel   14, 16, 17, 23, 77, 79, 82, 122, 144, 159, 161, 186, 187, 193, 197, 198, 207, 230 *see also* Church
Chivalry   29
Church   14, 26, 76, 78, 108, 144, 155, 158, 237 *see also* Chapel
Clare, Hugh de   159
Clare, Lady de   33
Clare, Margaret de   159
Clarence the Bastard   108
Clarence, Duke of   155
Clergy   19, 133
Closure theory   27
Cobham, Anne   114
Collars   38

INDEX

Collective-living buildings 1, 4, 23–4, 83, 93, 131, 133–4, 214, 215, 217
College master 131, 133, 215
Collegiate ranges 4, 19, 20, 22–3, 63, 83–6, 88–9, 92–5, 130–1, 133, 158, 176, 214
Collyer, Parson David 125
Collyweston 155
Communal living 4, 18, 20, 23, 57, 84, 86, 95, 133, 214 *see also* Dormitories
    garderobes 19, 56
Condor, Lord Grey of 39
Control 2, 10, 50, 115, 129, 131, 135, 136, 137, 140, 143, 174, 176, 177, 203, 208–9, 214, 216, 217, 218
Controller (occupation) 13
Conwy Castle 17
Cook (occupation) 119, 125, 128, 129
Corridors 16, 17, 19, 44, 60, 75, 87, 110, 111–13, 115, 154, 225
Cotehele House 52, 92, 94, 207, 230
Cotmead 75
Crests 37, 101, 141
Cromwell, Lord 141, 142, 146–9, 152, 154–5, 159, 173–4, 204–5, 231
Cross-passage 47, 66, 109, 149, 152, 171, 224
Cross-range 30, 78, 108, 109, 111, 148–9, 154, 156, 161, 162, 164, 168–70, 173–4, 177, 192, 193, 204
Cross-wing 22, 63, 109, 170, 224
Crow, William 125
Crypt 193, 197
Cubiculi 19, 60, 95, 131, 215

Dais 60, 61, 108, 119, 121, 130, 149, 168, 184, 186, 225
Dartington Hall 14, 27, 33, 52, 54, 57, 60, 62, 72, 76, 84, 87, 92, 94, 101, 130, 152, 156, 157, 169, 171, 172, 173, 193
Deincourt, Margaret 155
Devereux family 30
DNA 98
Documentary records 14, 19, 33, 34, 39, 40, 41, 60, 93, 215
    bias *see under* Gender
Doors, individual 4, 19, 27, 48, 51, 52, 57, 59, 60, 72, 82, 93, 95, 103, 115, 133, 135, 142, 165, 168, 175, 212, 213, 214
Dormitories 4, 18, 19–20, 23–4, 60, 69, 72–4, 94, 95, 105, 110, 111, 115–16, 126, 133, 148, 166, 175, 198–9, 204, 214–15, 230, 139
Dunstable Swan 185 *see also* Badges
Durham Cathedral 187

Edgecumbe family 207, 230
Edward I, King 17, 63, 145
Edward II, King 13
Edward III, King 30, 159, 187, 195
Edward IV, King 29, 108
Elizabethan period and houses 62, 130, 158–9
Epiphany Rising 66
Ethnicity 97
Eton College 22, 23
Execution
    of Edward Stafford 30, 91, 161, 177
    of John Holland 66

Fastolf, John 29, 86, 89–91, 93, 116–19, 121, 123–6, 127–9, 230
Fastolf, Millicent 117, 127
Fastolf, Thomas 119, 126–6
Fees, as a mechanism of bastard feudalism 35, 39 *see also* Cash
Fellows 19, 20, 84, 131, 133–4, 215 *see also* Students
Fenlands 99
Ferrars, Henry de 76
Feudalism 30, 34, 38, 46, 219 *see also* Bastard feudalism
    issues with term 30
Field of the Cloth of Gold 156, 161
Fitzranulph, Ralph 186
Fitzrauf 119, 125
Fleet Prison 114
Fortescue, Chief Justice 29–30, 32, 135
Fountains Abbey 54
France 99, 116, 117, 185, 187
French
    language 3, 53, 91
    wars 155
Furniture 73 *see also* Beds
    celures 119, 126
    chairs 87, 89, 90, 127

coverlets 119, 126
tables 87, 89, 90, 127, 183, 225

Gainsborough Hall 51, 52, 53, 55, 57, 61, 72, 74, 75, 84, 92, 94, 103, 106–16, 126, 129, 130, 131, 135, 136, 143, 157, 184, 185, 199, 216, 230
Gallery 22, 78, 114, 161, 166, 195, 196, 197–8, 203, 225, 229
Gardener (occupation) 119, 126
Gardens and parks 15, 161, 162, 193 *see also* Landscapes
  deer park 102
  lakes and ponds 102
Gatehouse 17, 18, 58, 63, 79, 118, 120, 121, 143, 145, 159, 161, 169, 173, 176, 179, 190, 192, 197, 205–7, 217–18, 229, 233, 234, 235
Gaunt, John of 64, 187
Gender 11–13, 15, 34, 44, 96, 97, 99, 100, 140, 215 *see also* Patriarchal society
  bias 11, 34, 215
Gentle servants *see under* Servants
Gentry 5, 9, 16, 17, 25, 28–9, 33, 37, 41, 78, 101, 116, 215
Georgian period and houses 130, 235
Gold Hole Tower 53
Goldstone, Prior of Christ Church 158
Goodramgate, York 19, 158
Gotch, John Alfred 130
Great house, definition 4–5
Guests 2, 12, 21, 50, 86, 88, 92–3, 96, 102, 116, 128, 129, 143–6, 152, 167, 168, 169–70, 173–7, 179, 186, 187, 206–7, 215, 219, 221 *see also* Visitors

H-plan house 170
Habitus 141, 167–9, 180
Haddon Hall 4, 14, 15, 36, 52, 53, 56, 57, 58, 60, 62, 72, 74, 76–84, 86, 88–90, 92, 94, 95, 116, 130, 154, 170, 192, 193, 198, 212, 220, 230
Hall, changes to 15
  aula 183
Hamblen-Thomas, Charles 125

Hastings family 30
Hastings, Lord William 35
Henry I, King 13
Henry II, King 185
Henry IV, King 185, 187, 195
Henry V King 39, 116, 155, 185, 187, 195
Henry VI, King 22, 29, 108, 116
Henry VII, King/Tudor, Henry 26, 39, 155, 191
Henry VIII, King 30, 78, 155, 175–6
Heraldry 139, 140, 156, 167 *see also* Badges
Herbert, William 29
Heriz family 146
Hickman, Frances 114
Hickman, William 113, 114
Hillier and Hanson 43–4, 143, 181
Holland, John 37, 63–4, 101, 171, 173, 193, 230
Homogeneity 2, 35, 115, 126, 136, 167–9, 212, 218
Hospitality 29, 34, 102–3, 145, 176, 177, 187
Hosting 102, 213 *see also* Hospitality
House
  courtyard plan 191–3
  growth of 7–16
Household
  growth of 7–16
  peripatetic 9, 92, 101, 192
House of Lancaster *see* Lancastrians
House of York *see* Yorkists
Howard, Henry 161

Identity
  and architecture 97–101 *see also* Uniformity, *see also* Sameness
  authority 2, 44, 47, 50, 84, 88, 96, 97, 100, 102–3, 105, 115–16, 126, 128, 130, 131, 136, 140, 144, 168, 170, 171, 176, 177, 212, 213, 214, 215, 216, 218, 219
  collective 129–36
  independence 96, 97, 115, 126, 129, 134, 137, 213, 214, 216

INDEX

individualism 2, 115–16, 126–7, 129, 136–7, 140, 214–16, 219
intangible displays 29, 34, 48, 101–3, 129, 183, 186, 213, 219
juxtaposed 115–16 *see also* Juxtaposed displays
permanence 29, 101, 140, 143, 212
personhood 125–9
power 129–41
privilege 11, 20, 101, 202
prestige 29, 30, 36, 37, 48, 101, 167, 170–1, 176
Ilchester, Richard 195
Illusions and illusory architecture 2, 3, 6, 63, 69, 140, 159, 169, 170, 172, 173, 175–7, 218, 221 *see also* Uniformity
Ince Manor 51, 52, 62, 74, 94, 230
Indentures 1, 34, 35, 39, 128, 131, 136, 167, 216
 between Richard, Earl of Salisbury, and Walter Strykelande 35
 between William, Lord Hastings and Ralph Longford 35
 between William, Lord Hastings, and William Bassett 35
 relationship 136
Individual and low-occupancy rooms 1, 16, 20, 23, 60, 73, 92–3, 95, 119, 125, 126–7, 131, 133–4, 158, 166, 168, 214, 215 *see also* Named rooms
Industrial Revolution 132
Inherited land, wealth and rank 25, 26, 31, 108, 159, 186, 187
Inner/outer
 nomenclature 24, 83–4, 95
 spaces 83–91
Inns 20–3, 63, 89, 96, 158
Inventories 86, 89, 91, 93, 104, 116, 117, 119, 121, 123, 125, 126–8, 131, 136, 159, 215
Ireland 99, 100

Jacobean architecture 130
Jewellery 9, 27, 37
Jobs 88, 97, 105, 126, 127–9, 131, 134, 214, 215

Juxtaposed displays 113, 115, 129, 131, 214, 216 *see also under* Identity

Kempe, Margery 135
Kinship *see* Social bonds
Kirby Hall 130
Kitchen 13, 14, 15, 17, 21, 66, 78, 87, 104, 106, 108, 109, 114, 152, 165, 186, 195, 198, 203, 206, 229
 kitchen children 87, 104
 kitchen clerk 87, 104
 sleeping in 87

Lady Row, York 158
Lambley 155
Lancastrians 26, 30, 32, 33, 78, 108, 131, 135, 155, 187
Landscapes 29, 53, 99, 101–2, 103, 141, 204 *see also* Gardens and parks
 prehistoric 143
Lawyers 88, 119, 125, 128, 129, 134
Lived experience 1, 2, 45, 50, 95, 98, 101, 103, 116, 127, 133, 136–7, 140, 179, 180, 182, 185, 205, 208, 212, 213, 216, 217, 219–21
Livery 1, 29, 34–40, 131, 136, 167, 183, 198, 205, 216, 219, 220
Livery robes *see* Livery
Lobbies 1, 60, 79, 82, 86, 154, 188, 189, 190, 225
Lodging ranges
 and social distance 198–205 *see also* Social distance
 and the great house 4–7
 definition 3–4
 development 17–25
 experiencing their aesthetics 169–76 *see also* Aesthetics
 features of 50–63
 fireplaces 52, 60–1
 function and use 103–6
 garderobes 52, 53–7
 individual doors 52, 57–60
 proto 17, 214
 size of rooms 91–4
 uniformity 52, 61–3 *see also* Uniformity
 use as accommodation 72–4
 use as bedchambers 83–6, 88–91

use as offices   83–8
windows   52, 60–1
Logier   3
London   25, 155, 156, 158
Lynde, William   123, 128

Machicolations   121, 161, 191, 224, 225
Magdalen College, Oxford   22
Maintenance   34, 35–6, 39, 218
Manor house, definition   4–5
Mareschal, Roger le   20
Marshal (occupation)   13, 87, 88, 104, 105, 187
Marshalsea   13, 14, 225
Marxism   10 n.24, 27
Meanings of buildings   2, 3, 28, 40–2, 44, 45, 50, 83, 98, 101, 103–4, 137, 139, 140–2, 145, 168, 169, 176, 177, 185, 191, 199, 211–13, 216, 218, 220, 221–2
Men   1, 10–11, 31, 33–4, 73, 129, 136, 155, 168, 192, 215 *see also* Gender, *see also* Sex
Merchants   28, 134
Mess hall   109, 131, 199
Middle class   3, 132 *see also* Middling
  myth of   132
Middleham Castle   38, 52, 53, 54, 56, 57, 61, 62, 72, 92, 94, 108, 179–80, 185, 186–92, 199, 200, 201, 202, 203–5, 207–8, 220, 221, 230
Middling   45, 132, 133, 134, 167
  definition of middling sort   132–3
  sort   3, 132–4, 215
Military   29, 48, 117, 218
  and retainers   18, 35, 126, 168, 215, 218
  service   2, 18, 29, 34–5, 126
Miniscularity, feeling of   62, 143
Monastic   40, 51, 108, 148
Morely, Isabella   33
Moreton Hall   93
Morris, William   40

Named rooms   93, 126, 128 *see also* Individual rooms
National Trust   40
Neville, Lord John   187
Neville, Lord Ralph, first   186–7

Neville, Lord Ralph, fourth   72, 187, 190, 204, 230
Neville, Lord Ralph, second   187
Neville, Lord Robert   186
New College, Oxford   84
Nobility   5, 9, 16–17, 25, 28–9, 33, 37, 41, 78, 101, 16, 215
Norman
  Conquest   186
  period   14, 18 n.67, 30, 195
Normandy   30, 127
Normandy, William of   30
Northern Ireland   6

Officer (occupation)   9, 13, 39, 123, 183
Offices   1, 4, 29, 83, 86–8, 88–91, 95–6, 116, 129, 134, 141, 148, 154, 183, 212, 213, 217 *see also under* Lodging ranges
Old Newnham   52, 54, 94, 231
Oriel College, Oxford   20
Ownership
  of retainers   37–8, 212, 213
  of space   57, 103–4, 115, 126, 129, 130, 140, 182, 212, 213

Pantry   13, 14, 17, 78, 108, 206, 224, 226 *see also* Services
Parlour   15, 17, 25, 78, 86, 88, 89, 106, 108, 131, 169–70, 206, 207, 213
  in inns   22
Partitions   29, 54, 57, 59, 74–6, 89, 92, 111, 152, 188, 189, 206, 212, 226 *see also* Screens, *see also* Timber
Paston family   117, 118, 121
Paston Letters   87, 91
Paston, Agnes   91
Paston, John   88, 91, 121, 125
Paston, Margaret   87
Paston, William   91
Patriarchal society   10–11, 31 *see also* Gender
Peasants and poor   6, 28, 41, 132, 133, 134
Penshurst   161, 176
Perfect house   130, 191–3
Perpendicular architecture   108, 119, 120, 125, 226
Phenomenology   44–5

INDEX

Pilaster 187, 226
Plummer, Charles 31–3, 34–5, 38–9, 134–5
Pollio, Marcus Vitruvius 145
Porch 37, 63, 64, 66, 69, 70, 110, 111, 112, 149, 155, 166, 169, 171, 172, 173, 174
Portcullis 162, 175, 179
Powderham Castle 64, 237
Prebendary 133
Privacy 1, 13, 16, 24, 43, 47–50, 57, 78, 83–4, 88–9, 91–3, 96, 97, 106, 113, 115, 117, 126, 131, 134, 161, 183, 213–15, 219, 221
  and garderobes 56
  and sleeping 21, 24, 73, 83–4, 91, 212, 213
Prodigy houses 62, 130, 158 see also Elizabethan
Propaganda
  architecture 145–6
  identities 139
Public spaces 16, 35, 49–50, 56, 83–4, 86, 88, 89, 95–6, 114, 154, 183, 189, 190 see also Privacy

Raby 186
  Castle 158, 187, 237
Rafman, John 123, 128, 129
Raglan Castle 29, 33, 237
Raglan, William ap Thomas of 29
Ratcliffe, Edward 26
Raymes, Robert de 17
Rector 126, 128
Rede, Bishop 229
Religion 97
  Protestant 25
Renaissance houses 43, 216
Retainer
  badges see Badges
  definition 31
  permanence in household 17, 23, 36, 129, 213
  service 1, 2, 11, 14, 25–6, 29, 30, 34–5, 39, 87, 127, 128, 134, 136, 155, 167, 170, 217
Retinues 17, 29, 32, 33–4, 36, 38–40, 48, 101, 104, 111, 115, 126, 129, 131, 135–6, 158, 167–8, 173, 185, 209, 216–17, 219, 220, 221

rivalling 135, 209
Richard II, King 37, 64, 101, 187
  emblem see under Badges
Richard III, King 38, 108, 113, 155, 175, 185, 188
  emblem see under Badges
Richmond Castle 53
Room divisions see Partitions, see Screens, see Timber
Rufford 74
Ruskin, John 40

Salon 25
Salvin, Anthony 161
Sameness in architecture, livery and identity 2, 37, 62, 74, 129–30, 134, 136, 157, 159, 216–17 see also Uniformity
Samlesbury 74
Scarborough Castle 114
Screens 69, 74, 76, 78, 81, 82, 84, 95, 144, 212, 227 see also Partitions
Scrope, Stephen 117, 123, 127–8
Senses 1, 44, 45, 140, 196 see also Vision
  noises 184, 202, 205, 220, 221
  smells 44, 202, 205, 220, 221
Servants 9–10, 13–14, 29, 31, 37–8, 56–7, 61, 72, 87, 93, 125, 128, 132–4, 143, 175, 203
  chambers 90
  gentle 49, 88, 119, 125
Services 6, 17, 18, 33, 48, 66, 75, 78, 87, 93, 105, 109, 121, 131, 149, 152, 162, 168, 184, 191, 193, 195, 198, 206–7, 224, 237 see also Buttery, see also Pantry, see also Kitchen
Sex (biological) 11–12
Sexuality 99
Shakespeare's Henriad 117
Sherriff Hutton 186, 187, 237
Shipdam, Watkin 86, 123, 128
Sittingrooms, in colleges 84, 86
Slaves 10, 10 n.24, 13, 37, 72, 87, 132, 134
Sleeping, and places for 15, 17–18, 20, 21, 73, 87, 90–1, 95, 104, 126, 199, 212, 215 see also Chamber

Social bonds and kinship 34, 36, 97, 126, 134, 213
Social distance 2, 50, 127, 180–6, 191–3, 196, 198–209, 213, 214, 215, 219, 220, 222
  and the great house 205–7
  represented by spatial distance 180–6
Social emulation 27–8, 134
Social hierarchy 14, 27–30, 31, 72, 106, 132, 134, 183–4, 203, 207, 215
Social mobility 2, 25–31, 101, 184, 217
Social order 127, 130, 191, 192, 202
  see also Spatial order, see also Architectural principles, see also Inner/outer
Society for the Protection of Ancient Buildings 40
Soldiers 31, 34, 35, 128, 213
Spatial analysis 42–4, 143, 180, 182 see also Access analysis
Spatial order 47, 123, 127, 130, 168, 212
  see also Social order, see also Architectural principles, see also Inner/outer
Squints or hagioscopes 144
St Augustine 192
St Bernard 203
Stables and barns 17, 21, 22, 66, 87, 126, 166, 167, 192, 206
Stafford, Countess Anne 33
Stafford, Duke Edward, third 30, 88, 91, 155, 159, 161, 166, 169, 170, 175–6, 177, 231
Stafford, Duke Henry, second 30, 155, 175
Stafford, Ralph 155, 159
Stairs 19, 22, 66, 69, 70, 71, 74, 82, 83, 111, 113, 119, 122, 123, 124, 149, 150, 152, 154, 156, 157, 158, 160, 162, 163, 165, 166, 170, 171, 173, 174, 188, 190, 199, 200, 226, 233, 237
  concealed, internal 60, 111, 188
  external 69, 188, 189
  newel 82, 108, 110, 111, 112, 113, 114, 125, 148, 149, 189, 190, 221, 226
Status, definition 48–50
Statutes of livery 39

Stewhouse 89, 123
Storage 9, 16, 17, 21, 148, 149, 152, 186
Strode family 231
Stubbs, William 32, 135
Students 20, 23, 84, 98 see also Fellows
Swansea 99
Sydenham, John 191, 229
Symmetry in architecture 22, 24, 25, 57, 59, 62, 108, 130, 157–8, 171, 173, 176, 216 see also Uniformity

Talbot, Anne 78
Tattershall Castle 155, 238
Taverns see Inns
Tenants 34, 50, 102
Tenements 114
Terraced houses 19, 84
Theatre, as a metaphor 15, 102, 139, 145–6, 154–9, 167–9, 177, 217–19
Thornbury Castle 27, 30, 51–7, 60–2, 69, 72, 76, 88, 91, 92, 94, 143, 146, 152, 154–66, 169–71, 173–7, 185, 217, 231
Thurbern, Robert 22, 23
Timber 19, 51, 54, 57, 60, 61, 69, 72, 74–6, 81, 82–4, 89, 92, 95, 112, 119, 148, 152, 167, 187, 188, 189, 202, 212, 223, 225, 226, 227 see also Partitions, see also Screens
  Timber-framed 41, 51, 60, 61, 69, 74, 75, 108, 111, 113, 194, 197, 223, 224, 226, 230, 236, 248
Tiverton Castle 64
Townhouses 25, 75, 83, 89
Towns 20, 21, 89, 114
Trade 25, 29, 134
Travel and Travelling 15, 20, 23, 35, 78, 92, 129, 131, 135, 203, 219
Treasurer 13, 14, 78, 141, 146, 148, 155
Tudor
  period 63, 73, 102, 133, 158
  architecture 73, 101, 108, 132, 158, 162
  household 73
Typologies 23, 41, 48, 73, 168, 214
  limitations of 23, 214

INDEX

Uniformity/Uniform architecture 2, 3, 4, 6, 22–3, 25, 27, 50, 52, 61–3, 66, 67, 69, 83, 112, 113, 123, 124, 129–32, 136, 153, 156–9, 160, 165–6, 168–73, 176, 189, 197, 212, 216, 217, 218, 221 *see also* Symmetry
  and habitus 168
  as decoration, fashion 26, 63, 158
  beyond the house 22–3, 158
  components of 62, 170, 176, 216
  in identity 2, 130–2, 136, 212, 216, 217, 218
  in livery 36
  in later houses 62–3, 130, 158, 216
  in room size 62, 157
  within the hall 130
Urban 34, 96
  buildings 20, 41, 100, 181 *see also* Townhouses
  centres 20, 21 *see also* Towns
  interests 29
  mercantile class *see* Merchants
  terraces 158

Vernon, Richard, fourth 78
Vernon, Richard, sixth 78
Vernon, Henry 36, 39, 78, 82, 230
Vernon, Richard de 76
Vernon, Roger 39
Vernon, William 36
Vicarial ranges 3, 7, 18–19, 23, 60, 63, 83–6, 88, 94, 95–6, 115, 130, 131, 133, 158, 176, 214, 215
  Vicarial house, York 19, 60, 96
  Vicars choral 3, 18, 19, 83, 83, 131, 133, 134
  Vicars' Close, Wells 19, 83, 84, 86, 94, 95, 96, 111, 115, 131
  Vicars' Court, Lincoln 85, 94
Vicars 19, 24, 60, 131
Viewer 53, 62, 102, 103, 104, 129, 141–2, 155, 167–70, 172, 173–4, 176, 180, 203, 218, 221–2 *see also* Vision
Viewshed analysis 143
Villagers 102
Vision 142–4, 176

visual deception 170, 173, 218 *see also* Illusions
visual relationships 2, 3, 19, 27, 28, 36, 37, 38, 51, 112, 131, 136, 141, 143–4, 157, 168–9, 170, 185, 192, 202, 207, 217
visuality 141–6, 146, 212, 220
Visitors 22, 63, 84, 140, 141–6, 159, 161, 168–71, 173–5, 177, 182, 205–8, 217 *see also* Guests
  royal visitors 113, 161, 175, 187

Wales 5, 6, 8, 41, 176
War 26, 29, 32, 48, 117, 135, 155, 187, 215
  Hundred Years War 108, 116, 155
  war and peace 1, 35, 39, 128, 167
  Wars of the Roses 23, 25, 30, 31–2, 38, 39, 114, 135, 184
Wardrobe 9, 10, 53
Wardrober (occupation) 9, 10, 13, 14, 15, 176
Warkworth Castle 33, 54
Warkworth Chronicles 135
Wells Palace 7
Wharram Percy 37
Widows 10, 34, 114 *see also* Gender, *see also* Women
Will and testament 91
Willoughby, Robert 26–7, 61, 229
Winchester (city) 21, 191, 193, 195
Winchester College 20, 22
Windsor Castle 14, 195, 238
Wingfield Manor 52, 54, 56, 57, 60, 61, 62, 69, 72, 76, 92, 94, 119, 121, 125, 141, 142, 143, 146–57, 159, 163, 169, 171, 173–4, 176–7, 185, 189, 204, 208, 231
Withdraught 90
Wolsey, Cardinal 176
Women 10–12, 15, 16, 31, 33–4, 73, 99 *see also* Gender, *see also* Widows
Worcester, William of 23, 123
Wotton, Henry 102, 145
Wykeham, William 22, 72, 195

York (city) 19, 60, 96, 158
York Minster 19
Yorkists 29, 30, 32, 35, 78, 108

ALREADY PUBLISHED

The Art of Anglo-Saxon England
Catherine E. Karkov

English Medieval Misericords: The Margins of Meaning
Paul Hardwick

English Medieval Shrines
John Crook

Thresholds of Medieval Visual Culture: Liminal Spaces
Edited by Elina Gertsman and Jill Stevenson

The Marvellous and the Monstrous in the Sculpture of Twelfth-Century Europe
Kirk Ambrose

Early Medieval Stone Monuments: Materiality, Biography, Landscape
Edited by Howard Williams, Joanne Kirton and Meggen Gondek

The Royal Abbey of Reading
Ron Baxter

*Education in Twelfth-Century Art and Architecture:
Images of Learning in Europe, c.1100–1220*
Laura Cleaver

*The Art and Science of the Church Screen in Medieval Europe:
Making, Meaning, Preserving*
Edited by Spike Bucklow, Richard Marks and Lucy Wrapson

*Motherhood and Meaning in Medieval Sculpture:
Representations from France, c.1100–1500*
Marian Bleeke

Graphic Devices and the Early Decorated Book
Edited by Michelle P. Brown, Ildar H. Garipzanov and Benjamin C. Tilghman

Church Monuments in South Wales, c.1200–1547
Rhianydd Biebrach

Tomb and Temple: Re-imagining the Sacred Buildings of Jerusalem
Edited by Robin Griffith-Jones and Eric Fernie

Art and Political Thought in Medieval England, c.1150–1350
Laura Slater

Insular Iconographies: Essays in Honour of Jane Hawkes
Edited by Meg Boulton and Michael D.J. Bintley

English Alabaster Carvings and their Cultural Contexts
Edited by Zuleika Murat

A Critical Companion to English Mappae Mundi *of the Twelfth and Thirteenth Centuries*
Edited by Dan Terkla and Nick Millea

Designing Norman Sicily: Material Culture and Society
Edited by Emily A. Winkler, Liam Fitzgerald and Andrew Small

Stone Fidelity: Marriage and Emotion in Medieval Tomb Sculpture
Jessica Barker

*Reliquary Tabernacles in Fourteenth-Century Italy:
Image, Relic and Material Culture*
Beth Williamson

Imagining Anglo-Saxon England: Utopia, Heterotopia, Dystopia
Catherine E. Karkov

The Rood in Medieval Britain and Ireland, c.800–c.1500
Edited by Philippa Turner and Jane Hawkes

*The Ashburnham Pentateuch and its Contexts:
The Trinity in Late Antiquity and the Early Middle Ages*
Jennifer Awes Freeman

*Late Medieval Italian Art and its Contexts:
Essays in Honour of Professor Joanna Cannon*
Edited by Donal Cooper and Beth Williamson

Printed in the United States
by Baker & Taylor Publisher Services